Merve Emre is associate professor of English at the University of Oxford and fellow of Worcester College. She is the author of *Paraliterary: The Making of Bad Readers in Postwar America*. Her work has appeared in the *New York Review of Books*, *London Review of Books*, *Harper's*, the *New York Times Magazine*, the *Atlantic* and other similar publications.

A *SPECTATOR* BOOK OF THE YEAR

Praise for *What's Your Type?*:

'A tremendous piece of storytelling and an acute analysis of the craving of the contemporary, secular imagination for certainties'
Bryan Appleyard, *Sunday Times*

'Emre is a masterful and nuanced storyteller. *What's Your Type?* is an impressive work of scholarship, not just a biography of two fascinating women but also a tightly argued and sweeping history of how the conception of personality changed throughout the upheavals of the twentieth century'
New Statesman

'The story behind the Myers-Briggs test proves an interesting one, and is told with considerable relish, vim and some savage comedy by Emre ... This is a very funny book, and properly angry about the stupidity of the entire exercise'
Philip Hensher, *Spectator*

'Emre's careful investigations of the tool's bizarre origins and alarming impact weave a compelling narrative that recounts the rise of twentieth-century managerial and personnel-theory science with the gritty wistfulness of a John Steinbeck novel'
Nature

'Emre's book begins like a true-crime thriller, with the tantalizing suggestion that a number of unsettling revelations are in store. Inventive and beguiling … the revelations she uncovers are affecting and occasionally (and delightfully) bizarre. This is history that reads like biography that reads like a novel – a fluid narrative that defies expectations and plays against type'   *New York Times*

'This is a sparkling biography – not of a person, but of a popular personality tool. Merve Emre deftly exposes the hidden origins of the MBTI and the seductive appeal and fatal flaws of personality types'
Adam Grant, author of *Give and Take*,
Originals and *Option B* with Sheryl Sandberg

'Emre's thought-provoking book is full of interest and she brings vigour to her investigation of Myers-Briggs'   *The Times*

'A brilliant cultural history of the personality-assessment industry'
Economist

What's Your Type?

THE STRANGE HISTORY OF THE MYERS-BRIGGS,
AND HOW PERSONALITY TESTING TOOK OVER THE WORLD

Merve Emre

WILLIAM
COLLINS

William Collins
An imprint of HarperCollins*Publishers*
1 London Bridge Street
London SE1 9GF

WilliamCollinsBooks.com

First published in Great Britain by William Collins in 2018
First published in the United States by Doubleday,
a division of Penguin Random House in 2018
This William Collins paperback edition published in 2019

1

Quotes on page 4, 42, 50, 78, 102 and 103 courtesy of the
Katharine Cook Papers at Michigan State University

A catalogue record for this book is available from the British Library

ISBN 978-0-00-820141-8

Printed and bound in Great Britain by CPI Group (UK) Ltd, Croydon CR0 4YY

MIX
Paper from
responsible sources
FSC www.fsc.org **FSC® C007454**

This book is produced from independently certified FSC™ paper
to ensure responsible forest management.

For more information visit: www.harpercollins.co.uk/green

For my mother

Contents

Speaking Type

To investigate the history of the Myers-Briggs Type Indicator, the most popular personality inventory in the world, is to court a kind of low-level paranoia. Files disappear. Tapes are erased. People begin to watch you.

In the fall of 2015, I was seven months pregnant and rifling through the archives of the Educational Testing Service (ETS) in Princeton, New Jersey. Many people are familiar with the ETS as the longtime publisher of the Scholastic Aptitude Test (SAT), but it was also the first publisher of the Myers-Briggs Type Indicator and the first institution to try to determine its scientific validity in the 1960s. Some months before, I had written a controversial article on the origins of Myers-Briggs, and it seemed my reputation had preceded me. In anticipation of my arrival, the staff had removed a folder containing letters from ETS staff to Isabel Briggs Myers, creator of the type indicator. When I asked to see the letters, there was a bit of hushed talk and a brief consultation with a lawyer before the archivist told me that he would not share them with me because of the "sensitive information" they contained. Later that day, a young male ETS employee who, I would later learn, was tasked with surveilling me during my visit, posted the following message to his Twitter account: "Today I'm creeping on a pregnant lady as part of my job." He seemed an ambivalent creeper or perhaps just an incompetent one. He proceeded to post a link to the article I had written and tagged me in his subsequent post. "Great article by the lady I had to creep on this morning," he wrote.

If anything, this sort of occurrence has been more typical than not of my journey into the world of personality testing. In the years that I have spent writing this book, I have encountered secrets and lies and various strategies of bureaucratic obstruction, some more obvious and objectionable than others. It started early in 2013—the moment when I started researching the life and work of Isabel Briggs Myers, about whom very little was known, other than that she was born in 1897, died in 1980, and with the help of her mother, Katharine Cook Briggs, created the type indicator sometime in between. After Isabel's death, her son had donated her personal papers to the University of Florida, which was a five-minute drive from the Center for Applications of Psychological Type (CAPT): a nonprofit research center that Isabel had helped found just before she died but that now served as the guardian of the type indicator's trade secrets and protector of its creator's legacy. Although her papers were technically the property of the university—and thus should have been open to public use—they required permission from CAPT to access. I applied to CAPT for permission, and twice I was assured by the university librarian, a gentle and apologetic man, that I would never receive it. "The staff is very invested in protecting Isabel's image," he warned me. In the past, they had done whatever they needed to do to keep people from scrutinizing her life too closely. Why her image should need protection, I did not yet understand.

After nine months of waiting to hear back about the status of my application, I was asked by CAPT to prove my commitment to Myers-Briggs by undergoing a "re-education program": a nearly two-thousand-dollar, four-day Myers-Briggs accreditation session that took place in the United Jewish Federation building on East Fifty-ninth Street in Manhattan. The accreditation session was led by a self-assured, fashionable woman in her fifties named Patricia, and she promised to teach me and my twenty-five fellow participants—Fortune 500 executives from the United States, United Kingdom, South Africa, and China, high school and college guidance counselors, dating coaches, a Department of Defense administrator, an astrologist, a retired priest—how to "speak type fluently." This was how Patricia put it, as if speaking type would soon become the most natural thing in the world to us. "This is only the beginning!" she said when we first filed into the room. "Just think of this as a language immersion program."

Among the various people and instructions that I observed at my re-education program, the most striking was Patricia's insistence that one's ability to "speak type fluently" depended on regulating with great care the language one used to describe the Myers-Briggs Type Indicator to the uninitiated. The first rule of speaking type, Patricia said, was that you had to memorize the history of type. Sometime in the 1940s, during the closing years of World War II, two women, a mother and daughter named Katharine Cook Briggs and Isabel Briggs Myers, designed a lengthy and ingenious questionnaire that assessed one's personality along four dimensions of ordinary human behavior: extraversion (E) and introversion (I); sensing (S) and intuition (N); thinking (T) and feeling (F); and judging (J) and perceiving (P). The categories were easy to understand and universally relatable, Patricia claimed. "Do you prefer to focus on the outer world or on your own inner world? This is called Extraversion (E) or Introversion (I)," explained the first slide she showed us. She clicked to the second. "Do you prefer to focus on the basic information you take in or do you prefer to interpret and add meaning? This is called Sensing (S) or Intuition (N)." The third: "When making decisions, do you prefer to look first at logic and consistency or first look at people and special circumstances? This is called Thinking (T) or Feeling (F)." And the final one: "In dealing with the outside world, do you prefer to get things decided or do you prefer to stay open to new information and options? This is called Judging (J) or Perceiving (P)."

How one answered the ninety-three items on the questionnaire would determine one's personality: one of the sixteen possible four-letter combinations that revealed your true self—your "shoes-off self," as Isabel liked to say—to you. We were told that both their questionnaire and their categories of personality (E/I, S/N, T/F, J/P) were based on the writings of Carl Gustav Jung, one of the twentieth century's most influential personality psychologists and author of the 1921 book *Psychological Types*. It was not necessary for us to know anything else about Jung other than his name. "Jung is a very respected name, a big name," Patricia told us. "Even if you don't know who he is, know his name. His name gives the test validity."

The second rule of speaking type was that you did not, under any circumstances, refer to the type indicator as a "test." It was a "self-reporting instrument" or an "indicator," Patricia explained. "People use the word 'test' all the time, but what you're taking is an indicator. It's indicating your personality based on what you told the test." Although her statement sounded tautological, Patricia assured us that it was not. Unlike a standardized test like the SAT, which asked the test taker to choose between right and wrong answers, the type indicator had no right or wrong answers—only two competing preferences. *"In reading for pleasure, do you (a) Enjoy odd or original ways of saying things; or (b) Like writers to say exactly what they mean?" "If you were a teacher, would you rather teach (a) Fact courses; or (b) Courses involving theory?"* And unlike a standardized test, in which a higher score was always more desirable than a lower one, there were no better or worse types. In a riposte to the long and punishing tradition of psychological testing in America, which had proceeded by separating apparently normal people from neurotics, psychotics, and sociopaths, all sixteen types were created equal. They each had their strengths and weaknesses and their special place in the world.

The final rule of speaking type was, to my mind, the most important and the most unsettling: you had to conceive of personality as an innate characteristic, something fixed since birth and immutable, like blue eyes or left-handedness. "You have to buy into the idea that type never changes," Patricia ordered us, and she asked that we chant after her: "Type never changes! Type never changes!" "We will brand this into your brains," she promised. "The theory behind the indicator supports the fact that you are born with a four-letter preference. If you hear someone say, 'My type changed,' they are not correct." Her insistence on a singular and essential self—a self whose moods and mysteries were crystallized by four simple letters—seemed to me impossibly retrograde amidst the cheerful promises of self-transformation through diet, exercise, travel, therapy, and meditation that I encountered in popular culture every day. Yet it also struck me as an irresistibly attractive fiction. There was a certain narcissistic beauty to the idea, a certain luminance to the promise that, by learning to speak type, we could learn to compress the gestures of our messy, complicated lives into a coherent life story, one capable of expressing both to ourselves and to others not just who we were but who we had been all along. What type offered us was a vision of individual identity in its most transcendent and transparent form. "Who are you?" the type indicator asked. "I am a clear ENTJ," Patricia answered. "I am an ISFP," the woman sitting next to me whispered in return. What other language afforded such clarity? Who would not want to believe in it?

That was the end of day one. The rest of the week was busy, crowded with tutorials and tests, group exercises and games. It ended on a rousing note with a sales pitch delivered to us by two executives who had flown into New York that morning from Sunnyvale, California, home of Consulting Psychologists Press (CPP), the current publisher of the Myers-Briggs Type Indicator. They urged us to use our accreditation status to purchase as many Myers-Briggs products as we could afford and to attend as many workshops as our schedules could accommodate. Then, in a graduation ceremony of sorts, they presented each of us with a pocket-sized diploma and plated metal pin with the words "MBTI Certified" embossed on it.

At the end of the week, my contact at CAPT informed me that, based on my performance at the accreditation session, they had decided not to allow me into Isabel's archive. In response to my request for more information about their decision, he cut off all further communication. His evasiveness raised the very question I suspected the organization would have most liked to avoid: What did they have to hide?

. . . .

Quite a lot as it turns out, but the most interesting secrets of the Myers-Briggs Type Indicator are not the secrets that the skeptics of personality testing might expect. For some time, it has been a well-known fact that the type indicator is not scientifically valid; that the theory behind it has no basis in clinical psychology; and that it is the flagship product of a lucrative global corporation, one whose interests sit at the shadowy crossroads of industrial psychology and self-care. For some time too, critics of typological thinking have issued scathing indictments of personality assessment's "liquidation of the individual," to quote social theorist Theodor Adorno. For Adorno, as for many skeptics writing today, type performs a rather insidious sleight of hand. It convinces people of their status as rounded and exceptional beings. Yet it does so by flattening human behavior into a static, predetermined set of traits, traits that often register the interests of the powerful institutions that use personality assessment to rationalize their daily affairs. By the late twentieth century, these institutions included corporations like Standard Oil and General Electric that used type to hire, fire, and promote employees; elite colleges like Swarthmore and Bryn Mawr that used type to admit students; churches that used type to ordain ministers; government bureaucracies that used type to appoint civil servants. Under the rule of type, the labeling of live human beings emerged as one technique for annihilating individuality—for treating people as interchangeable, and sometimes disposable, parts of an unforgiving social whole. Type was, in short, one of the bluntest and best-disguised tools of modernity: a wolf in sheep's clothing.

None of this is new. What remains unexplained is why, in the face of this knowledge, so many people—two million a year, in nearly all Fortune 500 companies and U.S. colleges and universities, in community centers and churches and couples' retreats, in the army, the navy, and the CIA—continue not only to embrace the type indicator but to defend its inviolability with the kind of ardor usually reserved for matters of the deepest faith. "Myers-Briggs is like my religion" is a familiar refrain one hears at accreditation sessions like the one I attended. "It helped me find myself." "It changed my life." "I was never the same again." What I have witnessed time and again, and what this book seeks to understand, is the unwavering belief in type's ability to comprehend who we are—why we work the jobs we work, why we love the people we love, why we behave in the apparently various and contradictory ways we do—a belief that persists despite how shamelessly type classifies individuals and conscripts them into the bureaucratic hierarchies of the workplace, the school, the church, the state, and even their own families. At the heart of this mystery is a set of questions fundamental to all human existence: What is a personality? Where does it come from? Why are we so intent on categorizing it? And, of course, the greatest question of all: Who am I?

Although they were not the only figures in the history of personality psychology to pose these questions, Katharine Cook Briggs and her daughter, Isabel Briggs Myers, were among the first to perceive how hungry the masses were for simple, self-affirming answers to the problem of self-knowledge. As proud wives, mothers, and homemakers with no formal training in psychology or psychiatry, they believed they could craft a language of the self that was free from judgment and malice; free from the coldness and impassivity that, in their minds, characterized the attitudes of professional clinicians. Their first subjects were the people they loved the most, their husbands and their children; their first workplaces were their homes. While they did borrow much of their language of type from Carl Jung, their relationship with him was vexed: at times mutually admiring; at times dangerously, even sexually, obsessive. No matter what obstacles or disappointments they faced, they believed they could overcome their amateurism with a stubborn, sometimes infuriating dedication to their cause, a belief that persisted even when it cost them their friendships, their marriages, their sanity. Their personal lives were everywhere bound up with the life of their invention, so much so that once it passed from the private into the public realm, they would eventually become eclipsed by it, in much the same way that the name "Frankenstein" has come to stand for the monster rather than his creator.

As I have pieced together the strange, bewitching lives of Katharine and Isabel, I have come to see that, implicit in the story of their lives, is an answer to my question about why we might speak the language of type with such a strong sense of purpose. Type, to borrow a phrase from French philosopher Michel Foucault, is a modern technology of the self: a system of personal interrogation that is as committed to self-discovery as it is to self-care. Learning one's type is a portal to an elaborate practice of talking and thinking about who you are, a discourse of self-understanding in which words like "extravert" and "introvert," "thinker" and "feeler" forge a common language for reflection and for acceptance of both yourself—the true you—and others. This language is spoken with veneration among strangers and friends, in families and in workplaces, and at the accreditation program I attended in New York. It appears everywhere in popular culture: in self-help books and online quizzes, in novels and on television shows, on dating sites where users specify that they are looking for "romantic ENFJs" or "rational INTPs." It strikes a delicate balance between the challenges of pure, trailblazing individuality and the comforts of belonging to a social class that surpasses the individual—a clan of people who speak the same language of selfhood, one instantly recognizable upon the utterance of a four-letter acronym.

As a technology of the self, the language of type does not just liquidate the individual. It liberates her too. Armed with a powerful vocabulary of self-consciousness, unshackled from conventions and inertia, she begins to understand herself—her personality—as the master and the arbiter of her destiny. In this sense, type is just the latest iteration of a human maxim as old as the letters carved into the Temple of Apollo at Delphi (γνῶθι σεαυτόν—"Know thyself"), the confessions of Saint Augustine ("Return to yourself; truth dwells in the inner man"), the epigrams of Shakespeare ("To thine own self be true"), and the philosophical meditations of Hegel ("Self-consciousness is the fount of truth"). Yet the scale at which type has ensnared the popular imagination is unprecedented and astonishing. Type is a $2 billion industry of the self that spans twenty-six countries and more than two dozen languages, from Afrikaans to Cantonese. Whether one encounters it among the ministers of Melbourne, the factory workers of Tokyo, or the psychoanalysts of Buenos Aires, the claim for its importance remains consistent: true self-mastery can proceed only through true self-knowledge. To learn how to speak type fluently is to learn how to wield this knowledge to cultivate a shared ethos of self-contemplation, an inward gaze that many people once looked to religious institutions and religious authorities to provide.

If the idea of self-mastery through self-knowledge has served as a linchpin of Western philosophy, from the ancient Greeks to Foucault, nowhere is it more apparent than in the biographies of Katharine and Isabel: two women of their own invention struggling to lead purposeful, creative, and self-directed lives amidst the upheavals of the twentieth century. The fact that they were wives, mothers, and struggling artists—and the fact that many proud "type watchers" I have encountered while writing this book are—is no coincidence. For men, especially Katharine's and Isabel's contemporaries, the road to self-discovery was paved with advantages: easy access to higher education and employment, freedom from the burdens of housework and childcare, a general atmosphere of social and political permissiveness. For women, who were often asked to place the needs of others above their own, the contemplation of the self and its desires often took more surreptitious or compromised routes. Katharine, whose life's work spanned the first half of the twentieth century, was attracted to type's mystical powers: the way it could grant her access to her soul and the souls of her children, bringing them closer to God and the man she took to be God's representative on earth, Carl Jung. Isabel, a novelist who assumed her mother's mission after World War II, gravitated to type's modernizing prospects: how it seemed to offer a perfectly rational, yet inspirational, system for managing people across very different domains of society, from her modest four-person household to the entire U.S. workforce. Throughout the history of type, the convergence of the mystical and the modern, the spiritual and the secular paints the illusory picture of what Jung called a "more perfect type of man": a man whose knowledge of himself directly serves the ends of society and its institutions.

In the quest for a more perfect type of man (or woman), the story of personality assessment exceeds Katharine and Isabel in fascinating, unpredictable, and disturbing ways. It collides with some of the twentieth century's most famous personality theorists and practitioners: Henry Murray, director of the Harvard Psychological Clinic; Edward Northup Hay, one of the first personality consultants in the United States; Donald MacKinnon, military psychologist and founder of the Institute of Personality Assessment and Research; and Henry

Chauncey, the founder and first director of the Educational Testing Service. It touches the lives of other forgotten women in the history of psychology, who also saw personality testing as an opportunity for individual empowerment. It perpetuates a very particular culture of capitalism, colonizing people's psychological livelihoods by encouraging them to work more and work harder by "working at the things that are right for them," as Isabel liked to say. It promotes many disingenuous and dangerous ideas about race, gender, class, and social perfectibility, ideas that have motivated, and continue to motivate, terrible forms of bias and discrimination.

Just as the type indicator leaves home during World War II to traverse America, from its East Coast boardrooms to its West Coast communes, so too does this book accompany type on its journey away from Katharine's and Isabel's homes and into the major institutions of modernity: the military, the corporation, the university, the hospital. It is in these institutions that type finds a captive audience before exploding into the popular consciousness in the 1980s and 1990s, when the acronym "MBTI," fully detached from its origins as Katharine and Isabel's brainchild, begins to take on an avid, cultish following. More than just a biography, and more than just a philosophical inquiry, this book narrates how two women's remarkable and uncharted lives prefaced the type indicator's exposure as a mass cultural phenomenon. Only by interlacing the private and the public histories of type can we begin to understand why, and in what forms, personality assessment endures to this day.

. . . .

I will confess that, at many points in writing this book, I wanted it to be a story of feminist triumph. There was a time, right after my son was born, when my initial stance of principled disbelief toward type and its communities began to soften. I experienced this first as a growing sympathy for my historical subjects, Katharine and Isabel. They were, after all, wives and mothers who yearned to transform their daily domestic labors into occasions for creative self-actualization—to make the home into an institution not unlike a psychiatrist's office or a scientist's laboratory, where their work could be taken seriously. I understood that impulse just then. I still do. Then there were the people I spoke with—mostly women, but some men too—who explained to me in no uncertain terms how type had saved their lives. It had rescued them from dead-end jobs and unhappy marriages. It had helped them come to terms with their parents and children. It had given them the courage to accept who they were and what they wanted out of the life that stretched before them, newly pregnant with possibility. Nearly all of them acknowledged that the liberation they felt was mass-produced but that they still felt it intensely and sincerely. I wanted to do justice to these experiences of individual transcendence, even if I found it hard to disentangle them from the dubious and often exploitative social histories of type that I had uncovered along the way. I wanted to tell all sides of the story in a way that was critical but fair and, most of all, disinterested. I did not want to be swayed.

Yet over time the desire to do justice to my subjects modulated into something more intimate, something more urgent. I watched my son grow. I watched him laugh his different laughs. I watched him play. I watched as he started to express his desires for certain things—a toy, a book, a room in the house—over others. I watched as these desires turned into demands, as these demands intensified and hardened into preferences. In short, I watched as his personality developed. Or maybe it just emerged. I could not tell the difference. And as I watched, I realized that the words drumming through my mind were the same words I had vowed to keep at a distance while I was finishing this book, the same words that had gripped my historical subjects almost a hundred years ago and had never let them go. "He's such an extravert," I observed one day to no one in particular, and I did not want to check myself, did not want to take it back. Even if I did not believe what I had just said—at least, not entirely.

When I relayed my slip to my husband, he pointed out that I had started my investigation of the indicator by committing the cardinal sin I had attributed to Katharine and Isabel's system of type: I had assumed that all people who encountered the indicator were either skeptics or true believers and that their type never changed. But people are more various than I had allowed. For there are times when, confused and lacking direction, we speak the language of type to affirm our understanding of ourselves and the people we love, and there are times when we want desperately to guard our individuality from type's sly encroachments, to hold fast to the distinct and irrepressible qualities that make you who you are and me who I am. I started and finished this book at moments of great change in my life—my second son will arrive any day now—and there were moments when, against my prior judgments, I found myself thinking and speaking the words my subjects used with a will to belief that I never thought possible. This book, then, is for the skeptics, the true believers, and everyone in between. Which is to say that this book, reader, is for you: you who cannot, and should not, be typed.

Part One

CHAPTER ONE

The Cosmic Laboratory of Baby Training

Katharine Elizabeth Cook, co-creator of the Myers-Briggs Type Indicator, never had much patience for scientific thought, though she had grown up in the heart of scientific America. She was born on January 3, 1875, in East Lansing, Michigan, on prime midwestern farmland that was home to Michigan Agricultural College, one of the first land grant universities in the United States. It was there that Katharine's father, Albert J. Cook, a distinguished professor of zoology and entomology, became one of the first educators to embrace the most scandalous scientific paradigm of the nineteenth century: evolution. Albert spent his days in the biology classroom, expounding on Charles Darwin's theories of natural selection and the survival of the fittest, while his colleagues, many of them good Baptists, looked on in disbelief. He spent his nights at home with his wife, Mary, a devout Christian, and their two children, Katharine and her older brother, Bert. Mary took no issue with Albert's teaching of evolution, for she was too deeply religious to be troubled by any scientific theory. "God was as real to her as her husband and children," Katharine would later recall of her mother's spiritual imagination. To Mary, Darwin's ideas were neither right nor wrong. They were simply unimportant. Biological evolution may very well have taken place for mankind, differentiating the first hominins from the great apes. But Mary believed in personal evolution—the kind that set "primitive men," as she referred to dark-skinned non-Westerners, apart from enlightened ones. For her, evolution was a matter for the individual soul, not the species.

Skeptical of her father's science and armed with her mother's spirituality, Katharine was, from the beginning, an unusually self-reflective child—a product, she claimed, of the debilitating nearsightedness that dulled her perception of the external world and turned her gaze inward. Thick glasses, knotted hair, a smile so shy it was barely perceptible—this was her uniform through life and she wore it with a perpetual sense of unease. When guests came over to the Cook house for dinner parties, they marveled at Bert, a chattering little monkey, while Katharine, "little Kate," was dismissed as a quiet child, moony, even a little bit stupid. Never mind that she was easily the more industrious of the two. Bert, who would leave for California after he graduated from Michigan Agricultural College in 1893, confessed to his sister that the high sun and the dry winds made him disinclined to do anything but play the occasional game of tennis, hunt, and chase after the "Western Girl," a "beautiful, indispensable darling being," the exact opposite in temperament of his "dear little Kate." Katharine, who, at the age of fourteen, had skipped several grades and enrolled in college alongside Bert, was not one for lazing about in the sun. "Even as a child," she remembered, "my capacity for loyalty and devotion to a goal was pronounced, so that my parents felt proud of what they called my stick-to-itiveness, without in the least understanding the psychology of it."

That stick-to-itiveness, so admired by Albert and Mary, would propel Katharine to the top of her class at Michigan Agricultural College by the time she turned sixteen. There she would experience what she described as her first crisis of faith. She found herself "wrenched and shaken," she lamented in her diary, by how the conflicting beliefs of her father and mother were writ large in a university system that had rapidly sidelined religious instruction for scientific research. Unlike many East Coast colleges, which had been founded to train spiritual leaders, the instructors at Michigan were devoted to the modern laboratory method: an empirical approach to learning in which sod-stained plants and wriggling insects were pinned down and operated on by curious students. "The microscope, the scalpel, the hammer, the test-tube, or the reagent is always at hand to aid in learning what the thing has to reveal," declared the school's president in his annual report of 1892—Katharine's junior year. After a lifetime of Mary's spiritual instruction at home, Katharine never lost her misgivings about giving herself over to the midwestern practicality of the microscope, the scalpel, the hammer, and the test tube. "I think science may lack the data that the soul possesses," she worried to her mother.

To ease her conscience, she sought advice from her elders, both at school and at church. Dissatisfied, she decided to search for an answer through prayer. "Being impersonal and objective, science cannot be expected to bring matters home to us," she concluded in her diary after a tearful day spent kneeling before her Bible, communing with her mother's god. The material world was especially ill-equipped to deal with what both Katharine and her mother identified as the greatest problem of their time, a problem that transcended her father's preoccupation with evolution, sexual reproduction, and even the survival of the human species—the "personal, passionate, subjective, and religious problem of personal salvation."

One had to deal with "the task of the individual," Katharine wrote, "who from his own microscopic beginnings must repeat in one lifetime the adventure of his whole race or go to Hell." She thought that salvation was to be found in cultivating one's personality, which she defined in the oldest, most basic sense of the word: the qualities or capacities of thought that made a person recognizable as a human being and not an animal—a "brute," as she deemed the less civilized orders of men. "We teach a lie when we teach that all men are equal," she wrote. "The lower orders of men are far closer to the higher animals than to the higher orders of men, and we ought to recognize that fact."

Although her tone brooked no argument, for some time she continued to wonder at her inability to love life, her status as a spectator of the present. The Cooks' family doctor prescribed all sorts of small diversions to help her connect with reality: a game of tennis with Bert when he came back home for a visit, an outdoor concert with her parents on a warm summer night, a birthday party with the neighborhood children. But she dismissed his suggestions as a waste of time and energy. She knew that she had to direct herself even deeper inward, not outward, if she were to save her soul in this modern world, a world that seemed to have no use for the soul at all. So she chose instead to dwell in her fantasies and her daydreams, detached from the ebb and flow of life around her, frequently alone.

Then she met Lyman Briggs, and they began to dwell in her dreams together.

. . . .

Lyman Briggs was a farm boy from Assyria, Michigan, whose ancestors had arrived in America on the *Fortune,* the first ship to follow the *Mayflower* to Plymouth Rock. The routines of his childhood would have been familiar to any midwestern pioneer. Every day he and his brother would rise before dawn and feed the chickens and pigs, gather eggs, drive the cows to pasture, and stock the kitchen wood box. When they were done with their household chores, they would walk several miles to the district schoolhouse their grandfather Briggs had built—rumor had it with his own hands—and then to the church he had founded for afternoon prayers. Yet unlike Katharine, who preferred the church pew to the laboratory bench, Lyman felt most at home among the physical materials of the world, treasuring the instruments men had designed to understand the inner and outer workings of nature. At the age of fifteen, Lyman arrived at Michigan Agricultural College. From the moment he saw the great glass cases in the physics laboratory filled with their marvelous apparatuses—the clouded beakers, the silvered coils—he knew he wanted to be a scientist.

At school, he was smart and well-liked and so delicately handsome that Katharine assumed he could have no interest in her. So she was surprised when, on February 14, 1893, she received four Valentine's Day poems drafted in his prim hand: "I write with love as the chief feature / To a co-ed darling creature / Write it full of binding love / Why the spirit did me move / To that pretty little dove / Dear Katharine, My Valentine." Their courtship was appropriately drawn out, and after they graduated from college—she at the top of her class, him a close second—they were married. As a wedding gift, her parents gave Lyman two hundred dollars, earmarked for his doctoral educa-tion at Johns Hopkins, where he was to study physics. For Katharine, there was no expectation that she would continue her education and thus no money to bequeath to her. There was only a carved chest of towels and linens to help her decorate her new home in the outskirts of Washington, D.C., where the new couple would live while Lyman took classes and worked part-time at the Department of Agriculture—a newly established executive agency under the presidency of Grover Cleveland. When Katharine traded the broad fields of Michigan for the railways, alleys, and monuments of the nation's crowding capital, she was just eighteen years old.

Their first child, Isabel McKelvey Briggs, was born in 1897 and greeted with paroxysms of love. Their second, Albert Briggs, named after Katharine's father, was born in 1899. When Isabel was two and Albert two months, Katharine started a diary to document the children's daily activities. She was awestruck by her daughter, who, although only a toddler herself, demonstrated a mature vocabulary and a budding sense of responsibility for her little brother's care. "This morning after bathing the boy and putting him down in his basket to sleep, I asked Sister to stay and take good care of him while I went to the kitchen for a few minutes," she noted in the diary. "Found the baby sleeping peacefully in his basket which was floating in a sea of pillows. Every pillow in the house was there, each one carefully placed where according to the best judgment of a two-year-old it would most effectively protect a baby of two months in case he should suddenly and unexpectedly decide to climb out." Sister—her nickname for Isabel after the Quaker tradition of referring to children as "broth-ers and sisters in Christ"—seemed to her to have an unusually curi-ous and inventive personality. "She is living in the midst of marvels which make of life a volume of mystery tales," wrote Katharine as she watched her daughter play with her dolls, boiling imaginary eggs for them in an imaginary saucepan that she had filled with imaginary water. When the dolls had finished eating, she gave the eggs she had saved to her little brother.

Her diary trailed off later that year, when Albert suddenly, terribly, died in his sleep. Katharine and Lyman were heartbroken, Isabel too young to understand the sorrow that had settled into the house. As the Briggs family mourned, the nineteenth century drew to its close. Buoyed by love for her daughter, extinguished by grief over the loss of her son, Katharine was confronted with her second crisis of faith. "Is life worth living?" she wondered as she approached her twenty-fifth birthday. "Does it mean anything? Is there any point to it? Why live at all? Why beget children who will beget children who will beget more children and keep the tragic life stream going on and on in futile struggle?"

Her existential despair may have seemed hypothetical. It was not. Her son's death had taught her how precious the lives of her children were, how closely their activities had to be regulated if they were to live long enough to cultivate their personalities and ensure their salvation. Under the shadow of death, she recalled the Darwinian education she had once spurned, the techniques of scientific manipulation she had practiced on lesser organisms at Michigan, poking and prodding and recording the behaviors of frogs and earthworms to see what would kill them and what would keep them alive. She wondered if she could learn to apply these same techniques to the problem of human life, both physical and spiritual. Could she conduct daily trials in living that would shape the outer and the inner worlds of the people she loved best? Could she reconcile her quest for personal salvation with the rational methods of the modern world? Could she make her home into a laboratory of personality research, an institution of scientific experimentation to rival Lyman's workshop at Johns Hopkins or her father's classroom at Michigan?

She believed she could. In 1901, after the death of yet another infant, a boy who left the world before she had the chance to baptize him, she began her experiments in personality in earnest with Isabel, her only remaining child. Together, mother and daughter would "seed the garden," as Katharine would later recall, for one of the twentieth century's strangest family businesses: the business of personality typing.

Although many forms of personality assessment retain some trace of their creators' personal preoccupations, the Myers-Briggs Type

Indicator was more intimately attuned to its creators' lives from the start. Katharine was a mother, and as a mother, she believed that children needed two things to mature into "civilized adults": "submission to necessary authority" and the "discipline of ambition," she wrote in her diary. She believed that the mark of civilized adulthood was "specialization." A parent had to direct a child to choose one line of work and pursue it zealously, not for personal fulfillment or financial success, but as a meaningful contribution to society—the kind of good deed that would ensure their salvation. "The architect fathers civilization when buildings are to be erected; actors and musicians father civilization when people require recreation or entertainment; the physician fathers civilization wherever people are ill," she proclaimed. If, as a wife and mother, Katharine could not specialize in something properly professional—if she could not "father civilization" directly—then she could make mothering into the lifeblood of all specialization. She could help children develop the psychological wherewithal to determine what kind of work was best suited to their personalities.

Her efforts would have spectacular repercussions. Half a century later, her daughter, convinced that her mother's ideas about specialization applied just as well to workers as it did to children, would make the same pitch for the Myers-Briggs Type Indicator, the questionnaire she would construct, as a premier "people sorting device."

. . . .

It is a truth seldom acknowledged that, when one conceives a child, one also conceives of that child's personality. What child is exempt from her parents' fantasies, their projections? What parent can ever truly accept the idea of her child as a tabula rasa—a blank slate? It is an idea far easier to swallow in theory than in practice. Or at least it was for the twentieth century's premier behaviorist psychologist, John B. Watson, who, against the objections of angry parents and concerned educators everywhere, claimed that the "unconscious protoplasm" of the infant mind was made of infinitely malleable material. "Give me a dozen healthy infants, well-formed, and my own specified world to bring them up in," Watson challenged readers at the outset of his 1925 book *Behaviorism.* "I'll guarantee to take any one at random and train him to become any type of specialist I might select—doctor, lawyer, artist, merchant-chief and, yes, even beggar-man and thief, regardless of his talents, penchants, tendencies, abilities, vocations, and race of his ancestors." If, on the one hand, there was something liberating about how thoroughly nurture trumped nature in Watson's philosophy of specialization, there was, on the other hand, an element of existential dread. Could one's child grow up to be anyone? Anyone at all?

The age-old question of nature versus nurture, which shadows many of the hopes and fears that preoccupy the parents of young children, was the same question that motivated many of the first behaviorist theories of personality in the United States. In the 1900s, many of these theories were formulated not by men of science but women of childbearing age. The earliest personality primers were written for mothers by mothers at a time when the very concept of motherhood was undergoing a dramatic change. Gone were the overindulgent, sentimental mothers of the Victorian era and their fat, cherubic babes. In their place was a new class of professionalized caregivers: mothers who treated parenting as an occupation—systematic, rational, labor-intensive—rather than an unruly biological impulse. They designed strict regimens of diet, sleep, and exercise for their offspring. They disciplined. They punished. They saw in all the tedious work of motherhood the possibility for freedom and creativity, and they judged those mothers who, through excesses of cooing and coddling, had become slaves to their tiny, whimpering overlords. "There are few sights more pathetic than that of the nervously exhausted, physically weakened mother," wrote Rachel Kent Fitz in her 1906 parenting guide *Problems of Babyhood: Building a Constitution, Forming a Character.* For women like her, the home could function as a domestic institution not unlike the other institutions—schools, corporations, hospitals, federal bureaucracies—in which the study of personality would flourish throughout the twentieth century.

After the deaths of her children, Katharine Cook Briggs was determined to anoint herself a leader among the twentieth century's new class of professional mothers. She cordoned off the living room of her house as a "cosmic laboratory of baby training," a place to do God's work only with greater rigor. There she began to conduct small experiments on Isabel and, once Isabel had outgrown her mother's methods, on the children of neighbors and Lyman's work acquaintances who, impressed by Isabel's behavior and frustrated by their own offspring's whining and tantrums, sought Katharine's advice. There was eight-year-old Jane W. and seven-year-old Eleanor G., as well as Eleanor's younger sisters, Lois, age three, and Pauline, age two. There was Donald A., Roger P., and Robert C.—all two years old, all the sons of military bureaucrats whom Katharine had befriended through her husband's circle of influence in Washington, D.C. There was little Louis Jr., just shy of six months and barely able to hold his head steady. These children and a dozen or so more were Katharine's first test subjects, and they held the answers to her crisis of faith. They helped transform her home from a private domicile into a quasi-public space where she could lavish upon the children "the highest order of intellectual education"—a phrase she borrowed from one of her favorite writers, utilitarian philosopher John Stuart Mill, who was himself the product of a labor-intensive regime of home training.

She was never extravagant in her methods, although others certainly were. The early days of American child study—or "child psyching," as skeptics called it—were rife with extremists both inside and outside the home. Renowned psychologists at Harvard and Stanford hypnotized their own children, muttered at them in Latin and ancient Greek to plant the seeds of philological genius in their drowsing minds. Private schools charged parents exorbitant fees to train their children as Pavlov had trained his mutts, conditioning them to respond with good behavior to bells and whistles and gongs. "For your child, we guarantee a loveable personality!" one school advertised. "Not only psychologists, but otherwise intelligent people, quickly become consummate jackasses when they are asked to develop a child's character," observed Donald A. Laird, the director of the Colgate Psychological Laboratory, in an article that appeared in the Briggs family's daily newspaper, the *Sunday Star*. Laird, who openly mocked the idea that one could shape a child's personality at all, proudly subscribed to the school of "neglect and hard knocks from the real world." He held up his own son as an example of the virtues of laissez-faire parenting. "He is still out of jail, is in his right mind, has an appetite, knows enough to come in out of the rain, and still lifts his hat to the ladies."

Katharine, who clipped Laird's article from the *Sunday Star* with anger, bristled at his suggestion that parents could simply let their children be. "As if every child were not, because of the very nature of the situation, an experiment from the moment of birth!" she wrote. "As if everything done for him or left undone, from feeding formula to discipline, were not an experiment, every parent an experimenter, and his home an experimental station!" Absent the microscopes and plants of her formal education, Katharine's home laboratory was nevertheless designed to see what kinds of growing conditions might permit her to control the little lives that, as she had recently discovered, were not hers to control at all. When Isabel was a toddler, she began with "No! No!" drills. Katharine would place her child in front of a bright, tempting object—a glass bowl, a flickering flame—and chant "No! No!" when the child would try to touch it. If Isabel reached too close and too fast, as most toddlers are wont to do, Katharine would slap her hands or spank her with vigor to reinforce the rule. "No! No!" drills were followed by "Come here!" drills, "Don't touch!" drills, and "Just touch!" drills, which mother and daughter repeated nearly every day, of every year, until Isabel turned five.

She rewarded Isabel's obedience with stories. Katharine animated household objects so that they whispered to Isabel of their origins. There were the tables and chairs that had begun their lives in faraway forests, only to end up in the Briggs family kitchen; the rugs Isabel toddled upon that unspooled their histories as silken threads, visitors from the Far East. She conjured up imaginary kittens and sheep to keep her daughter company after her siblings' deaths, and she spent hours watching Isabel shear wool from the air. When Isabel cut her finger, her mother wrote her a story called "The Blood Myth" to explain how blood clotted. Myth begat mythology. When Isabel shivered, there was "The Fire Myth" to teach her how humans regulated their body temperatures, and once, when her daughter did not think to come in from the rain, "The Dew Myth" to trace the science of the raindrops that clung to her hands and to her hair and to the spiderwebs that stretched in the corner of the Briggses' garden fence. "Imagination is now our favorite plaything," Katharine wrote. "There is nothing we cannot pluck from the vines in our wallpaper."

It was, by all measures, an extraordinary childhood, made even more extraordinary by how carefully the relationship between mother and daughter was calibrated and controlled. From 1901 to 1910, Katharine recorded Isabel's responses to her drills and stories in a notebook titled "The Diary of an Obedience-Curiosity Mother." Obedience and curiosity were the most important traits one could instill in a child, Katharine believed, though it never occurred to her that they were diametrically opposed to each other. Demanding obedience to authority may have kept a child in line, but it also stifled her curiosity, her sense of mischief and play. When the two forces came into conflict, as they often did in Isabel's favorite storybook, Rudyard Kipling's

Isabel, five years old, clings to Katharine's neck. While many mother-and-child portraits from the 1900s feature mothers gazing into their children's eyes or holding hands, Katharine and Isabel look straight into the camera: Katharine with pride; Isabel with docility and incomprehension.

The Jungle Book, Katharine, like Kipling, urged her daughter to err on the side of authority. "Now these are the Laws of the Jungle, and many and mighty are they," she read to her daughter from Kipling's poem "The Law of the Jungle." "But the head and the hoof of the Law and the haunch and the hump is—Obey!"

Her child was not the only person from whom she expected obedience. To the mothers of her other test subjects, she sent a monthly questionnaire to gauge how her methods had affected their children's personalities. "Any mother who believes in and uses the Obedience-Curiosity idea in the training of her babies can make her work of permanent value to other mothers by recording her results," she implored them. "Each mother is urged to make her report frank, impartial, and accurate, bringing out her successes, her difficulties, and the personality of her child." Most of the questions she posed required that her subjects choose from one of only two possible answers, (a) or (b). It was her first forced-choice questionnaire and a precursor to the type indicator to which she would lend her name decades later.

1. Is he placid or intense?
2. Is he calm or impulsive?
3. Is he markedly observant and imitative or imaginative and original?
4. Does he show timidity or fear or is he markedly confident?
5. Is he markedly talkative or quiet?
6. Is he affectionate or reserved?
7. Is he venturesome or cautious?
8. Is he mischievous or careful?
9. Has he any tendency to self-consciousness?
10. Does he try to "show off?"

She had no tolerance for mothers who inflated their children's sense of self-importance. Nor could she abide mothers who, claiming an excess of maternal feeling, refused to spank or slap their children as she had spanked and slapped Isabel. "The futile, unauthoritative mother," she declared, "is simply ridiculous." When one mother recoiled from her suggestion that she spank her son Davy when he ran out of her arms and into the street—"I will never use physical violence on my child," she vowed, her voice trembling with indignation—Katharine responded with cool antipathy. "Nonsense," she said to the woman. "You use physical violence on your child every day of his life. You used physical violence just now when you picked him up and brought him kicking and screaming out of the street. You use physical violence every time you wash his face, clean his nose, or give him a dose of medicine. For a baby of his age a spanking is medicine. It's the only way to get across to him certain vitally important truths."

For Katharine, emotional women like Davy's mother had obstructed the progress of society with their unwarranted praise, their excessive fawning over their average or below-average children. The ultimate purpose of baby training, she believed, was first to identify "slow" children whose emotional and intellectual development lagged their peers and help them catch up, and then to transform the "average" children into high-functioning adults, each one capable of specializing in a profession based on his personality. Otherwise these children would grow up into adults with no purpose in the world. "Multitudes of people are utterly worthless or worse than worthless, having no just claims whatsoever upon the civilization which they burden with the dead weight of their existence," she wrote in "The Diary of an Obedience-Curiosity Mother." "This is a sound, incontrovertible judgement, which has to be shunned, because our feeling for the 'underprivileged' is so strong that such truths can hardly be mentioned. Our feeling revolts against it."

In Katharine's quest for social perfectibility through child-rearing, we can hear echoes of the Darwinian paradigm she had absorbed from her father, only now with a dark, utilitarian twist. In the first decades of the twentieth century, Katharine was not the only thinker who believed that a society's path to perfectibility depended on modifying its offspring's personalities so that only the strongest, fittest individuals would thrive. In his best-selling textbook from 1914, *The Eugenic Marriage: A Personal Guide to the New Science of Better Living and Better Babies,* Dr. William Grant Hague explained that "eugenics, simply defined, means 'better babies.' " Better babies meant better men, which, in turn, meant a better nation, poised to assert its superiority in a rapidly changing world. For Hague and other eugenicists, promoting strong personality traits and weeding out weak ones was a crucial reproductive ideology—a way to accelerate natural selection through selective breeding. One could not change a child's personality even "one particle after conception took place," Hague wrote. Whatever "innate character" the father or mother possessed was "transmitted to the child at the instant of conception and that innate legacy constitutes the working instrument of the child for all time."

Katharine was sympathetic to Hague's eugenic imagination. The child's personality—her "working instrument," as Hague called it— may have been fixed at the time of birth, but that was no reason it could not be honed, made slick and sharp by good parenting so that it might cut down the "primitive mediocrity" of the modern era. But her philosophy of specialization also offered a rationale by which parents could accept and cultivate their children's preferences or abilities rather than attempt to change them, a balm for a child struggling with a task that did not come naturally to him, paralyzed by failure or by choice. For every child had innate preferences, just as every child had "a right hand and a left hand, both of which he uses constantly, but one of which he uses more handily than the other, feeling more secure in the use of it," Katharine wrote. (Inspired by her mother's writings, Isabel would later use right- and left-handedness as her default metaphor for explaining the notion of personality preferences without judgment.) The consolation parents could derive from Katharine's philosophy of specialization was one way for her to temper her frequently brutal judgments of her young subjects.

. . . .

Isabel Briggs did not grow up to be a genius, at least not according to her mother's assessment of her child's abilities. A genius was someone whose talents were concentrated on one activity, like baby Mozart plunking away at his piano or baby Einstein scribbling at his figures. Isabel, by contrast, grew into a generally competent child, a well-rounded and high-achieving specimen. By two, she spoke in full sentences. She read from the Bible at five. When she turned ten in 1907, she begged Lyman to explain to her the physical properties of the sun and the stars. "My child is not a genius," Katharine insisted time and again. She was merely obedient and curious. Her personality may not have been original—how could it be when it had been programmed from the beginning?—but it was the ideal product of her mother's experimental machinery.

She excelled at everything her mother directed her to try. She was her piano teacher's star pupil, even though her mother decreed her ear "only ordinarily accurate." She spent hours interrogating her father about his love of plants and animals, delighting him with her eagerness to discuss the problems of science "as man to man." At twelve, she displayed a real talent for stenography; at thirteen, for metal making. She picked up German, French, and Latin on her own, with no apparent difficulty, and she impressed the local high school's English department with her knack for fiction writing, publishing six short stories in local magazines by the age of sixteen. Katharine did not see her daughter's lack of specialization as a failure but as proof of the pliability her obedience-curiosity training had wrought. "Like everyone else who has ever worked intimately with her, I feel that my daughter would do very well to specialize in my line," she wrote in a diary entry tinged with pride and envy. "What a housekeeper that child would make!"

She was in and out of school according to Katharine's whims. "I made a convenience of school, sending her just enough to satisfy her, the teachers, and myself that she didn't need it," Katharine wrote. Skeptical of Progressive Era reforms in mass education and the blighted "sheep" produced by a rapidly democratizing public-school system, Katharine kept Isabel at home. There, with little help from anyone other than her mother, she seemed to thrive. "My good primitive proceeded to educate and civilize herself," Katharine recorded. As rumors of Isabel's unconventional education pricked the ears of envious and admiring neighbor mothers, even more started calling upon Katharine to ask her for advice.

"I want you to tell me all about your wonderful little girl," demanded one woman who showed up unannounced on the Briggs family's doorstep. "Is it true that she has had to spend only two months in each grade?"

"I didn't believe half the stories about her until I saw her on the streetcar the other day," confessed another when she ran into Katharine on the street. "We discussed Kipling and Scott all the way home, and now I am ready to believe anything."

It was not long before news of Isabel's accomplishments spread beyond the neighborhood. One spring night in 1910, several months shy of Isabel's thirteenth birthday, Katharine and Lyman had Lyman's old friend Ray Stannard Baker and his wife, Jessie, over for dinner. Although he had also graduated from Michigan Agricultural College, Baker had long since abandoned the silence and sterility of the laboratory to get his hands dirty on the front lines of investigative journalism. As a staff writer at *McClure's Magazine,* he had made his reputation as one of the nation's fiercest crusaders for social justice—a "muckraker," Teddy Roosevelt would sneer—and now, along with his fellow muckrakers Ida Tarbell and Lincoln Steffens, he had purchased *American Magazine,* a culture and lifestyle publication that had great need for new, outspoken columnists. Upon meeting Isabel and hearing Katharine expound on her theories of baby training, he felt inspired to offer her a steady job. "It occurs to me that you might be willing to give us some idea of your methods in training Isabel," he wrote to Katharine. "It might give an added impressiveness to this line of thought." While the field of child study had no shortage of men opining on maternal responsibilities and child psychology, what it lacked, and what Baker knew would sell magazine subscriptions, was a young mother's uncompromising voice.

The evening with the Bakers marked the start of Katharine's career as one of America's most controversial sources of parenting advice. Using the observations that she had amassed in "The Diary of an Obedience-Curiosity Mother," she presented Isabel's personality as her "experiment in education," and while she acknowledged that one could not "prove scientific facts with a single experiment," one could "learn much, and point the way to further experimentation." In the spirit of further experimentation, she provided readers of her first column with a checklist for transforming any child into an obedient and curious one:

1. Be consistent and persistent.
2. Punish only one thing—the disobedient spirit, as manifested by direct face to face disobedience and tantrums.
3. Punish only once.
4. Punish sufficiently.
5. Never threaten or warn of punishment. To warn a child is to teach him that prompt obedience is unnecessary.
6. Don't talk too much.
7. Make only such commands as are worth enforcing.
8. Reward the child with exploration and enjoyment.

There was always the problem of public exposure. Child-rearing was a hotly contested issue, and Katharine's methods, while nowhere near as unorthodox as hypnosis or reflex training, were still quite unusual for her time. She recalled a neighbor of hers who, upon hearing Isabel read aloud from *Pilgrim's Progress* at the age of five, had warned Katharine that her child might die of brain fever in her early teens or else become neurotic and stupid as she approached maturity. "You're making a terrible mistake!" her neighbor had cried. "You simply shouldn't allow her to be so precocious." (The woman's own child, a girl named Mary, had failed first grade. She would later appear in Katharine's article "Ordinary Theodore and Stupid Mary.") Katharine feared for her child. She worried that her critics would seek out her remarkable girl and assail her with their scorn, borne of their misunderstanding and envy. It was Baker's idea to cloak both mother and daughter with pseudonyms. Isabel was called "Suzanne," while Katharine would become known to mothers across the nation as "Elizabeth Childe—the mother of Suzanne."

Over the course of a decade, her career as the mother of Suzanne netted her $1,230—this at a time when women were almost never paid to write—and bylines in *American Magazine,* the *Ladies' Home Journal, Woman's Home Companion,* and *The Outlook.* Her output was prolific. "The Diary of an Obedience-Curiosity Mother" contained "such good bits," according to Edward Bok, editor of the *Ladies' Home Journal,* that every major lifestyle magazine in the country demanded excerpts from it. "A Mother's Excellent Platform," the titles of these excerpts read. "The Woman Who Feels 'Tied Up,'" "What the Mother Leaves Out," "When We Punish a Child," "Why I Find Children Slow in Their School Work," "The Mental Vision of the School Child." And, in December 1914, there was on the cover of *Woman's Home Companion* an article with the headline "The Case for the Homemaker," which begged readers to acknowledge the women who, like Katharine, did the important, if largely invisible, work of raising children. "The women who count most of all, who are really doing the things worthwhile for the world's progress, are a quiet lot," she wrote. "Go to any public school, visit any room, and ask the teacher to introduce a child who is well cared for; who is polite; who is considerate of others. Go home with that child and meet one of the women who counts, who really counts."

. . . .

When did she stop counting? In September 1915, when Isabel left for Swarthmore College in Pennsylvania, over a hundred miles away from her mother's daily ministrations. "Suzanne, my only child, went to college last September, and so the educational experiment which for eighteen years has been the chief interest of my life has come to an end," wrote Elizabeth Childe in the final article she ever published, a eulogy to the life and the career she had created as the mother of Suzanne. The house grew quiet. Lyman was at work from morning to night, and while between husband and wife there remained an indistinct feeling of fondness, he asked little of her, and she demanded nothing from him in return. "Mine is just the old, old story of the mother whose life begins to crumble when the children grow up and don't need her—when she must choose between releasing them from their childhood or becoming the 'terrible mother' and poisoning their lives," she wrote. She knew the right choice to make. She gravitated to the wrong one.

Yet her reluctance to free Isabel from her childhood did not make Katharine a "terrible mother." Nor did it poison her daughter's life. The consequences were further reaching than whatever private misfortunes she imagined. Over the next two decades, Katharine would transform Isabel from an unwitting laboratory subject into a dedicated collaborator, an intimate ally in her pursuit of a better, more specialized social order. Soon the notion of "releasing" Isabel would seem like an impossibility, especially once mother and daughter were bound together, forever, by the Myers-Briggs trademark.

CHAPTER TWO

Women's Work

According to official school records, Isabel began her freshman year at Swarthmore College as "Isabel McKelvey Briggs" and graduated at the top of her class as "Mrs. Clarence Gates Myers." Her change of name was not unusual. Plenty of women happened to stumble onto the men they would marry while away at school, and most, if not all of them, took their husband's last name. But Mr. Clarence Gates Myers—Chief, to all who knew him— was not her only option in the years she lived beyond her mother's reach, attempting to reconcile the peculiarities of her childhood education with the personal and professional demands of adulthood. "College of course will be the test of our individual training," Katharine warned her daughter as Isabel boarded the train for Swarthmore at Washington, D.C.'s Union Station. She left her mother standing on the railway platform, eyes dry, impassive, her face obscured every now and again by the crowd's raucous waves goodbye.

For some time, Isabel believed she was free from her mother's obedience-curiosity training. She was no longer quizzed on the books she read, no longer forced to recite passages from the Bible for the expectant neighbors, no longer cloistered from children her own age like a princess in an impenetrable tower. And, of course, there were boys. High school had ended for Isabel in June 1915, and with it that summer came the beginning of five affairs. Each boy was impermanent enough to warrant only a single identifying initial in her diary: "A," "C," "F," "H," and "J." They were types, these men were, and while she had them in her thrall she confessed that she couldn't fall in love with any of them "in this world or the next." "F" was the religious type; "B" the British type; "H" the temperamental type. "J" was nondescript, a bore, and "C" was the type of man you liked well enough but who liked you more. The asymmetry of his affections made her feel guilty, at least until college started with its infinite distractions and possibilities, and then none of them mattered as anything but the wrong type of man for her. When she looked back at her first type system, designed to organize her childish affections, it was hard to imagine that these men had been real to her once.

But Chief was real, a farm boy from Iowa who had never heard of Swarthmore College until he had won a scholarship to attend it. He was tall and redheaded and rather extraordinary looking, at least according to the photographs of him that remain, which emphasize the Nordic cast of his features, his dark, unrelenting eyes. The night Isabel met him was an otherwise tiresome night taken up by a compulsory college mixer, a freshman-junior dance. She was a freshman, he a junior. He asked her to dance and dance they did, drifting through the hours until the other couples dispersed and the musicians put down their instruments and Isabel went home to write about him in her diary. She called him "Myers," and she thanked God first for his height—all six feet four inches of it—then for his dancing abilities, and finally for his "realness." "I can talk to him about real things, not kidding," she wrote. They argued about many things, including whether women were inherently fickle, governed by their feelings. She did not know it, but he had a girl back home in Iowa who loved him, a girl he was destined now to disappoint. He did not know it, but for the next year, Isabel would fill up the rest of her diary with his name—Chief, Chief, Chief—repeating over and over again until she ran out of pages.

What makes a person more than just a type—an initial on a page, a four-letter acronym? Why do we write some names in our notebooks, pressing them hard into every line on every sheet, while others we never bother to write at all? These questions worried Katharine, who, upon visiting her daughter at school in the fall of 1916, stressed to Isabel that the type of man she wanted her to marry would have "strength" and "control" and an uncompromising "moral code." Isabel, in turn, confessed to her mother that she wanted someone bigger and stronger than her, someone who wouldn't seem like "a nice little boy all the time." But how could one reconcile real people to either mother's or daughter's generic descriptions of human beings? Over the years, this question would resurface, for the two women, as one of the greatest mysteries of both personality type and love: the ways in which one's world, and the people who wandered in and out of it, could morph from individuals to representations and back again, each helping to make sense of the other. At any time, a person could materialize before their eyes as a singular human being, worthy of name, or just a string of descriptors; in 1915, the hotheaded type ("H"), the British type ("B"), the religious type ("F"); later, the extravert (E), the introvert (I), the thinker (T), the feeler (F). Invariably, what one referred to as personality seemed to emerge in the subtle quiver, the almost imperceptible sway, between these two ways of understanding the self and others.

"We know not the complexities of personality, the smoldering emotional fires, the other facets of the character-polyhedron, the resources of the subliminal region." These were the words of pragmatist philosopher William James writing in *The Varieties of Religious Experience* (1902), the first book that Chief gave to Isabel when they started dating and the first book that Katharine tried to dissuade her from reading. Until Isabel left for college, her daughter's literary education was something Katharine had managed with great care. In addition to the Bible and *The Jungle Book,* she had allowed Isabel to read *The Swiss Family Robinson, The Life of Hernando Cortes,* and Washington Irving's *Sketch Book,* which Isabel decreed "the stupidest book" she had ever read. "At fourteen, she knew all that I knew and could find out," Katharine wrote of her child's education, which she had extended to include matters more delicate than nineteenth-century sea tours and shipwrecks. "We discussed marriage and its possibilities and duties exhaustively. She was interested in men from the women's logical point of view. What kind of husband and father would he make? It made her critical of men and boys, but I feel safer about her than if she were merely judging them by their clothes or their dancing or their particular 'line' of conversation. I can't quite imagine her falling in love with an undesirable man."

For Isabel Briggs, handsome, clever, and rich, with a comfortable home and a happy disposition, the possibility that she might disappoint her mother was almost unthinkable. But Katharine's daughter did, in fact, fall in love with a man based on his height and his dancing and his "particular 'line' of conversation." Yet none of this was as threatening to Katharine as the ways in which Chief promised to undo her eighteen-year experiment in obedience and curiosity with his modern literature about personality. There was a sense in which a man's undesirable book promised a far more subversive undertaking than a man's undesirable advance, and William James's *The Varieties of Religious Experience* was, from Katharine's perspective, utterly undesirable. James argued that religion was "the feelings, acts, and experiences of individual men in their solitude, so far as they apprehend themselves to stand in relation to whatever they may consider the divine." In his view, every person, by virtue of her mysterious inner world—her personality—could summon up a realm of religious experience that had no traffic with religious institutions (like the neighborhood church), religious texts (like the Good Book), or religious types (like the obedient child). The emphasis on solitude and self-apprehension, the valorization of individual subjectivity over social typologies represented a stunning retreat from Katharine's thinking about the relationship between personality, specialization, and salvation. For James, an individual's personality was the source, not the product, of her religious experience.

Katharine had raised her child to believe the opposite in her cosmic laboratory of baby training, where obedience, especially to one's mother and father, was one of the pillars of growing up as a good Christian type and a productive member of society. "We are no longer a Christian nation," she lamented after she had snatched *The Varieties of Religious Experience* from Isabel's hands. "In discarding Christian values, the very substance of the old religion, we have discarded not only the Fatherhood of God, but with it the American way of life," she cautioned. Reinstituting the American way of life meant striking the right balance between the individual's personality in all its strangeness and singularity and the demands of a larger spiritual and social order.

Still, her daughter must have cut a pretty picture reading James's forbidden book—fingering the fresh-cut pages with anticipation, pulling strands of curly auburn hair from her face, alert to her mother's approaching footsteps. Whatever Isabel might have thought of it, *The Varieties of Religious Experience* remained a sticking point between Katharine and Chief, whom she reprimanded when they first met for giving her daughter the book. He responded with the first of many irritated remarks he would lob at his future mother-in-law. "Your attempt to preserve the literary innocence of your precocious infant reminds me of an attempt I once made to lock up my brother in our barn," he told her in a half-folksy, half-snarky tone she would soon come to know well. "I slammed the door, locked it, drove some nails into the casting, and rolled a couple of barrels up against it, and when I went around the corner to find more barricading materials, I found him sitting on the ground making a kite, quite unconscious of all my efforts." His prophecy to Katharine, that soon she would fade into the background of her daughter's life, was shocking enough for Katharine to erase Isabel and Chief's entire courtship in the letters she would later write to their two children—her grandchildren. "Your mother grew up and went away to college, and then there was a world war and she married her soldier, you know," she summarized, leaping across the grim years between 1915 and the early 1920s, when Chief would enlist in the United States Air Force and Isabel would graduate from Swarthmore and make a life for herself as his wife.

When Katharine's cosmic laboratory was displaced by another domestic institution—the institution of marriage—it added variables to her homegrown experiment that she could neither control nor accept with equanimity. There was a man whose ideas she did not sanction, a daughter newly susceptible to love's bad influences. Perhaps romantic love, and not college, was the real test of her training as a mother. What happened when two people as different as Isabel and Chief collided, threatening to unmake their past selves to make a shared future? How to minimize the damage that would inevitably

WOMEN'S WORK | 25

accrue? If people could specialize along professional lines, then they could surely specialize along romantic ones; each person could play a distinct role in a relationship, preserving his or her individuality while strengthening the union. The trick was to marry someone whose differences complemented you, whose type resonated with yours. ("People with complementary Myers-Briggs personalities get along best," echoes Project Evolove, a dating site that derives its matchmaking algorithm from Katharine and Isabel's type theory.) Marriage, Isabel would later tell Katharine, was a "domestic typology laboratory." The intimate experiments that took place within its confines were as crucial to the development of the Myers-Briggs Type Indicator as her mother's baby training—and sometimes the stakes were even higher.

. . . .

What changed for Isabel in the years when her personality enjoyed freer rein? For the first time in her life, she wanted to have fun, to go wild, to "shake things up," she wrote in her diary during her summer of love. Of course, she was not far enough removed from her mother's influence to really and truly unbridle herself. She remained as competent and as studious as her mother had trained her to be, although every now and again she staged small acts of resistance to her upbringing. At the end of her freshman year in 1916, she won the Anson Lapham Scholarship, a two-hundred-dollar prize awarded to the student with the best examination results. She came in second in the freshman gym contest, a testament to her agility in jumping through hoops and somersaulting over the horse. Whooping, she landed on her feet. It was very unladylike—no doubt her mother would have disapproved. In her sophomore year, she joined the Swarthmore comedy troupe and was cast in a skit that mocked the bad food service at the local church. She dressed up as a piece of lettuce. "Lettuce pray," she quipped, feeling lucky that her mother was not there to witness such sacrilege. She was sympathetic to the European communists—her mother would have had her committed—and after the Russian Revolution in March 1917, she gave a speech to her classmates on May Day entitled "Industrial Preparedness." "For the greatest efficiency," she argued, "the great industrial army of the United States must have proper food and shelter, and decent hours. The government must conserve both its natural and its human resources, and particularly realize the limitations on the physical powers of men." Chief, a leftist himself, watched from the wings and smiled at her conviction. Later that year, he escorted her to the May Day dance. Holding hands, they circled each other tightly, weaving a net of orange, red, blue, and green streamers above them.

When Katharine first met Chief, her objections to him were predictable ones. Her child was too young to love seriously. Men were not to be trusted, especially this man. In addition to his dubious taste in reading material, he had displayed a typical adolescent male's "plays of doubt." She confronted Chief about these "doubts" in a lacerating letter that warned him to stay away from the child whose life, she believed, was still hers to control. She did not yet ground her reservations in Myers-Briggs type theory—that would come some years later—but she felt that between Chief and Isabel there could be only dissatisfaction. And she knew, as only a mother could, that she would be doing her child a great disservice if she allowed her to become "Mrs. Clarence Gates Myers" before Isabel had achieved any of the marvelous things she had trained her to accomplish.

A weaker man than he might have been deterred by Katharine's warnings. But Chief's response demonstrated emotional savviness of the highest order. He wrote back to Katharine and invoked a language that he knew she alone would appreciate: the language of scientific experimentation as it applied to human relationships. "Isabel seems to stand the test of all the uncomplimentary criticism I can mass, in my own mind, against her," he concluded. "She has character, personality, brains, imagination (exact, piercing, subtle—yet unromantic, and very real and practical). She's not an ethereal dream creature, but a very real and useful person. It is impossible to give any adequate summary of my impression of her, except to say that I've weighed her in the most brutal of scales, applied the acid test so to speak—as far as is possible in ordinary human relations—and find in her a most unusual and lovable girl."

To some, this profession of love would have seemed cold, exacting. To Katharine, it was wonderfully, reassuringly cerebral, and while it did not allay all her doubts, she gave Chief permission to pin her daughter as a sign of their commitment to each other. His fraternity pin, imitation gold inlaid with cheap gems, was set aside for the occasion. In a giddy letter from Isabel written toward the end of her sophomore year, Katharine would learn that she fixed the pin to her "undermost underthings" by day and, by night, when she undressed and thought about Chief's arms wrapped around her arms, his lips on her lips, she would let the pin's jeweled edges rest on her naked body. Katharine was shocked but also relieved. Even though their relationship was strained by distance and defiance, between mother and daughter there were no secrets.

They were engaged on April 2, 1917, the same day President Woodrow Wilson convened an emergency session of Congress to advise the United States to declare war on Germany. Already World War I had savaged Europe. Millions lay dead in the trenches. More were starving on the streets. Isabel felt it was not the appropriate time to flash rings or to plan parties. Better to stay guarded, to wait and see whether the draft would usher in the possibility of a long and dreaded separation. In Katharine's youth, secret engagements were still scandalous affairs. Chafed by her daughter's breach of propriety in refusing to make the engagement public, she sent Isabel the following letter and, since old habits die hard, ordered her to commit it to memory: "It is the PRIVILEGE of parents of grown children to make suggestions; and it is the DUTY of the children to give serious consideration to these suggestions. It is the PRIVILEGE of grown children to make their own decisions; and it is the DUTY of the parents to respect and acquiesce in these decisions." Isabel, now a junior in college, was still as unaccustomed to making her own decisions as she was to incurring her mother's criticism. She deferred to Chief. He had graduated from Swarthmore in the spring and was idling about town, waiting to see what the draft would bring. Would he go to war? He told Isabel that he longed to hurl his 180 pounds of "bulk" at the "half-human stuff" of the German army. Or would he avoid the draft and start law school at the University of Pennsylvania, his studies funded by a loan he had accepted from Katharine and Lyman? He was appreciative about receiving such a large sum of money from his future in-laws, but he refused to pay his debts to Katharine by allowing her to meddle in his relationship with her daughter. "The fact that your precious has not been the dutiful child she usually is, that fact, I say is *me,*" he boasted to her. Shortly thereafter, he registered as an army aviation officer and left Swarthmore for flight training school in Dallas, Texas.

They were married on June 17, 1918, the same month the Spanish flu quietly killed more soldiers than the war itself and the Germans planned their final offense into Allied territories. He was in uniform. She wore a new dress, dark blue and pleated with a wide, open collar, one hand holding a bouquet of wildflowers tied with a stray piece of tulle—something left over from her childhood perhaps or borrowed from her mother's chest. "Isabel Briggs, who was slated to hold various important offices this year, was married to Clarence G. Myers," announced the Swarthmore student newspaper, *The Phoenix.* The ceremony took place in the parlor of the Briggses' family home, the same parlor that, not so long ago, Katharine had filled with myths of fire, blood, and rain while recording every detail of her daughter's life. In the same home where she had once discussed marriage's duties and responsibilities with her daughter, she wrote a letter to her son-in-law about "the most intimate of relations," the carnal act that made people "truly married." She urged him to make love to her daughter that very evening, on the overnight train they would take from Washington, D.C., to Memphis, Tennessee, where the couple were to spend the summer. There Chief would begin his training as a bomber pilot at the flight camp twenty miles outside the city. It was a short drive from the boardinghouse where Isabel would live while she looked for a summer job.

If inclined to historical thinking, we could trace the earliest stirrings of the Myers-Briggs Type Indicator to this boardinghouse in Memphis during the summer of 1918. It was in this house that Isabel woke up every morning, fixed her hair, ate a modest breakfast, and made her daily pilgrimages to the United States Employment Agency and the Girl's Club, the organizations she cleaved to so that she might find a job that best fit her needs—twelve dollars a week to cover rent and basic living expenses—and her desires, which were harder to calculate. She raised the problem of specialization in a letter to her mother. "What are the right things for me?" she wondered, debating whether to take a job as a typist at the Fischer Lime and Cement Company. Her instinctive answer was "being my man's helpmeet," but Chief had encouraged her to pursue her own passions, to seek happiness independent of his happiness. Although her husband's beliefs were unusually progressive for the time, Isabel was less certain that she should be—or that she wanted to be—anything more than a good wife and mother to the six children she planned to have: three boys and three girls whose due dates she plotted assiduously in her diary. "I think that under the spur of necessity a woman *can* do a man's work as well as *he can*. But I'm perfectly sure it takes more out of her," she reasoned, her certainty inoculating her from the patent sexism of her assumptions. "And it's a waste of *life* to spend yourself on work that someone else can do at less cost," she continued. "I'm sure that men and women are made differently, with different gifts and different kinds of strengths, and it ought to be that there is just as much woman's work as there is man's work. There ought to be some highly intelligent division of labor that can be worked out, so everybody works, but not at the wrong things." The idea of working at the right things would emerge as a mantra for the Myers-Briggs Type Indicator and its promise that it could match workers to the jobs that were best suited to their "different gifts." (In a nod to her summer in Memphis, Isabel later titled her first and only book about the Myers-Briggs Type Indicator *Gifts Differing*.) But it started out as a mantra for marriage—a way of figuring out what specialized tasks men and women were best suited to perform in the business of romance.

Here was a potentially radical insight buried under the weight of historical circumstance. It was true that men's work—the work performed outside of the home—often did take more out of a woman than a man. This was not because men and women were made differently but because the married women whom Isabel observed in the summer of 1918, toiling away in Memphis's new grocery stores and sawmills and factories while their husbands were fighting in the trenches overseas, could not simply stop working when they came home, exhausted, at night. There was still dinner to cook, still dishes to wash, still kitchens to tidy up, and, for many, still children to feed and bathe and put to bed. By the end of the summer, Isabel was one of the nation's eight million married women who now worked outside her home, and she prided herself on her ability to juggle the different varieties of physical and emotional labor that she performed. On Friday afternoons when she finished her week at the cement company, she rushed to see Chief at flight camp, where she spent the weekend entertaining her husband and his army buddies with all the charm she could muster. It was tiring work, but she persisted in it until the end of the summer, when she returned to Swarthmore to start her senior year. "Though she came back to us with a new name, she proves to be still the same old Isabel," reported *The Phoenix*. "She told us how she had been very much attached to the army during the summer, and had seen the work of amusing the soldiers from their point of view. She told us one of the hardest things in the world was to amuse a soldier who had nothing to do, and surely, she should know. 'If we can keep them smiling,' she concluded, 'it's worth every last dollar we've got.'"

To her eager classmates, Isabel presented a smile as a commodity: a good that could be manufactured, bought, and sold. By this logic, her personality—the raw material that went into eliciting smiles from soldiers—was an asset. It was an investment, something worth cultivating. When she graduated from college in June 1919, the same month that her mother's home state of Michigan made history as the first state to grant women full suffrage, she wondered how she could continue to improve herself now that she had exhausted the offerings of higher education. She and Chief moved to Philadelphia so that he could start law school, and on cool mornings in September and October, after her husband had left for class, she cleared the breakfast table, put on her workday outfit—a dark hat wreathed by white chiffon ribbons, a clean blouse, a loose belted coat—and rode her bicycle for hours throughout the city and its surrounding fields, wondering how best to occupy the time that remained until he came home. On weekdays, she quizzed Chief on tort law and helped him type up his papers. On weekends, they taught Sunday school together at the Unitarian Church of Germantown and talked politics.

Much to Katharine's horror, law school had turned Chief into a more vociferous socialist just in time for the victory of Vladimir Lenin's Red Army and the Red Scare of 1919–1920. He believed that the social good was "infinitely more desirable" than any individual's desires or plans, he told his mother-in-law, rebuffing her philosophy of specialization and its overly simplistic separation of the world into "primitive" and "enlightened" people. "There should be something more than just equality of opportunity for the clever and the unclever—lest the clever succeed in hogging the whole earth," he wrote, sounding ever more like Eugene Debs, leader of the Socialist Party of America. In his free time, Chief wrote philosophical tracts with titles like "Nationalized America," "Industrial Democracy," "Labor and the New Social Order," and "Lincoln or Lenin," which he delivered to social clubs around the rapidly industrializing city of Philadelphia.

But Chief's politics no longer appealed to his wife, who now worried about having enough money to support their six hypothetical children. She expressed to him her mature belief that social and political improvement originated with exceptional and enlightened individuals, not with a revolution in the means of production. "Professors, legislators, governors, and presidents—they are all such *mere people,* when their jobs call for something special," Isabel complained as she and Chief watched the uninspiring 1920 election contest between Ohio senator Warren G. Harding and Ohio governor James M. Cox. (Debs was on the ballot too, but she did not acknowledge him.) After an interlude of adolescent rebellion, a brief flirtation with socialist ideas alongside the man she loved, Isabel had returned to her mother's ideology of human progress not as Katharine's laboratory subject but as her fellow spokeswoman. The quest for a better social order, she informed her husband, began with the personalities who were—or who ought to have been—at the top of the political and economic hierarchy: politicians, intellectuals, the titans of industry, the men who were the best, the fittest for the job of leading America. She felt sure that the most urgent task facing society was to design the tools that would identify who these men were, even if these tools relegated women like her, homemakers with college degrees, to the role of their man's helpmeet. Her husband responded subtly, expanding his lecture series to include a talk that laid out the many psychological benefits women derived from working outside the home.

Theirs was a home rife with contradiction, a marriage between two very different types of people, Isabel later concluded. She was an emotional wife whose decisions betrayed modern feminist ideals, he a logical husband who had emerged as an unlikely—and unwanted—feminist ally. Isabel warned Chief that it was only a matter of time before his well-reasoned radicalism would get him in trouble, either with her family or the university. Chief was "bats," Katharine complained when she received his letter championing the "social good." His professors seemed to agree. When he was denied a teaching assistantship at the law school the next year, she did not gloat, did not remind him that she had told him so. But she did not comfort him either. Instead, in the third and most difficult year of her marriage, she moved back in with her parents to save money while he finished his studies.

. . . .

She found her mother in a terrible state. Katharine had fallen into a deep and inexorable depression when Isabel's education, "once the hope of the world," had become "an old, dead project," she wrote in her diary. This was not precisely true; her squabbles and negotiations with Chief had kept Katharine well occupied during Isabel's college years. But her day-to-day life had lost the intensity that had accompanied her total immersion in her daughter's affairs. In a letter that she drafted but never sent to Isabel, she lamented, "No one over fourteen years old really wants a mother, or ought to want one."

As an unwanted mother, she had done her best to keep busy. In 1918, she invented things: a removable tray for traveling bags to keep coats and skirts unwrinkled, a purse compartment for toiletries and stationery. They were patented but never made. In 1920, she signed up for a correspondence course on screenwriting and, in 1922, writing under another assumed name ("Katharine McKelvey," a combination of her first name and her daughter's middle name), she produced a script called *The Ninth Name*. It was sold to a small Hollywood studio but never produced. For some time, she tried her hand at writing short stories. But the magazine editors who had once vied for her parenting columns now returned her manuscripts with tepid rejection notices. In 1923, she celebrated her forty-eighth birthday and lost all remaining interest in her home and marriage. She spent most of her waking hours playing solitaire. She wondered if she was losing her mind. "Can a person understand hell as a state of mind unless he has been there?" she asked her diary.

Her daughter's return did not pull her back from the abyss; after all, depression rarely lifts on cue. But Isabel's unfalteringly spirited presence did reanimate some of Katharine's interests, chief among them reading and clipping the latest articles on personality science and child-rearing from newspapers and magazines. One day in November 1923, as she leafed through the latest issue of the *New Republic*, she saw an article by behaviorist psychologist John B. Watson titled "Jung as Psychologist." It piqued her interest. She had read Watson during her baby-training years, and like many people at the time, she had heard of Sigmund Freud and his various complexes, but she did not know who Jung was or what made his system of psychological thought distinct from those of his contemporaries.

She started reading and, by the end, she suspected that Dr. Carl Gustav Jung's type theory, his categorization of people as "introverts" and "extraverts," "thinkers" and "feelers," might resurrect her "old, dead project" of specialization and salvation. In Jung's writings, she would find a captivating and emphatically modern vocabulary to express to others her theory that people's personalities were innate, stable, and easily classifiable, thus making individuals amenable to professional and personal specialization. In the figure of Carl Jung— the man himself—she would find a new and dangerous private obsession.

CHAPTER THREE

Meet Yourself

There exist conflicting accounts of what happened when Katharine Briggs discovered Carl Jung's *Psychological Types*. The first account, the one Katharine recorded in her diary, is a conversation she had with "Dr. Stone," a local psychologist whose help she sought when her depression proved unmanageable. To him, she claimed that before she had started reading Jung's work, she had started developing her own theory of types once Isabel had moved back home. From her observations of her family, and from the biographies she had studied of important historical figures like George Washington, Benjamin Franklin, and Jane Addams, Katharine had concluded that mankind could be divided into four mutually exclusive categories of people: meditative, critical, sociable, and spontaneous. "I loved the ideas that came welling up, thought I was making them myself," she reflected, confident that she had articulated a wholly original schema for helping people choose the lines of work or the relationships best suited to their personalities—and, by extension, the advancement of civilization. "I found myself working rather feverishly, as if the fate of mankind and the entire evolutionary adventure of the race were somehow at stake."

She had already spent some months drafting a book that explained her theory of types, classifying all her family and friends, as well as characters from history and fiction, on the day she read John B. Watson's review of Carl Jung's *Psychological Types*. Never a fan of psychoanalysis, Watson had begrudgingly come to accept it as "common scientific property" after Freud and Jung had traveled to the United

States in 1909 to lecture at Clark University. The men had seduced American psychologists with their prurient tales of female hysterics and sexual neurotics, their exotic theories of infantile sexuality and psychic repression. Yet when the "smoke of mystery had been cleared away," Watson observed, "it was found that most of its new principles were not so new after all." Psychoanalysts could not peer into the soul and read its secrets. They were not augurs or oracles. They could do only what most behaviorists already did: wait, watch, and listen to their patients, issuing diagnoses based on what they observed.

Psychological Types represented a step back from the then common consensus that psychoanalysts were "behavior diagnosticians and teachers and not magicians," Watson complained. The book sought to reinstate the psychoanalyst as a spiritual healer, a god among mortals. To do so, Jung had invented the frustratingly opaque notions of "type" and "type pairs" to suggest that the "souls of men" could be classified along three binaries: extraverted and introverted types, intuitive and sensing types, and thinking and feeling types. Watson dismissed the whole enterprise as nonsense, a metaphysical ruse so flimsy that it defied serious critique. "One cannot go into a criticism of Jung's psychology," he spewed. "It is the kind the religious mystic must write in order to find justification for certain factors his training has forced him to believe must exist."

There was no proof for Jung's type theory; as a matter of method Jung did not believe his conjectures ought to be validated by modern empirical methods. "According to Jung, objective psychology can go only a little way toward giving an adequate picture of the human 'soul,'" Watson wrote. Rather, the soul found its deepest treatment in religious, philosophical, and literary texts that stressed the importance of polarity to ancient and modern civilizations alike: the Greek myth of brothers Prometheus (foresight) and Epimetheus (hindsight) and the Yoruba legend of creator gods Obatala ("peacemaker") and Oduduwa ("warrior"); the Sanskrit idea of *dvandva* ("the pair of opposites") and the Chinese concept of *Tao;* the writings of Abelard, Luther, Zwingli, and Schiller. Such were the sources that Jung drew upon to make his nearly seven-hundred-page argument that the whole world was populated by opposite and opposing spirits of nature that manifested in people's souls. *Psychological Types* was a loose, baggy monster borne of "unproven assumptions about inborn dispositions and inherited constitutions," Watson concluded his review. It offered no tools for the scientific study of personality.

Katharine was skeptical of Watson's opinion. He was, after all, a behaviorist, and she knew that behaviorism could never provide a full account of the personality differences she had observed among her young subjects; science, as she had once observed, lacked the data that the soul possessed. She ordered Jung's book at once and, when it arrived in the final days of 1923, she consumed it in a feverish, uncomprehending daze. So awed was she by her first impression of Jung's type theory that she set her notes and her book aside; Jung's extraverts and introverts superseded her meditative, critical, sociable, and spontaneous types. She spent the next five years contemplating her soul, trying to understand how Jung's dichotomies explained the currents of her life: her childhood disdain for pleasure and play, her adolescent suspicion of scientific training, her adult attachment to her child, and now, her midlife crisis.

This was her self-reported story. Then there is the account she would offer Isabel during her return home, the account that would become family lore. After reading Watson's article, Jung had appeared to Katharine in a dream. He had knocked on the door of her house, which, due to her neglect, had become dusty and disordered, and he had sat down in the living room to help Isabel and Albert, who was still alive, cut out paper dolls. When he finished, he refused Katharine's invitation to stay for dinner and showed himself out, riding away on a large horse. "Dr. Jung symbolized a psychological reality— something within me, something that actually had called upon me!" Katharine wrote. Upon waking, she lay in bed for some time, then lit a fire. "I took all my notes, the work of months, and laid them upon the fire in the living room without a regret," she wrote. "They had served their purpose."

Destruction by fire—it was the last and perhaps the most powerful myth she would offer her daughter, a fitting conclusion to the end of her life as a baby trainer and the beginning of a new calling. She imagined she could rise from the ashes reborn as one of Jung's disciples. She could take his dense, ponderous meditations on the soul and distill them into something simple and buoyant, beating back skeptics like Watson who believed *Psychological Types* offered nothing profitable for the study of man. Twenty years later, this is precisely what the Myers-Briggs Type Indicator did: it refracted Jung's ideas through the hazy prism of Katharine and Isabel's philosophy of specialization, and, in doing so, it made his work eminently useful.

. . . .

Katharine spent the next five years doing little else but scrutinizing every word of Jung's book, copying paragraphs from it into her notebooks with the quiet determination of a monk in his cell. The darkness that had consumed her since Isabel's departure for college lifted, slowly at first and then all at once. Now she took an interest in her home, stocking it with biographies of historical figures whose personalities she admired: Charles Darwin, Alexander Hamilton, Daniel Webster, Henry Clay, John C. Calhoun. Now she looked at her husband as if she had seen him for the first time, chronicling his daily routines and his nightly dreams with the same diligence she had once recorded Isabel's childhood. She recalled the words of William James in *The Varieties of Religious Experience*: that there existed a "hot place in a man's consciousness," a group of ideas to which he devoted himself, and that these ideas, more powerful than theological or ecclesiastical belief, would become the "habitual center of his personal energy." Whereas these words had once threatened her religious sensibilities, so much so that she had tried to prevent her daughter from reading any further lest she stray from the model of an obedient Christian type, they now offered her a way to reconcile her spirituality to the urgent, intimate pull of Jung's type theory. "For five years, five of the most exciting and interesting years of my life, friends laughingly referred to Jung's *Types* as my Bible," she later recalled. "And indeed I did use it much as my father and mother had used the Good Book—as a means of salvation—always understanding my life a little better because of what I read, and my reading a little better because of what I had lived."

Jung became her "personal God." She referred to him with tremendous reverence as "the man from Zurich"—as if he were the only man to walk the streets of that great glittering city where the discipline of analytic psychology was born. His realm, she taught Isabel, was the world beyond the conscious world, a world in which the unknown, shapeless material of the mind flowed into dreams and fantasies. Each dream, each fantasy was part of an unfolding process called "individuation": a dawning awareness of the self and its possibilities. The purpose of analytic psychology was to help men and women realize their full potentials as aware, integrated, and whole selves—their psyches developed, their contradictions resolved, their relationships balanced, their souls intact. The process of individuation was a way of adapting to the parts of herself that did not seem, at first, to belong to her: her irritation toward her daughter's husband; her resentment toward her husband; her constant and confusing desire for public recognition as something more than a homemaker, though she should have taken comfort in how thoroughly she had specialized. "In offering me this study of types," she wrote, "my Maker and author of my dreams was meeting my urgent need by thrusting upon me a spontaneous study of the different ways of living and loving life."

At the time, her exaltation of Jung was, in part, a compensatory measure. To many Americans in the 1920s, the name "Sigmund Freud" would have made a far greater impression than "the man from Zurich," especially after Freud's momentous lectures at Clark University in 1909, followed by the English publication of *The Interpretation of Dreams* in 1913. This reputational imbalance was something Katharine attributed to the fact that Jungian psychology was "less highly spiced, more wholesome" than Freud's scandalizing theories of sexual repression. "Psychoanalysis, which with Freud leads to sexuality, with Jung leads to something very like religion," she observed. While Freud's complexes and psychosexual stages were "easily exploited in popular fiction," Jung's theories about mankind's dichotomous personality functions—extraversion and introversion, sensing and intuition, thinking and feeling—had proven too "mystical," too "metaphysical," and, in short, too "unscientific" for skeptical American minds. If Freud was preoccupied with sex, then Jung was preoccupied with the soul.

She was drawn to the language he used to describe the soul, terms like "introvert" and "extravert," which had very different meanings in 1923 than they do today. What defined Jung's introvert was not quietude, solitude, or indecision (as many summaries of the Myers-Briggs types would later claim) but her interest in the self, or what Jung, writing in more technical language, called "the subjective factor." What made an introvert an introvert was her belief in the superiority of her singular orientation to the world—her subjectivity—over and above the expectations and desires of those around her. To the extravert, the introvert came across as "either a conceited egoist or a crack-brained bigot," for the extravert's behavior was governed by pure objective conditions. To illustrate the contrast between the two, Jung offered a simple example. On a blustery winter day, the fact that it was cold outside would prompt the extravert to don his overcoat, while the introvert, the person who "wants to get hardened," Jung wrote, "finds this superfluous." Whereas the extravert resigned herself to the simple fact of the cold, the introvert sought to overcome it by toughening the very fiber of her being.

And while the introvert was committed to cultivating herself in whatever way she deemed fit, no matter the circumstances, the extravert fretted over the arrangements of his various "personae": a term Jung had appropriated from the theater, where it referred to the many distinct characters (dramatis personae) that one actor could play in front of an audience. The extravert was as chameleonic as any seasoned actor, forever adapting himself to suit the stages and scenes of life. The extravert "does what is needed of him, or what is expected of him, and refrains from all innovations that are not entirely self-evident or that in any way exceed the expectations of those around him," Jung summarized. If the self-focused introvert ran the risk of excessive egoism, the extravert ran the risk of excessive normality. The extravert was the weak-willed one, pathologically disconnected from his inner world, lacking in self-possession.

Katharine was a self-diagnosed introvert and proud of it. She was on a "quest for the Self," she announced to her husband and daughter in 1925, and as such, she believed she was incapable of moving through the world in a conventional manner. "I have never been imitative. Quite the contrary," she wrote. "The fact that everyone else is doing something gives that thing an aspect of routine, cut-and-driedness, barrenness, which is acutely distasteful." In an exercise that she designed to test her relative preference for introversion over extraversion, she listed all the personae she had played throughout her infancy, her youth, her adulthood, and now her middle age on the back of a loose piece of paper: "Pleasure-seeker; Opportunist; Friend; Executive; Citizen; Neighbor; Financier; Wife; Mother; Mother-in-Law; Daughter-in-Law; Housekeeper; Employer; Hostess; Amateur Psychologist; Writer."

She used *Psychological Types* to make sense of the various roles she had inhabited, some against her better judgment, over the course of her life. Looking back on her college years, she began to understand her early crisis of faith in Jung's terms as a conflict between the sensing type and the intuitive type. The curriculum at Michigan, she realized, had been keyed to a purely sensuous reality: what students could see through the lens of the microscope, feel with the blade of the scalpel, sniff along the rim of the test tube. For many of her classmates, the sensations produced by the material world were not only useful for scientific discovery but also pleasurable. Like Jung's sensing type, they reveled in material delights, in smart outfits and bright, rich smells. And like Jung's sensing type, they often seemed to degenerate into pure pleasure seekers, unscrupulous aesthetes. The sensing type was someone who, as Jung described him, "dresses well, as befits the occasion; he keeps a good table with plenty of drink for his friends, making them feel very grand, or at least giving them to understand that his refined taste [entitled] him to make a few demands of them. He may even convince them that certain sacrifices are decidedly worth while for the sake of style." But she identified herself as the very model of Jung's intuitive type, someone who prized her unconscious predilections more dearly than whatever pleasures the object world could have afforded her. She would never have sacrificed her inner world for anything as crude as sensory—or sensual—reality.

Examining the twenty-five years she had spent as a wife and mother, she reasoned that the hardships she had suffered—the crushing losses of her children, two to death and one to life—had led her to realize the full extent of her preference for thought over the unruliness of feeling. The former she celebrated as the cornerstone of modernity, a way of objectifying her children so that she was not hurt by their disappearances. The latter she dismissed as a fundamentally ungovernable way of binding people to one another, better suited to gangs and tribes than enlightened suburban parents. Most women, she thought, must naturally be inclined to feeling: How else to explain why they were the ones responsible for looking after their homes and their children? But even among women, and among mothers in particular she had observed degrees of sentimentality. Some mothers were more emotional, more primitive in their dealings with their children. Others were rational like her.

The primitive versus the rational mother was a contrast that Katharine would map onto Jung's thinking and feeling types. "Thinking totally shuts out feeling if it ever wants to reach any kind of pure results, for nothing is more liable to prejudice and falsify thinking than feeling values," Jung wrote. Jung's thinker was a discoverer of facts, a creator of new worlds in which "intellectual formulas" were "quite indispensable for the salvation of mankind." For the thinker, anything that got in the way of his rational designs had to be purged from existence. For Katharine, that was the specter of the primitive mother: the mother overcome by her emotions. That she had loved her daughter there was no question, either when she was an impressionable child or now that she had grown into her own woman. But over the years the shape that love had taken was contorted, hardened by the knowledge of great loss.

Suddenly, she was so busy writing that she barely had time to eat—or worse, she confessed to Isabel, to do the shopping so that Lyman could eat. "This new religion is the new part of my life, the domestic side is the old part," she announced to her hungry and confused husband, and she explained the change that had come over her in the new idiom she had learned from *Psychological Types*. "When Isabel no longer needed the powerful sum of libido I had for years been bestowing upon her and her education I saw that I owed it to her and to Chief to withdraw it in order not to be an interfering and officious mother and mother-in-law," she wrote in a letter addressed to Lyman that she may never have shown him. "But I failed hopelessly in the attempt at transference. I found no objective interest to which I could transfer that energy. I suffered an involuntary and purposeless introversion, about which I said nothing to you because it was unspeakable. My island shrunk to nothingness, became submerged, and when you were not at home I all but went under." To clarify the transition from her old life to her new life, she also wrote him a poem called "Routine":

Hodgepodge and fires
And growing things,
And telephones
And orderings;

Tea towels and friends
And poetry,
And food and clothes
And bills to pay;

The urgent task;
The distant goal;
Symbols and dreams
To feed my soul—

From these and all,
God help me bring
This winging hour
Its real own thing!

Reminiscent of Emily Dickinson's beloved lyric "'Hope' is the thing with feathers — / that perches in the soul—" "Routine" looked with reverential longing to "this winging hour": the emancipatory moment when Katharine's "symbols and dreams" would feed her soul, showing her how the daily monotony of "food and clothes / and bills to pay" could yield its own real thing. But she did not wait for God to help bring about the deeper purpose she sought in domesticity. Near the end of her five-year period of deep contemplation, she turned her attention outward and began designing a set of tools to bring Jung's theories to the masses, attempting, for the first time, to regiment the experience of self-discovery.

. . . .

Her first magazine article in nearly a decade, "Meet Yourself: How to Use the Personality Paint Box," spoke to readers of her conversion experience to Jungian psychology. The article appeared in the *New Republic* in December 1926, its title a combination of the profound and the prosaic. One could hear echoes of the maxim inscribed in gold letters on the Temple of Apollo at Delphi—"Know thyself"—and the dawning of a deep and revelatory self-consciousness. One could also hear an invitation to a children's game of arts and crafts. To meet oneself, she explained, was to embark on an epic journey of self-discovery whose end was not some abstract notion of truth or freedom but one of Jung's sixteen personality types—"sixteen ways of growing from infancy to maturity," she wrote. Each type was represented by a different shade in the "personality paint box" of life. To discover the shade that best suited you, Katharine urged her reader to write down each type and its traits on a 3″ × 5″ index card, spread the cards across a flat surface, and arrange them vertically from most descriptive to least descriptive.

Later, Isabel would further standardize the work of self-discovery with a questionnaire, but for now, Katharine believed that her readers possessed enough self-awareness to navigate her descriptions of Jung's types on their own, sliding index cards up and down their dining room tables. The extraverted (E) sensing (S) type was an "extreme realist," she summarized, "valuing above all material possession and concrete enjoyment." The extraverted (E) intuitive (N) was an impatient and fickle-hearted "explorer, inventor, organizer, or promoter" who sought opportunity and adventure. Introverted (I) intuitives (N) could be found among the world's "philosophers, religious leaders and prophets, artists, queer geniuses and cranks." Their impulsive attitudes were counterbalanced by the practicality of the extraverted (E) thinkers (T), the "reformers, executives, systematists, and men of applied science." If her reader recognized himself in one of these descriptions, he was to move the index card to the very top of the table, where it would stay until it was displaced by another, more appropriate type description.

In its insistence on self-discovery as a civilizing form of self-mastery, "Meet Yourself" modeled a new genre of writing known as popular psychology: self-help in an era when the public demand for psychological counsel far outstripped the number of psychologists available to provide it. In the decade after Freud had published *The Interpretation of Dreams,* hundreds of newspaper columns and radio programs sought to address the problems they perceived as common to American society in the Roaring Twenties: inattentive spouses who drank on the sly; misbehaving children who bobbed their hair and hemmed their skirts and listened to jazz; professional ennui and personal paralysis in the face of a rising consumer culture. For Katharine, such advice might have once come from a trusted member of her church. But modern people, she observed, did not want judgment, repentance, or absolution, the rigmarole of religious instruction. They wanted understanding and they wanted it on their own terms. "Fortunate are they who can use the path of prayer," wrote Joseph Jastrow, president of the American Psychological Association and author of the nationally syndicated column Keeping Mentally Fit. "There is little need to advise that path for those who tread it; for they do so of their own accord. But the psychologist, like all other men, knows many who find their codes and creeds in other directions; so he must speak to and for all."

To find one's codes and creeds—this was the promise of meeting yourself through Jung's type theory. Type was no parlor game, no frivolous exercise designed to sort people into simplistic and overdetermined categories. It was an opportunity to articulate a grand system of self-governance, a system beyond conventional notions of good and evil, beyond God, and beyond the laws of the land. It was a system in which one's personality—one's self—was the ultimate arbiter of what was right and what was wrong. The only person who could judge you was you, and you, Katharine reassured her readers, had little "choice or control" in the matter. She knew from her observations of her children that type was set at birth, forged in the dreamlike chaos of infancy. "Every one of us is born either an extravert or an introvert, and remains extravert and introvert to the end of his days," Katharine wrote. To meet oneself was to cast aside all other codes and creeds and to acquire a new conception of "wholesome living," a new basis for the happy acceptance of one's life.

In writing "Meet Yourself," Katharine had placed her finger on the nerve center of type's appeal: the promise that, within each person, there lived a coherent individual who was master of her own life. This was by no means an original sentiment. Western philosophy had, for centuries, set forth a similar argument, from the Socratic dialogues to the writings of the Cynics, the Stoics, the Epicureans, and even the early Christians. In 1734, Alexander Pope had started his poem "An Essay on Man" with the command "Know then thyself, presume not God to scan, / The proper study of mankind is Man." In 1750, Benjamin Franklin, one of Katharine's heroes, had quipped, "There are three Things extremely hard, Steel, a Diamond, and to know one's self." In 1831, Ralph Waldo Emerson, the poet whose work had inspired William James's theory of a personal religion, urged each person to "know thyself" so that he might find the "God in thee." Katharine's article was just the most recent node in a long intellectual tradition that stretched across the Atlantic and back. But in the pages of the New Republic, the idea of meeting yourself was presented in a tone of definitive, cheerful accessibility that made the journey to self-discovery seem accessible—

fun, even. The unearthing of one's personality was no laboratory science, no serious invitation to navel-gaze. It was a human art of the most pleasing kind, and it could be practiced by just about anyone. "We may now assemble our personality paint box," Katharine concluded, "and try to discover just how we, our families, and our friends have managed to mix the colors."

Katharine's personality paint box was literalized in the figure of a 2 × 2 box—the first and simplest type table, a precursor to the now famous 4 × 4 grid of the sixteen Myers-Briggs types. "One need not be a psychologist in order to collect and identify types any more than one needs to be a botanist to collect and identify plants," Katharine comforted her readers, lest they felt intimidated by the specialized language she had used to populate her type table. One had only to learn to recognize the different characteristics of extraverted and introverted sensation, intuition, feeling, and thinking to determine which function served as "master" over one's personality. Once a reader had located her "primary function" in the personality paint box, then she could identify her "childish function" in the box directly opposite, the function that was "sometimes useful, sometimes a liability, sometimes a revolting anarchist."

Of all the shades in the personality paint box, one appeared brighter to Katharine than all the others: intuition. It was a wholly abstract concept to her. One could not touch or taste or see intuition at work, she thought, and yet one often heard people declare with great certainty that intuition was the key to genius. "A new idea comes suddenly and in a rather intuitive way," proclaimed Albert Einstein in 1926, the same year Katharine gathered her courage and wrote the first of many letters she would send to Jung. The letter did not read like a conventional fan letter. It was serious, probing. She asked him to clarify what precisely intuition was and why, on page 547 of *Psychological Types,* he had referred to it as "the noblest gift of man." His partiality to intuition had struck her as a moment of unrestrained passion in his writing, a rare slip in his persona as a clinician.

His lack of restraint had thrilled and puzzled her, she confessed to him, not because she believed herself to be an intuitive type, although

THE PERSONALITY PAINT BOX

If you are able to locate your primary function below, your two balancing functions will be in the diagonally opposite quarter of the box, while your undifferentiated and childish function will be touching corners with the primary in the quarter of the box directly opposite.

EXTRAVERTED SENSATION

Makes the extreme realist, very observant, living in the present, and most at home in the enjoyment attitude. Untroubled by theories, guided by custom and convention, valuing above all else material possessions and concrete enjoyment.

INTROVERTED SENSATION

Impressionistic and visionary, observant, but seeing everything differently from other people. At home in the enjoyment attitude, but very uncommunicative, often appearing perplexed. Sensitive to atmosphere, valuing above all else his own subjective impressions.

EXTRAVERTED INTUITION

Makes the explorer, inventor, organizer or promoter, living in the expectant attitude, always ready to sacrifice the present for the immediate project, enthusiastic, impulsive, keen-minded, impatient and often fickle, valuing opportunity above all else.

INTROVERTED INTUITION

Makes philosophers, religious leaders and prophets, artists, queer geniuses and cranks, living in the expectant attitude, with a passion for understanding, impulsive, eager for some new view of life, valuing inspiration and insight above all else.

EXTRAVERTED FEELING

Makes interpretive artists, orators, philanthropists, supporters of cultural movements and activities, living in the personal attitude and strong in the art of friendship for its own sake, sociable and tactful, but too fluent to be brief and businesslike. Valuing harmonious social relationships above all else.

INTROVERTED FEELING

Makes a reserved and inaccessible personality, silent and deep, outwardly reposeful or even cold, with no desire to impress or influence others. At home in the personal attitude, but intensely averse to violent display of emotion. Values above all else the inner emotional life for its own sake.

EXTRAVERTED THINKING

Makes reformers, executives, systematists, and men of applied science. Stubborn, dogmatic, sceptical, practical and dominating, living in the analytical attitude strictly in accordance with an intellectually derived formula, and expecting others to live by it. Strong in will-power and practical achievement, but weak in æsthetic activities and the art of friendship. Values above all else the concrete facts of life.

INTROVERTED THINKING

Makes the scholar, theorist, and abstract thinker in science, mathematics, economics, philosophy, etc. Dogmatic and egotistical if he mistakes his world of ideas for his own personality, but more often inclined to undervalue himself and his own mental processes. Lives in the analytical attitude, but is more tolerant than the extraverted thinker, less critical, and less inclined to force his judgments upon others. Values understanding.

Katharine's Personality Paint Box was the earliest blueprint for MBTI's famous 4 × 4 type table.

she suspected they had that in common, but because she thought she had caught a glimpse of his soul across the thousands of miles that separated them. Perhaps, she speculated, it had something to do with his special esteem for women's intuition. This was a psychic factor she had started thinking about in relation to her old project of baby training: women always seemed to know when the people they loved were in danger. Perhaps intuition was as evolutionarily encoded as loving one's children. Perhaps it was the intuitives, like him and her, who would inherit the earth.

She never expected an answer to her questions, so she was surprised when Jung wrote back, a long letter from his home at Küsnacht, Switzerland, three pages overflowing with his wide, slanted hand. How different his penmanship was from Lyman's cribbed little letters, his perfectly measured lines! And yet how authoritative, how uncompromising, his words seemed! "Dear Madam," he began. "I understand sensation and intuition as being perceptual 'functions.' Sensation would be sense perception of external processes, intuition would be perception of internal processes." These internal processes, he noted, were partially psychic and partially physical, and they included all aspects of life that the sensorium had failed to register: telepathic phenomena and fantasy activity, the mirage series of the unconscious. "Intuition can see through walls and round the corners and into the deepest obscurities of the human heart," he wrote. It may not have been properly scientific for him to call intuition a "nobler" function than the others, but reflecting on his dreams, his fantasies, and all they had made possible in his life had appealed to his "feeling side." "And thus it came that I made that emotional exclamation," he explained to her. "I am not yet so dried up that I could not wonder any more at the amazing facts of human psychology."

. . . .

To say that Katharine Briggs became obsessed with Carl Jung is to understate matters. Ordinary obsession—the passion of a distant admirer—exists in the realm of daydream and wish fulfillment. Katharine's obsession with Jung was alive, active, purposive. It was the stuff of her waking life and her wandering dreams, and it started innocuously enough. Her next and final piece for the *New Republic,* which she titled "Up from Barbarism," celebrated Jung's romantic preference for intuition with a subtlety that only someone attuned to the details of their correspondence could discern.

In it, she detailed the lives of four children who had demonstrated different type abilities. Henry, who specialized in sensing, had a penchant for observing and mimicking others, demanding first a toy broom with which to imitate his mother, then a toy car with which to imitate his father. Ethel, who specialized in feeling, wanted to make and keep as many harmonious relationships as possible. She craved attention and she found people who talked about things other than her "very tedious." Frank, who specialized in thinking, aimed to live the perfectly reasoned life, no matter how tactless or temperamental his logic could make him. Henry ended up a conformist, Ethel a narcissist, Frank a bad husband and father.

Then there was Hebe, the intuitive baby, "so full of initiative that no one could predict what she would do next." "Her play was imaginative rather than imitative," Katharine wrote. "She had little need for toys or playmates, so easily did she fill her life with imaginary friends, kings, queens, mythical palaces and make-believe adventures. With the quick understanding of the intuitive child, she learned to read long before reaching school age, adding to the world of imagination in which she lived. Her amazingly intelligent questions covered a wide range, so great was her interest in the new and unknown." Here was a portrait of Isabel, the creative intuitive. (In early drafts of the piece, "Hebe" was called "Irene," which Katharine changed when she realized how similar it sounded to "Isabel.") Although she learned with rapidity, she ignored the "fundamental enjoyments of life." She was "persecuted by vague and spasmodic cravings for the very satisfactions she scorned." Here too was Katharine's portrait of herself, the repressed intuitive.

As Katharine wrote the article, she wondered how she might satisfy the cravings for pleasure she had stifled as an introverted and intuitive type. She turned first to writing fiction, staying up late to compose private, erotic stories about Jung and the practice of analytic psychology. Her longest one was a novella titled *The Man from Zurich,* and it was narrated by a character she referred to as "Sterling": a handsome, cultured resident of Washington, D.C., who had fallen into a deep depression. After a near suicide attempt, he had been saved from permanent institutionalization at Saint Elizabeths Hospital by the unexpected kindness of a stranger: an analytic psychologist who was visiting Washington from Zurich, an attractive European named Dr. Markus. "In the beginning, he was 'the man from Zurich'—then Dr. Markus—now simply Markus," Sterling thought. "He doesn't know how easily I could spell G-o-d—or does he? Thanks to his gospel according to the Zurich school of modern psychology, I've been 'born again.' Why shouldn't I think of him as my creator at least?" In the novella's first half, the doctor and patient cohabited Markus's one-bedroom apartment with joy and ease, accompanying each other to parties and plays, dining out and drinking in each other's company, "steering pretty clear of the rocks of homosexuality." But the tension between them grew almost unbearable in the second, climactic act. "I must break away from Markus," Sterling concluded before initiating the patient and doctor's long, agonized goodbye in the novella's closing scenes. Katharine sent the story to several publishers but only heard back from one, a disgruntled editor who told her that her intimations of homosexuality were undignified and her digressions into Jungian psychology were boring. After his harsh rebuke, she stopped writing novels altogether.

Discouraged by the narrative arts, she turned to song and prayer to express her devotion. She started by rewriting the lyrics of show tunes that she knew by heart, adapting the most popular fox-trot of the early 1930s, "Song of the Vagabonds," into a hymn she called "Hail, Dr. Jung!" The verse and chorus went:

Signs and symbols reading
Jung gives proof exceeding
He knows all humanity
Understands old Adam,

Not to mention Madam,
Wise old owl, so wise is he

Upward, upward, consciousness will come.
Upward, upward, from primal scum.
Individuation
Is our destination
Hoch, Heil, Hail to Dr. Jung!

She tried the song out on her living room piano. Her fingers skipped to the familiar one-two-three beat of the waltz as she gave voice to her new lyrics, pausing every now and again to change a word. But who would sing the songs she had written? Where would she find a chorus to lift its voice in ecstasy?

No one, it seemed. Lyman was at work, as ever, and now Isabel too was gone. Katharine had shared her notes on type and child-rearing with her daughter just before Isabel left her mother again, this time to move back in with her husband, who had saved enough money to buy them a pretty gabled house in Swarthmore. Katharine assumed her daughter would find happiness there as a wife and, soon, a mother. "Her pronounced femininity suggested strongly that she might never care for any but the domestic career, in which case I determined to bequeath to her these records to do with as she sees fit," Katharine wrote. She encouraged Isabel to use the language of type to improve herself and her household relations with Chief, who she believed was a thinking type rather than a feeling type, like Isabel.

Isabel took the message to heart. Before she moved out, most likely at her mother's behest, she started a diary that she titled "Diary of an Introvert Determined to Extravert, Write, & Have a Lot of Children." In it, she kept notes on her daily routine as her mother had once done for her, using the language of type that she had now inherited from her mother:

Keep complete job list and do one every day.
Housekeep till 10 A.M.

Two hours writing.
One-hour outdoors.
One-hour self-development—music, study, friends.
Wash face with soap every night.
Never wear anything soiled.

CHAPTER FOUR

An Unbroken Series of Successful Gestures

onsider a different list for self-improvement, this one courtesy of modern American literature's most famous con artist, Jay Gatsby. In plotting his transformation from James Gatz, penniless North Dakota farm boy, to Jay Gatsby, East Coast millionaire, he writes the following daily routine down on a stray piece of paper that is discovered shortly after his death.

Rise from bed
Dumbbell exercise and wall-scaling
Study electricity, etc.
Work
Baseball and sports
Practice elocution, poise and how to attain it
Study needed inventions

Written in 1924, around the same time that Isabel started "Diary of an Introvert Determined to Extravert, Write, & Have a Lot of Children," *The Great Gatsby* offered its readers a glimpse into the largely invisible work that went into making one's personality cohere as a unified entity. "If personality is an unbroken series of successful gestures, then there was something gorgeous about him, some heightened sensitivity to the promises of life, as if he were related to one of those intricate machines that register earthquakes ten thousand miles away," Fitzgerald wrote of Jay Gatsby, perhaps the most enigmatic fictional personality of the twentieth century. By Fitzgerald's account, one's personality was neither innate nor inert but seismographic: a transcription of the millions of precisely calibrated actions and activities one undertook from day to day, an etching into human form of one's deliberate encounters with an unpredictable and unforgiving world. Personality was something you practiced over and over again like dumbbell exercises or elocution drills or a tricky baseball play, running faster, stretching farther, until the ball no longer eluded your grasp. It was a tone to be struck, a pose to be held until every movement of every muscle appeared natural and effortless.

For Gatsby, personality was also a necessary fiction, a gimmick that served a very particular purpose: the accumulation of wealth, power, and prestige. Like Isabel's labor-intensive amusement of Chief and his fellow fighter pilots during the summer of 1918, *The Great Gatsby* afforded its readers a remarkably vivid example of putting one's personality to work, trading "those rare smiles with a quality of eternal reassurance in it" for an elaborate house on the Long Island Sound, careless champagne parties, and the jangle of money, a cymbal's song, in his long-lost-love Daisy's voice. It all ended quite badly for Gatsby, of course—his curated personality was, ultimately, a dangerous, deadly gimmick. But Fitzgerald's story about personality's intangible, imaginative dimensions showed how one could, over time, assemble and disassemble the self until it was virtually indistinguishable from something inherent, something eternal, something true.

In the early decades of the twentieth century, most psychologists drew a sharp distinction between character and personality, wherein the former connoted a stable, unified, and interior self and the latter the mutable expression of that self across different social circumstances. "Personality is more than character. It is character forcefully expressed," claimed psychologist Norris Arthur Brisco in a 1920 tract. But in the fiction of the time, the very concept of having a personality was deeply, irretrievably entangled with the art of inventing and reinventing yourself as a compelling character—a quintessentially American art. One could trace it from Gatsby all the way back in time to Katharine's second favorite book, Benjamin Franklin's 1791 rags-to-riches autobiography, in which he provided his readers with a checklist of the thirteen virtues—temperance, silence, order, resolution, frugality, industry, sincerity, justice, moderation, cleanliness, chastity, tranquility, humility—that could help them develop their personalities in the earliest days of the republic. Like Franklin, Gatsby would become famous as an emblem of the self-made American man. "The truth was that Jay Gatsby, of West Egg, Long Island, sprang from his Platonic conception of himself," Fitzgerald wrote. In this sense, his fictional character, and his fictional character's fictive personality, were no different from any other American, man or woman, who believed that his or her personality could be a product of the imagination. Like a well-ordered home and a well-ordered marriage, a well-ordered novel could institute its own fantasy of what a personality was and how it ought to be discovered and cultivated.

Isabel and Katharine both read *The Great Gatsby* shortly after it was published in 1925; Isabel in her new home, Katharine in her old one, now empty again. One could imagine Isabel catching glimpses of her mother's project in Fitzgerald's novel, taking note of James Gatz's list and reproducing it for herself. She had always been a good imitator, and there was, after all, an intimate relationship between the creation of an artwork and the creation of a personality. A good novelist, Fitzgerald had once written in a letter to his editor, expressed a character's personality by highlighting his penchant for certain memorable things: shirts of sheer linen and thick silk, dressing rooms swathed in rose and lavender silk. From exterior preferences, one could deduct interior states. It was an aesthete's approach to personality.

A good theorist of personality reverse-engineered the work of the fictional imagination. She tallied a person's memorable preferences—silk over cotton, rose over burgundy, East over West—and compressed them into a complex yet integrated vision of the self, a different kind of fictional character. "There is probably no one who has a better understanding of human character than the successful fiction writer," Katharine observed. "Perhaps there is no better way of developing the understanding eye than to attempt the creation of fictitious characters which shall be true to life and step out of the covers of a book as the well-executed portrait seems to step from the canvas." She put

Fitzgerald's novel down and returning to Jung's *Psychological Types* with a renewed commitment to discovering one's type as a creative labor. "Let us imagine ourselves about to write the great American novel which has been simmering in the back of our mind for years," she wrote to her daughter.

Like the craft of creating a well-rounded character, the practice of personality typing was an aesthetic preoccupation in the most classical sense of the term. It privileged the creative pursuit of beauty, symmetry, and wholeness over the ugliness and irresolution that splintered people's lives. Like the novel, its medium was language, a language whose style ranged from the sentimental cadences of *The Great Gatsby* to the clinical novels of personality that Isabel would start writing after her mother introduced her to Jung's work. Hers were not the "great American novel[s]" her mother imagined as the companions to *Psychological Types.* They were detective stories and workplace novels, genres that her mother dismissed as insubstantial and unserious when compared to her own spiritual and philosophical writings on type.

Yet Isabel's use of type as a guide for her creative writing foreshadowed the character-building exercises she would urge people to do upon learning their Myers-Briggs type. The indicator would entrust people with a native language of the self, encouraging them to narrate their life stories in an idiom that felt fresh and freeing and true. Threading words like "extravert" and "introvert" through people's daily acts of self-consideration, the indicator would merge the impulse to self-discovery with the will to self-creation; its subjects would emerge, or seem to emerge, as the authors of their inner and outer worlds. But in learning how to speak type, they would unfurl as characters of Katharine and Isabel's design, vessels for the ideas about specialization that the two women would popularize in and out of the fictional realm.

. . . .

Like Jay Gatsby and Benjamin Franklin, Isabel was a character of her own making. Her desire to transform herself from a housewife into a novelist swelled at precisely the same time she read Fitzgerald's novel and logged her first, imitative entry in her "Diary of an Introvert."

She had tried her hand at writing before and always with some modest success: a letter to Edward Bok, her mother's editor at the *Ladies' Home Journal,* published on her fourteenth birthday; some plays and a poem placed in *Life* when she was still in college; and a series of short stories for a children's magazine called *Scattered Seeds,* written while she waited for her own family to grow and multiply. By 1925, she had been pregnant three times, and she had suffered two miscarriages and one premature birth—a daughter named Ann who died just as soon as she had been placed in her arms. "Very blue. Oh, little Ann," read the one-line entry in her diary. It was followed by the draft of a sonnet titled "The Toy Balloon," the sad story of a little girl who begged her mother for a toy balloon to hug and that ended with the lines "It hit Mother's hatpin and quick as a wink / My beautiful bubble was dead." Isabel sought some small consolation in her writing, but all the poems and short stories she had drafted were rejected by the magazines to which she sent them. "I have the rest of my life to write books, but only just now for bringing up my little people," she reasoned. Motherhood had to come first.

And, for some time, it did. After an anxious pregnancy, her son Peter was born in 1926. Her daughter, whom she also named Ann, followed in 1927. She raised the children as her mother had told her a faithful obedience-curiosity mother should—spankings when they spoke out of turn at the dinner table, stories when they asked permission to sing nursery rhymes before bed. Her regimen elicited the approval of Katharine, who visited her grandchildren often to observe their budding personalities and type them, this time without the use of the questionnaire she had distributed to the mothers of the neighborhood children. She identified Peter as an extraverted thinking type and Ann as an introverted feeling type just like Isabel. "Your father and mother are both introverts, while one of you is an extravert, the other an introvert. That was obvious when you were babies," she wrote in a letter to Peter and Ann, whom she referred to as "child number one" and "child number two" respectively and as "my little human puppies" collectively. "When number one was born, the type stood out plainly from the first. Before the end of the first month, I told your mother she had an extravert child, and it was the same with number two. In the first month, I told your mother she had an introvert child." She thought her daughter would be happy now that her irrepressible femininity had found its proper outlet in the creation of her little people.

But Isabel could not find the right time or place to confess to her mother that the children were not enough. Now that she had everything she thought she had wanted—one child of each sex, one child of each type—a restlessness stole over her days. She recalled the accomplishments of her childhood and her adolescent years, and she wondered what had happened to that version of herself: the girl who had made all A's (except in physical education, which surely did not count); the girl who had held the most important extracurricular offices at Swarthmore; the girl who had dressed up like a piece of lettuce to mock the church; the girl who had defended the rights of industrial workers in a breathless, thrilling speech delivered before the man she desired. That girl had wanted to be a playwright one day and a political scientist the next, not merely someone's wife and someone else's mother.

She realized she no longer wanted to spend her days as her husband's helpmeet, as she had once thought in the idyllic glow of her early marriage. She yearned to be something special again, an exceptional person who would make her mark in the world. She yearned to put words on paper again, and while they would not be the words for which her name would eventually become renowned—extravert and introvert, thinker and feeler, sensing and intuitive type remained her mother's idiom—they represented a first step toward merging the art of character creation with the work of personality typing.

In August 1928, she read an announcement in *New McClure's Magazine* for its first ever mystery novel contest. The entrant who wrote the best mystery novel would receive a $7,500 cash prize, the largest ever awarded for a literary contest—more than $100,000 today—and a book contract with the premier New York publishing house of Frederick A. Stokes. At first, the idea of winning merely distracted her from the care of her children and her household chores. She spanked Peter out of turn and absentmindedly; she burned the roast. Then, slowly, it consumed her whole, until she resolved to write an entire book in five months to make the submission deadline. She tried to write during the day, but there was always one restless toddler or another fighting to sit on her lap, punching the typewriter's keys, impeding her progress. "Even thE most feaRsome paSSage lacks impresSiveness WHen wRitten like thiS," she joked in a brief, nervous profile of herself she sent to the magazine along with her submission. Most of the drafting had to be done at night once the house had been swept, the dishes rinsed, and Chief and the children were asleep. "Between nine and three stretched six heavenly, uninterrupted hours—if I could stay awake to use them," she wrote. "Mostly I stayed awake, though many a time my head bumped the typewriter in the middle of a sentence." The longest, darkest hours of the night were her "winging hour"— the moment when the symbolic realm, the world of the imagination, would liberate her from the duties of childcare and housework.

Isabel called her novel *Murder Yet to Come*. It featured a team of three amateur detectives, fictional characters inspired by Isabel's brief stint of summer work in Memphis and her marriage to Chief, the two experiences that had made her eager to find a way for people to work at the things that were right for them. There was lean, lazy, and graceful Peter Jerningham, a playwright, and his shadow, a detail-oriented secretary named John MacAndrews whom Jerningham had hired to type his notes and respond to his letters, a top-notch stenographer who harbored secret literary ambitions. Together, the detectives Jerningham and MacAndrews offered a striking self-portrait of Isabel: a sophisticated, sentimental, and artistic type who had chosen to do the menial work of organizing someone else's life. Then there was the third detective, Carl Nilsson, a former marine, a "true Viking" who bore more than a passing resemblance to Chief: "a superbly built blond giant, broad in the shoulders and lean in the waist, blue-eyed and square of chin, slow of movement except in emergencies, slow of speech except in wrath, slow of thought compared with Jerningham, but moving steadily from one solid conclusion to another." Together, the three set out to investigate some strange goings-on at a creaky Gothic mansion called Cairnstone House, which was inhabited by a cast of characters ripped straight from the potboilers of Sir Arthur Conan Doyle and Wilkie Collins: a sadistic old copper merchant named Malachi Trent, whom the detectives would pronounce dead by chapter 3; Malachi Trent's lovely niece Linda, who stood to inherit all his money; Mrs. Ketchem, an old crone of a housekeeper; and Ram Singh, a Hindu servant who had borne witness to his master's dealings in cursed jewels in the East Indies.

Her mother dismissed Isabel's drafts as predicable and bland, using them as further evidence that Isabel was not a literary genius but a genre writer: someone capable of applying formulas in a diligent manner but not improving on them. "Had she produced a work of genius instead of merely what her father calls 'a corking good yarn,' it would contradict rather than support my contention of mental vigor versus genius in her care," Katharine wrote in her diary of *Murder Yet to Come.* "A literary work of genius comes out of the unconscious like a dream. It is subtle, meaning much more than it says, much more than the casual reader quite grasps, often more than is fully grasped by the writer himself."

Yet she should have appreciated—or perhaps she resented—how the novel's characters served as direct receptacles for the theory of type specialization that she had passed on to her daughter. Each member of the detective team possessed what Isabel had once described to Katharine as "the different gifts" of women and men. Gray-eyed, red-haired Jerningham (an introverted, intuitive type) had the "quickness of insight" to uncover the murderer of old Malachi Trent, while Nilsson (an extraverted, sensing type) took "smashingly effective action" to apprehend him. MacAndrews (a thinking type) plotted the "slow-solid decisions" that protected the beautiful Linda from scandal. The men's friendships and working relationship were always invigorated by their personality differences, never strained by them. Each was happy to accept his personal limitations and cede authority to the others when necessary. It may not have been a great novel, but it was a prescient one, a fantastical blueprint for how, a decade later, Isabel would champion the type indicator's ability to treat real workers like characters in a workplace novel, assigning men and women to the jobs that were right for them. (Today, the novel is advertised on the Myers-Briggs website as an artifact of Isabel's thinking. "Great mysteries are driven by great characters, and Isabel Myers' mastery of personality served her well," announces the site, where one can buy *Murder Yet to Come* for $15.00.)

When the editors of *McClure's* judged the contest in 1929, they awarded first place to a novel called *The Roman Hat Mystery* written by a young man named Ellery Queen—a pseudonym for two cousins from Brooklyn who would soon become the most famous mystery writing team in America. But just before they announced the prize, *McClure's* went bankrupt and was absorbed by the *Smart Set*. Though it had debuted short stories by F. Scott Fitzgerald, Eugene O'Neill, and Sinclair Lewis in the early 1920s, the *Smart Set* had rebranded itself recently as America's "Young Woman's Magazine." The contest was judged again, and this time, the jury was instructed by the *Smart Set's* editor to select a female winner, one whose voice and background would appeal to the magazine's dominant subscriber base of married women over the age of twenty-five. "You want to hear about me?" Isabel asked in the profile she had written to accompany her novel. "Well—I am thirty-one, and I am married, and I have two babies, and that in itself is such a blissful state of affairs that I sometimes have difficulty believing it. You see, I know my luck." The vote was unanimous. The jury awarded *Murder Yet to Come* first place, the cash prize, serial publication in the *Smart Set*, and the publishing contract.

On February 26, 1929, Isabel came home from running errands in the snow to find her husband sitting in the kitchen, clutching a telegram that Western Union had accidentally handed to their neighbor. It contained just one sentence, a sentence intended only for Isabel, which Chief had already read a half-dozen times: YOU WIN STAKES MCCLURE PRIZE CONTEST CONGRATULATIONS. The celebration started later that night—"I am your worshipping servant," Chief whispered to his wife once they had sent the children to bed—and extended into the early weeks of the spring. For Isabel, these were weeks filled with love and admiration, with endless telephone calls and notes of praise, with two extravagant shopping excursions to

Philadelphia to purchase the white fox stole and cinched blue suit she would wear when the reporters came to town, which they did in the summer of 1929. The *Brooklyn Daily Eagle* published a snapshot of Isabel sitting on a chair in front of her house, a typewriter on her lap, her arms around Peter and Ann, who each sat atop one of the chair's arms, glowering. The accompanying caption read, "$7,500 Is a Lot of Money . . . Peter and Ann will help her spend it." In their Books and Authors column, the *New York Times* issued a tribute to the author's literary and domestic accomplishments: "Isabel Briggs Myers is the wife of Clarence G. Myers, a Philadelphia lawyer. They were married in 1918 when Mr. Myers (then Lieutenant Myers) was an army flier. They have two children and live in an ivy-covered Colonial house in Swarthmore, Pa. Mrs. Myers wrote 'Murder Yet to Come' in five months, most of it at night when the children were asleep."

Happy to have her friends refer to her as a "minor celebrity" and a "distinguished authoress," Isabel received well-wishes from everyone except Katharine, who never quite warmed to her daughter's success and shared only her cool criticisms of the novel. When Isabel asked for her mother's help compiling some biographical materials to send to her publisher, Katharine produced a twenty-two-page abridged version of "The Diary of an Obedience-Curiosity Mother," hoping her old, dead project of baby training might prove useful for understanding Isabel's success. "I shall be glad to tell you what I can," she wrote to Isabel's publicity manager. "It has been lots of fun to be her mother."

Debuting as a two-dollar paperback, *Murder Yet to Come* garnered mixed reviews. "Good to the last word! . . . It will make your hair frizz," proclaimed the Philadelphia *Ledger,* a sentiment echoed by the *Honolulu Star-Bulletin:* "Though all the old hokum of East Indian servants, a ruby stolen from an Indian goddess, poisoned arrows, hypnotism, and all the rest are here in abundance, the hokum is so adroitly presented that it has the fresh aroma of something scented for the first time." The British papers were less enthusiastic about Isabel's recycling of the same old tropes they had grown up with in the stories of Sherlock Holmes and Hercule Poirot. "It is a sound, businesslike example of the thrilling, as opposed to the scientific type of detective story and as such continues to hold some interest to the end," wrote *The Spectator*. "It must, however, be admitted that the reader will have solved the mystery long before this." "The surprises are a little too abundant to be entirely surprising," complained *Country Life*. What really mattered, however, was that *Murder Yet to Come* tore through seven print runs in six months, even after the stock market crash of October 1929. By the time the United States had plunged headlong into the Great Depression, it had topped the best-seller lists in both the United States and the United Kingdom, and Isabel had been feted around the women's clubs of Pennsylvania and New York in a manner befitting the minor celebrity she now saw herself as.

A shame, then, that she had entrusted most of her prize money to stocks that did not survive the financial crisis, investing in conglomerates with generic names like "United Founders" or "Manufacturers Investment Company" whose symbols had disappeared overnight from Wall Street's ticker tape. Seventy-five hundred dollars may have been a lot of money for one person to spend, but it was a rounding error for the American economy, which lost $30 billion over the course of two days in October. As President Herbert Hoover tried in vain to reassure a panicked nation, Isabel watched her money evaporate along with her plans to reinvent herself as a professional writer, a wild success in her chosen vocation—the right thing for her. Gone were the nanny and housekeeper she had intended to hire to care for the children and the house while she spent entire days at the typewriter in a room of her own. Gone was the playroom she had wanted to convert into a "real kingdom" for Peter and Ann, a consolation prize for the writing retreats and speaking engagements she had planned. Of course, she had it much better than many other Americans. The Depression, which would last until the end of the 1930s, would strip millions of people of their homes, their jobs, their livelihoods. For Isabel, it only stripped her of her dreams.

Chastened by her bad luck and embarrassed by her hubris, she turned to her mother for advice and to her father for money. As Lyman signed a check over to his worried daughter, Katharine reminded her to eat, to sleep, and to never forget Jung's teachings. "I have some psychological advice as important as the physical," she wrote. "Watch out for ego inflation. It can take possession of you from many directions and very subtly—not as egotism at all, but as excitement." To exalt her ego was to "insult the greater intelligence which is really handling your life."

. . . .

What was the "greater intelligence" handling her life, and what, if anything, was it guiding Isabel to do? After an unpredictable end to the Roaring Twenties—the whirlwind success of *Murder Yet to Come,* the financial blow she had suffered during the Depression—Isabel felt "done. Emptied. Finished. Not another idea in my head," she confessed to her mother. She never expected to write another book. She did not know if she could.

Yet her New York publisher, who had made a good deal of money from *Murder Yet to Come*'s seven print runs, had signed her to a two-book contract. Now he was eager to know when her next novel would be done. "The work goes far more slowly than I had hoped, and it is impossible at this point to promise when it will be done," she complained to him in 1930. She insisted that the children were taking up more and more of her time, but the children were, if anything, easier to manage: two towheaded, impossibly handsome, impossibly charming creatures who were in school for some of the day and no longer tearing around the house yelling "Mother, *Mother!*" Whether she realized it or not, what she was really suffering from was a terrible case of writer's block.

She wondered to what degree her accomplishments were heartfelt and to what degree they were a reflex, an unwitting extension of the training that had been imposed upon her as a child. Perhaps she had no passions—nothing that really and truly distinguished her personality from anyone else's. Perhaps her mother's repertoire of personality drills and exercises, the obedience-curiosity typology she had instituted in her daughter since birth, had backfired, programming Isabel to spend her life as a nonspecialist, a dilettante, flitting from one line of work to the next just to prove that she could do whatever she wanted to do in the moment. She wished she had some way of discovering the right thing for her. "I want to write books," she insisted to a friend from Swarthmore. "I want to write plays. I'd like to be Chief's wife in a thorough and artistic fashion, not just with what is left of me after a long day spent wrestling with a recalcitrant scene or chapter." Yet her ambition was laced with uncertainty. At heart, she confessed, she was "a lazy person." Her love of leisure could be "overshadowed by taller desires but never rooted out."

In the summer of 1931, she vowed not to be lazy. She had sequestered herself and her family in the woods outside of Philadelphia to work on a murder mystery play she had titled *Death Calls for Margin*. Her agent had already sold it to Lawrence Shubert Lawrence Jr., great-nephew of Lee, Sam, and J. J. Schubert, the brothers single-handedly responsible for transforming New York's run-down Broadway district into the epicenter of its bright lights, big city theater industry. Lawrence Jr. had announced his plan to expand the family empire by testing new plays in Philadelphia "with the idea of making this city a center of original productions somewhat after the style of New York, Chicago, or Boston," he had boasted to the *Philadelphia Inquirer*. Isabel's agent had sent him her script, another well-crafted potboiler whose plot echoed Dashiell Hammett's *The Maltese Falcon*: the story of a romance between a private detective and the beautiful young woman who hires him in act 1, makes love to him in act 2, and double-crosses him by act 3. Isabel had debuted the play at the Players Club of Swarthmore, where she had assumed the role of the dark-eyed, dark-haired femme fatale opposite Chief's handsome, hard-nosed detective. It was one way to fulfill her wifely duties "in a thorough and artistic fashion." There was nothing quite as delightful, she thought, as unleashing new personae into the world and watching one's fantasies come to life.

Now Lawrence Jr. wanted to stage a proper opening at the Buck Hill Falls Laurel Blossom Festival, the Midsummer Eve celebration that lured thousands of people, including the mayor of Philadelphia and Queen Elsa I, the sixteen-year-old reigning beauty queen of the Poconos, into the woods to carouse during the longest day of the year. Isabel, too nervous to play the female lead in front of Lawrence Jr., had asked Barbara Pearson, a striking, golden-haired graduate from the Yale School of Drama, to perform opposite Chief. On a hot and suggestive opening night, Isabel watched from the wings as her replacement stalked across the stage and purred her lines ("I don't know what I would do without your help") at Chief in a voice shot with all the seduction of youth and beauty. She was Isabel's antithesis in almost every respect: young, fair, unattached, and extraverted, her future rich with promise and possibility.

Eying her understudy, Isabel recalled her mother's writings on type, a spiritual dalliance that she had been happy to encourage without making any deep commitments to Jung's codes or creeds. Now it struck her that there, right before her eyes, was a character situation more vivid, more urgent than any she could hope to invent through her fiction: a "domestic typology lab," she would call it when, several decades later, she was asked to identify the origins of the type indicator. Here the comedy and tragedy of human life played out almost daily. Marriage and its temptations offered a "perfectly marvelous" scenario, she thought, for exploring what the differences between two people's desires might reveal about their psychological types. The people whose intimate, interior landscapes one knew best of all—one's husband, one's children—were the best testing grounds for Jung's theories.

Soon she would set the play aside, citing the lack of funding for theater productions at the height of the Depression, and rededicate herself to her original profession of choice: the good wife. "Marriage? Big Job! Start It Early" announced the Philadelphia *Ledger* in a 1932 profile they published of Isabel, in which she introduced herself "not as author or playwright, but as wife and mother, with a background of experience that has nothing to do with fiction or the stage." She appeared to the newspaper's readers not as the successful, independent female writer of the Roaring Twenties, straight-backed and resplendent in the fox fur stole she had once donned for her author photo, but as a "thoroughly modern yet intrinsically old-fashioned young woman"—hair bobbed, collar high, pearls blinking from her ears and neck. "Being the happy wife of a thoroughly satisfactory husband and the doting mother of two charming children means far more to her than all the glory that has attended her phenomenal entrance in the literary field," reported the article, which proceeded to showcase Isabel's theory that, if a woman could not or did not want to work outside the home, marriage presented her with a job equivalent to any other kind of labor. "I worked for my marriage: I ranked it as the very most important thing in my life," she explained to the newspaper's readers. "And I think that if people do that earnestly enough, putting as much thought and effort into it as a man puts into making a success of his business, it is bound to be happy." Yet if success in business was the responsibility of the man, then success in marriage was primarily the responsibility of the woman—"nature herself" had decreed it so. "I am a strong believer in the theory of types," Isabel told readers. "Most women are by nature cut out for the job of looking after personal relationships."

The ideas were not her own. She had taken them from the notes on domesticity her mother had given her before she had moved out of the house for the second time—notes that her mother was constantly adding to. "A philosophy of marriage must almost of necessity be also a philosophy of life," Katharine had written in 1930 before her daughter had decamped for the Poconos. "I am about to state a thesis which I know will be controversial, but I am prepared to defend it. Science is dependent on the masculine mind, marriage upon the feminine mind." Even in the shadows of first-wave feminism and women's suffrage, some general observations about the state of affairs between men and women struck Katharine as unimpeachably true in the early 1930s. "Success for mankind in general demands an impersonal attitude toward the hard facts of external reality; while success for womankind in general demands personal influence over men," she argued. Men like her husband and Chief were good at logic and figures; women like her and Isabel excelled at the emotional management of themselves and others. Every marriage represented the marriage of Jung's thinking type to Jung's feeling type: "The marriage of a fish to a canary," Katharine put it prettily, as if she were writing a new fable for her adult daughter's enjoyment.

But the typological division of the sexes was more than just a way of assigning roles that individual men and women would play within their marriages. For Katharine, it represented a more universal "division of labor necessitated by the inescapable division between the sexes": the division between the creators of life and the creators of culture. "Woman creates mankind, and man creates civilization—with women's assistance," she wrote. "The Shakespeares and Beethovens and Michelangelos, usually with their needs tenderly watched over and supplied by an inconspicuous but devoted mother and sister, or wife or mistress, are free to pour the entire stream of creative energy into their art—freedom which no woman artist can ever attain." By her account, a woman's desire to sweep floors, make beds, wash dishes, do laundry, breed and bear and baby children reigned as the chief attraction of her psyche, its pull as certain and as calculable as the force of gravity dragging Newton's apple down from its tree. Every "normal woman" wanted children more than she wanted anything else in the world, "not only wanted them, but needed them," Katharine claimed. Women who chose creative paths either suppressed their desires to have children or had to cope with the "even greater handicap of motherhood" on their artistic ambitions. There was no virtue in having it all. There was only hardship and failure and, worst of all, private conflict—psychic disintegration, in Jungian terms.

For Katharine, the same natural type distinctions that kept women at home and sent men to work also ensured that marriage stayed fun. She believed that there came a point in any marriage when the tensions that kept a couple interesting to each other began to slacken, and they risked passing from a state of love—mad, mysterious, consuming—to the state of boredom that invariably came from knowing each other a little too well. All happy families were alike in that they kept the necessary degree of tension intact, with both spouses working hard to preserve the mystery of each other's inner worlds. There was no need for Chief to understand the intricacies of Isabel's emotional responsibilities, just as there was no need for Isabel to advise her husband on his law practice. In Katharine's marriage fable, the moral was never to mistake the fish for the canary, never to judge the thinker for his lack of emotion or the feeler for her lack of logic. Otherwise both would suffer by comparison. Yet to acknowledge and accept each other's types was to bind themselves, freely and gladly, to the division of labor between the creators of life and the creators of civilization, exerting one's control over a biological inevitability that was as applicable to "business relationships, personal and vocational and education problems, as to the problems of marriage."

Katharine's notes had shaken Isabel's confidence in the idea that she could do everything she wanted: write books, write plays, be a wife, be a mother. She knew she had to choose and, gazing at the children as they ran through the house playing, laughing, jumping on her husband when he came home from work, she knew what her choice would be. But she took her last, half-hearted stab at fiction writing, more for contractual reasons than creative ones. She resurrected playwright Peter Jerningham and his secretary John "Mac" MacAndrews for the second novel she owed her publisher, a sequel to *Murder Yet to Come* that she titled with the imperative *Give Me Death*. In *Give Me Death*, Jerningham and Mac's services were requested by the Darniel dynasty, a wealthy, hotheaded southern clan whose male heirs had started committing suicide after their wedding nights. Sifting through the family's interminable blustering about Confederate honor, esteem, and Virginia pride, the detectives were to discover a long-repressed secret in the form of a suicide note written, it would appear, by Gordon Darniel, the family patriarch and first suicide: "It has been proved to me beyond hope of question that there is in my veins a strain of Negro blood. To prevent exposure of this fact, I am—shall we say—going away," he wrote. The note would turn out to be a plant, but the mere suggestion of a marriage tainted by miscegenation was enough; each esteemed Darniel man would hold the family's antique handgun to his head and pull the trigger, leaving behind a trail of contaminated blood and shameful secrets. In 1934, when anti-miscegenation laws were still enforced in many states, Isabel knew that the possibility of racial impurity—of discovering in oneself or one's spouse not a distinct personality type but a different race altogether—would strike fear into her readers' hearts.

Her critics were not sympathetic to her eugenic imagination.

"Isabel Briggs Myers is one of those fabulous people who won a large prize for writing a first mystery story and now she comes along with a second, 'Give Me Death,'" announced the *Chicago Daily Tribune* before it launched its sarcastic review of the novel. "Pretty nearly everybody in a family of southern extraction commits suicide, or maybe they do and maybe they don't. Anyway, you know why southerners, confronted by a shameful secret, feel called upon to kill themselves, so that element of the mystery will begin to clear itself fairly early in the game." For the reviewer at the *Washington Post,* Isabel's "epidemic of suicides" "throbbed too much" with racist apologia, while the London *Observer* begged the author to stop leaning so heavily on "a matter of possibly dying prejudice." "I would ask her not to launch a splendid ship on a ha'p'ort of tar," he concluded.

But the criticism hardly mattered; now that she had decided not to be a writer, the bad reviews counted for nothing. Freed from her obligations to write, she was happier than she had ever been—happy just to observe how her husband and her children were growing and changing; happy to pour her energies into being a wife and a mother, as Katharine had suggested, rather than a woman artist, neglectful of her household duties, besieged by feelings of guilt at home and at work. She believed she had made peace with her specialty in life, and, for the next several years, she would remain unencumbered by the kinds of psychological burdens that descended upon her mother and her amateur practice.

CHAPTER FIVE

Desperate Amateurs

Like many analytic psychologists in the 1920s and 1930s, Katharine Briggs was fond of analyzing people's dreams—indeed, she had developed a thoroughly scientific method of doing so. Every morning, she would remove a 3″ × 5″ index card from a stack she kept by the bed and turn expectantly to Lyman, who would then relay everything he remembered of the people, places, and events that had impressed themselves upon his sleeping mind. Katharine would then list the "dramatis personae"—the characters—in Lyman's dreams before ascribing to each of them a deeper, more incisive meaning. If one of Lyman's dreams struck her as especially revealing, she would type up her notes in the morning and spend the rest of the day clipping images from Depression-era newspapers, magazines, postcards, and recipe books to illustrate his visions. In the years leading up to World War II, she amassed dozens of scrapbooked dreams, loose-leaf testaments to her husband's unconscious.

In one strange and memorable dream from the mid-1930s, a dream that Katharine titled "An Embarrassment of Femininity," Lyman had found himself tucked into bed with Katharine and three of her female friends, each of whom he had felt obliged to "peck" in front of his quietly amused wife. After he had fulfilled his kissing duties, he awoke and was instantly overtaken by shame. Yet when he narrated the dream to his wife, she rejected any obvious sexual explanation for the presence of her friends in her and Lyman's bed. The women were not to be taken literally, she explained to him, for they represented the inferior functions of Lyman's psyche—the aspects of him that had been neglected for years, had started to atrophy, and now demanded his attention. The first friend stood for intuition, yearning to be embraced. The second and third both symbolized feeling. Lyman was a sensing and thinking type, she explained. It was only in his dreams that he could cheat on his personality—on himself.

To illustrate her point, Katharine glued a black-and-white photograph of the *Mona Lisa,* smiling her famously ambiguous smile, onto an image of a shockingly pink flower in the throes of full bloom. Next to the flower, she pasted a drawing of a well-groomed couple, all silk and pomade, fondling each other in a rose garden. For a dream that she had refused to interpret according to "scandalizing" Freudian protocols, the collage Katharine created to represent Lyman's unconscious emitted a bizarre, beautiful, and frustrated creative energy. This

Katharine's collage for Lyman's dream "An Embarrassment of Femininity"

energy, this unholy trinity of sex, love, and amateur dream analysis, was what sustained Katharine's devotion to type.

She was an amateur in the most promising and the most dangerous sense of the word: "amateur," from the Latin verb *amare*, "to love," but in a glancing and superficial kind of way. She loved dream analysis and she loved Jung's system of type, but when it came to practicing it, she was, by her own reluctant admission, a dabbler, an autodidact. To continue her education after her assignments for the *New Republic* came to an end, she started writing to the women who had studied under Jung or retained his services as a psychoanalyst, requesting that they send her records of their private sessions with him. She wrote to Mary Foote, the famous American portrait painter who had closed her New York studio in the late 1920s and moved to Zurich to become the transcriber and publisher of Jung's seminars. She wrote to Rosamond Clark, a wealthy, waspish Bostonian who, along with psychoanalysts Esther Harding and Eleanor Bertine, had hosted Jung on Bailey Island, a secluded summer community off the coast of Maine where Jung had led a six-day seminar titled "Dream Symbols of the Individuation Process." She wrote to Dr. Kristine Mann, founder of the Analytical Psychology Club of New York and one of the first practicing Jungians in the United States, to ask if Mann would accept her as a patient, confident that the surest way to learn how to analyze others' types was to subject herself to analysis. "I and my two colleagues have been analyzing people in New York for nearly twenty years now," Mann wrote back. "Our price is $20 for each consultation of an hour. But we all try to bring our fee within the reach of those who are seriously anxious to take up analysis."

Katharine does not appear to have responded to Mann's offer. Instead she coveted Mann's position as a self-anointed Jungian analyst; if Mann could offer analysis sessions out of her living room, there was nothing to stop Katharine from doing the same thing. Ethical concerns did not enter her mind, and there is no reason they should have; her ambitions predated the emergence of licensing and certification programs for psychologists by two decades. Even if she had wanted to remake herself as a professional, there was no way for her to do so. All Katharine thought about was the ease with which she could transform her cosmic laboratory of baby training into an institution of psychoanalytic care: the "Maker's Cosmic Laboratory," as she called it, differentiating her newer and loftier aspirations as a psychoanalyst from her more immediate goals as a mother.

She would outfit the Maker's Laboratory with all the tools, material and ideological, that would prove crucial to her and Isabel's design of the Myers-Briggs Type Indicator over the next half decade. There were the 3″ × 5″ index cards on which Katharine would chronicle her subjects' dream motifs ("Phallus," "Eczema," "Nakedness," "Garage," "Ship," "Peacock," "Pig," "Plow," "Rape of the Mother," "Rebirth," "Resurrection") and link them to innate preferences for introversion and extraversion, sensing and intuition, feeling and thinking. There were the exercises from the dream study club she organized for her friends, a group of neighborhood women who frequented Katharine's home once a week to discuss their unconscious visions and to understand, with Katharine's guidance, how their inferior personality functions could be enhanced so they might live an "enriching and complete life." There were dozens of copies of the type tables she had debuted in the *New Republic* and now passed out to anyone who asked for one. Above all, there was Katharine's unshakable belief that the good intentions of an amateur could make up for the lack of scientific rigor in her analytic process. Later, when the Myers-Briggs Type Indicator would come under fire from scientists and statisticians, the same spirit of amateur can-do would buffer Isabel from her harshest critics.

Katharine found the transition from mother to analyst to be easier than she had anticipated. Personality typing was more intuitive than *Psychological Types* made it out to be, she reasoned. "You could always try an interpretation any way—using it tentatively as a working hypothesis," she wrote in her notes. When Lyman dreamed of a lithe dark-haired girl, a Spanish dancer, who was teaching him some new steps, Katharine interpreted the figure of the woman as "his soul working in the interest of neglected sensation." "A little pleasure now and then, a little living in, and enjoyment of the present for its own sake certainly wouldn't hurt," she told him. To encourage his indulgence in sensual pleasures, she had the attic redone in knotty pine and made into a billiard room for his Christmas present. "Whatever new steps he was to learn from the lady of his dreams was between him and his own soul and no business of mine," she sniffed. "But by getting an inkling of his dream life I was able to give him the most successful Christmas present I have ever given to anybody." Lyman, who retired to his attic immediately after dinner and only descended late at night, happily continued to act the part of his wife's subject when he woke in the mornings. He knew that her will to type him would always outpace her judgment of his desires, however suspicious they might have been.

Soon, however, Katharine realized that her greatest goal—to hasten the evolution of human civilization one personality at a time—would not be achieved by experimenting on her accommodating husband and well-adjusted neighbors. She wanted to surround herself with people whose "souls were diabolical—starved, crippled, ruined," she wrote in her diary, people possessed by "an almost overwhelming sense of mystery" that she alone could solve. Not only were these people the ones who needed her help the most, but they were also the people she needed to advance her understanding of type beyond Jung's theoretical abstractions, to understand how it looked, sounded, or felt when someone suffered from "introversion neurosis" or "extraverted hysteria." Just as she had opened her home to hapless mothers, demonstrating to them how her experiments could lead to better babies and better students, so too would she impress her practice of analysis onto those who had not yet discovered how learning their type could drag them out of "the primitive scum" of modernity and into an enlightened state.

This time, out of necessity rather than choice, her experiments would begin with someone else's child.

. . . .

Sixteen-year-old Mary Venable Tuckerman of Montgomery County, Maryland, had an IQ of 140 and an aversion to good hard work. Hers was an old story. She was the rebellious daughter of a respectable bourgeois family. Her mother, Una, was a scholar of Wordsworth. Her father, Louis, was a researcher in the thermometer testing division of the National Bureau of Standards. Most mornings, Mary refused to go to school. When she did go, she was inattentive and dreamy, burying her head in one of the many fantasy books she had checked out from the library. Year after year, she failed her classes. She had no friends, she hated her parents, and she resented her little brother, Louis Jr., a budding, brilliant mathematician who took after his father. She was, in short, all the things that difficult teenagers tend to be: stubborn and disrespectful and quite possibly depressed, the imperfect child of parents so buffered by their own accomplishments that they simply could not imagine what to do with her.

At the Bureau of Standards, Louis reported to his friend and superior Lyman Briggs, to whom he had confided his problems with his daughter. Katharine, who had met the Tuckerman family at a party in the spring of 1930, had taken an unusual interest in Mary's activities. A wayward child, Mary seemed the opposite of Isabel, but she was nevertheless a "valuable personality" in her own right, Katharine told Una and Louis. According to her type table, Mary was an extreme introvert, someone in possession of a brilliant mind whose withdrawal into the childish mysteries of fantasy and fairy tale signaled an unevolved primitivism. Some aspect of her personality had failed to integrate properly.

Using her type tables and child-rearing questionnaires to guide her, Katharine diagnosed Mary as threatened by a "serious introversion neurosis"—a total retreat from reality. The only cure for it, she told Mary's parents, was for Katharine to "entangle her in life." Before she could begin, however, she wanted to get Jung's opinion on the matter. "Without professional training or experience, and guided only by my none too perfect understanding of analytic psychology, I feel very deeply the responsibility I have taken upon myself," Katharine wrote to Jung of Mary Tuckerman. "Indirectly, through my effort to understand and apply your teachings, she is in a certain sense your patient."

But she was too eager to wait for Jung's approval—or perhaps too fearful that he would deny her the contagious pleasure of helping others under his auspices. Within the next week, Mary, frightened and tense, was installed at the Bureau of Standards as Lyman's summer intern. Una did not know how to drive, so Mary took the streetcar to work every morning. But every afternoon, Katharine picked her up. She motored through the surrounding parks or the Bethesda countryside, delaying Mary's return home so that she and Katharine might get acquainted. Slowly, Mary warmed to Katharine's company and began to confide in her as she had never confided in her parents. "I'm behind in my school work, the biggest girl in the class, and I just die of shame to see those little kids doing things I can't do!" she wept to Katharine one day, slumping low in the passenger's seat. "I haven't the nerve to ask for help, show my ignorance, be laughed at! I'd a million times rather they think me bad than know I'm a fool." Touched by the girl's tears, Katharine took to calling Mary "my little friend Tucky." She believed her conversation to be Tucky's reward for a hard day's work, a generous offering to a child whose parents did not have the time or the wherewithal to support her journey to meeting herself.

In her next letter to Jung, Katharine reassured him that she was attempting no analysis whatsoever, none, that is, except the most straightforward and unimpeachable kind—nothing that anyone could call reckless. She had simply encouraged Tucky to share with her the dreams she had, until then, kept inside, so that Katharine might determine how Jung's types could illuminate the unconscious elements of Tucky's personality. And what remarkably mythological dreams Tucky had! They seemed to have come straight from the pages of a picture book, bursting with golden heroes and holy lands and monsters lurking in the dark. There was one dream that Katharine titled "The Prince," in which a sun god hatched from an egg and built a dazzling city in the deepest caverns of the earth, a home for all the winged immortals who would one day rule the world. There was another called "Brothers," a dream Tucky had forgotten upon waking but that later impressed itself on her conscious mind in the form of a poem. On the afternoon that she received her first paycheck from her internship, she opened the door to Katharine's car in a state of great agitation, determined to recite the poem to her.

"I have a poem!" she exclaimed to Katharine. "It's right there, but I can't get all of it out! It's coming—Oh, I want to write it down!"

Katharine said nothing. She began driving the car in circles, slowly, so that Tucky might turn her mind inward, gain access to her unconscious, and recall the verses of "Brothers." Beside her, the girl grew unnaturally quiet and unnaturally still—as if in a trance, Katharine thought—and Katharine pulled the car to the side of the road. She retrieved a pen and $3'' \times 5''$ index card from her bag and waited for the symbols and images that would come. As the sun set over the hills of Bethesda, its red-gold light streaming into the Briggs family's car, Tucky began to chant her poem in a cold, abstracted little voice:

A boy from the depths of the ocean
A boy from the mountain heights—
We met by the side of the water
And pledged our friendship there.

There is nothing that can part our friendship
Or destroy our brotherhood,
For we are sons of the ages
And our tie is of more than blood.

Though race and time and space and death
May part us from each other
We are brothers still till the end of time,
Going arm and arm together.

We were born of different races
And neither understood
Yet we met and gave without asking
The pledge of Brotherhood.

Katharine was dumbfounded by "Brothers." Image for image, its verses echoed a strange vision that Isabel—an introvert herself—had had at the dinner table earlier that month, when she and the children were visiting her and Lyman. Peter had requested that his mother save a fried chicken leg for him to eat later. He did not want it then, but he could not bear to have anything so good wasted.

"Don't worry," Isabel had said with a reassuring laugh. "Nothing will be wasted." Then she had stopped talking, stopped moving, stopped breathing. She told her mother that the phrase "Nothing will be wasted" had touched something deep inside her. She had seen before her eyes not the Briggs family's dinner table but the shore of an ocean on a narrow, boulder-strewn beach. There, at the water's edge, stood two boys, gripping the shaft of a strong staff between them. One was dark haired and dark eyed, his skin tanned by the sun, his only clothing a khaki loincloth. His hair was knotted with vines and leaves—a testament to the untamed jungle from which he had descended to the seashore. His companion was golden and slender. He laughed often, and as he did, he splashed the other boy with his two wet, webbed feet, sending drops of water into the sky where they hung and glittered like stars. "He gives the impression of princely aristocracy, culture and spirituality," Isabel told her mother, who had written it all down for Isabel on her $3'' \times 5''$ index cards. "He smiles up at the boy whose home is in the heights, but who is nevertheless his friend." Katharine had told Isabel the light boy was a symbol of introversion and intuition; the dark one a symbol of extraversion and sensation coming to meet and complete him.

Could it be, Katharine wondered, that the lives of her two very different introverts were somehow connected across time and space, that Tucky's expression of her dream had opened a conduit between them? Absent any physical connection between the two young women, she believed she could still perceive the entanglement of Mary's and Isabel's souls in the shared mirage series of each girl's unconscious. It was even possible, she thought, that there were more people who had had this vision: a brotherhood—or, in this case, a sisterhood—of introverts, signaling to one another across immeasurable distances, like whales scattered across the ocean. Communities could be organized around personality types. She stopped her mind's racing long enough to start the car and drive Tucky home. When she stepped out of the car, the girl was still holding the 3″ × 5″ card with Katharine's transcription of "Brothers" on it.

When Katharine came home that night, she sat down at the kitchen table to write Tucky a letter. The time for circumspection had passed, she thought. Tucky had to know what was happening inside her. "My very dear Tucky," she began. "I like your little <u>Brothers</u> poem more than I know how to tell you, but I am going to try to explain how and why I like it." The poem was far more meaningful than Tucky could ever know. Katharine asked her to think of it as a pretty little purse, one filled with a secret compartment in which there were hidden any number of priceless jewels—an irresistible metaphor for a girl whose inner life had once seemed impoverished and irredeemable. Her job, as Tucky's friend, was to open the purse's secret compartment so that Tucky might have the pleasure of possessing the jewels, to interpret the poem using Jung's language of type so that Tuckey might gain access to her more evolved self, which Katharine could make hard and glittering and valuable at last. "I believe that your poem is an allegory, given to you by the author of your dreams much as Jesus gave the parables to his disciples," Katharine concluded. "I believe it to be both a promise and a prophecy. I believe it tells you the intimate story of your soul life." The poem spoke of a change to come, a rebirth that would release Tucky from her life of neglect and disappointment as the big girl, the sad girl, the stupid girl, the bad daughter. Surely, she thought, Jung would not object her methods.

Their drives continued as before, only now when Tucky opened the car door to walk home, she and Katharine would grasp hands for a moment, each mutely contemplating the other's presence. One week before Tucky was to start her junior year in high school, Katharine took her on a road trip. As the highway stretched before them at night, black and infinite, they played a little Jungian game that Katharine called "imagery." She would speak a word into the dark and Tucky would describe the images the word evoked. Then she would speak its opposite and wait to see which word in the pair had a greater effect on Tucky's imagination.

"Immortality," Katharine said.

"It is dark," Tucky answered, "with just enough light to see; there are rocks jumbled about; one pile is bigger than the rest. There is a man sitting on this pile. He is strong and fine and there is a feeling of peace and quiet which is so strong and so much a part of the picture that the picture would be empty without it."

"Death."

"There are two pictures. One is an ugly heap of human skeletons, falling apart and crumbling in a black, damp, stagnant, musty-smelling hole. The other is of the Prince. He is lying with his left arm holding his shield, and his right hand is lying by his side. His eyes are closed and he is sleeping."

They stopped at the summer camp in the Pocono Mountains where Isabel, then struggling to write her follow-up to *Murder Yet to Come,* had retreated on her long vacation with her husband and children. Mother and daughter observed Tucky, who, at the age of sixteen, was neither an adult nor a child and had to decide whether to run with Peter and Ann through the laurel blossoms or to sip a cool glass of lemonade with the adults, who would talk about serious things in serious tones. She chose the adults. When Katharine and Isabel took her to lunch that afternoon, her face glowed as she announced to them a revelation of sorts. "I'm changing!" she cried. "I'm different!"

Here was the evolution that Katharine had imagined her Maker's Cosmic Laboratory could bring. Isabel took careful note of it. Decades later, the imagery game her mother had played in the dark with Tucky would form the basis for one of the last sections on the Myers-Briggs Type Indicator: the word pairs, which gave the test taker two opposed words (like "immortality" and "death") and asked her to pick the one that most appealed to her personality.

. . . .

Katharine and Tucky left the Poconos as the laurel blossoms started to wilt. They spent a long, languorous week on the road in each other's company, oblivious to the August heat waves and the droughts, the changing currents of a world on the brink of another great war. Then they motored back to Bethesda so Tucky could prepare for the school year.

"Do you ever feel like kissing Mrs. Briggs?" Una Tuckerman asked her daughter when Katharine finally brought her home.

"No!" Tucky protested. "That would spoil it all."

But Una had grown wary of the relationship that had developed between Katharine and her daughter. She knew that she had been cast as the villain in Tucky's tragedy of psychological self-discovery. "I was fond of Tucky because she let me see her soul, which though somewhat spoiled was lovable and terribly troubled," Katharine wrote. "Her parents and teachers saw only the bluffing, naughty persona, which was one of the most defiant superiority complexes I ever saw." In place of the blood ties between mother and daughter, Katharine had asserted the far more intimate, more intense connection between an amateur psychologist and her unwitting patient. Meeting yourself, she had warned Mary, could be a profoundly lonely endeavor. As it liberated you, so too did it sever the bonds you had established with other people, other ways of living and loving life. Meeting yourself meant assuming a great and solitary responsibility for your actions, a responsibility that could leave one feeling appallingly alone. Yet Katharine was here to share that responsibility with her and to delight in the new and frightening pleasures that Mary's self-understanding might bring.

Una did not welcome the cultish kidnapping of her daughter by Katharine. At her most anxious, she demanded a stop to it. "She naturally loved me and hated me for helping her child," Katharine informed Jung in a letter she wrote updating him on her progress with Tucky. The evening car rides, the late summer excursions, the unfolding of Mary's dreams in the dark—all of this was looked upon by Una with suspicion, which Katharine attributed to her jealousy and paranoia. As Mary was pulled back into her family life and out of reach, Katharine started writing desperate letters to Jung, begging for his help. She revealed to him a very different Tuckerman family than the one she had introduced him to in her earlier correspondence. Lyman's friend Louis was no top-notch scientist, she said, but a "very neurotic man," "one of those brilliant but impractical people who hate and shirk responsibility—the introverted thinker I should say, to the nth degree!" Her friend Una was no longer a woman of cultural refinement but a lunatic, a household tyrant, an unhappy woman trapped in an unsuccessful marriage from which there was no escape—only misdirected anger toward Katharine. And even Mary, Katharine's dear little friend Tucky, was an "outrageously bad mannered girl," "self-centered and arrogant," "tiresome to be around," "wholly lacking in graciousness and tact," she raved. Yet at the same time she insulted the family in her correspondence, she continued to approach them, offering her help even as it was repeatedly rebuffed. The less they wanted her, it seemed, the more desperately she wanted them.

Concerned for her daughter, Una forbade Katharine from seeing her and took Mary to a psychiatrist—an "extravert Freudian who had a deadly hatred for me," Katharine complained to Jung. She believed that she and Jung were fighting Una and Freud for Mary's soul, a fight in which she was on the side of the righteous—the side of her god and other introverts—and Una, her mind scandalized by Freud's suggestions of sexual impropriety and deviance, was on the side of evil. "I witnessed the battle between god and the devil, and had the shocking experience of seeing the devil win," she wrote, wondering how much her heroic interference had served as the catalyst for the struggle. "I fear I am myself the storm center of her psychosis, the devil persecutor, who has brought all this on her."

It never occurred to her that her interference in the Tuckerman family's affairs could constitute a risky and profound ethical violation—the kind the American Psychological Association sought to prevent two decades later by indicting the spirit of amateurism that Katharine championed and would continue to embrace as she and Isabel started their work on the type indicator. "It is unethical for a psychologist either to claim directly or to imply professional qualifications that exceed those he has actually attained," the APA would write in 1953. "A psychologist engaged in clinical or consulting work, where sound interpersonal relationships are essential to effective endeavor, should be aware of the inadequacies in his own personality which may bias his appraisals of others or distort his relationships with them, and should refrain from undertaking any activity where his personal limitations are likely to result in inferior professional services." But in the early 1930s, when the field had yet to articulate its professional protocols, let alone share them with the public, Katharine could see no cause for withholding her application of type theory to help Mary. "In the absence of psychoanalysts," she wrote, "anyone with a reasonable power of introversion or the gift of prayer may seize upon some important elements of truth in almost any dream." If anything, the only problem was that she was, inevitably, a poor proxy for Jung, her god. "If I could wish just one wish for humanity it would be for some half million Dr. Jungs scattered at convenient intervals over the face of the earth," she wrote to him, awaiting his instructions for what she should do with the Tuckerman family now that she had invested so much in their lives.

When his letter arrived, she was hurt by how severely he reprimanded her for her intrusiveness. "It is indeed an unfortunate end to your attempts, yet an almost unavoidable one," he wrote, refusing to absolve her of her bad behavior. "Your attitude was altogether too Christian. You <u>wanted</u> to help, which is an encroachment upon the will of others. Your attitude ought to be one who offers an opportunity that can be taken or rejected. Otherwise you are more likely to get in trouble. It is so because Man is not fundamentally good, almost half of him is devil." Only the blind mistook entanglement for liberation. She could not have known the hypocrisy that lay behind his admonition— that he, too, had often failed to acknowledge the "inadequacies in his own personality" that made him susceptible to intimate relationships, especially with his female patients. All she knew was that she had been scolded by the only person whose praise she truly desired. Compounding her larger sense of embarrassment was a small but sharp jab that he included at the end of his note: she had failed to provide sufficient postage for her letter, and he had had to pay the difference.

"If you should write another letter to me," he concluded, "please take into consideration that a letter abroad costs more than two cents."

Her pride hurt, she tried to defend her amateurism as mitigated by her faith—not in Christianity but in his teachings. His suggestion that the Tuckermans were victims of her "too Christian zeal," she argued, had come as a "good deal of shock." She had presented herself to the Tuckerman family as nothing more than "a studious home-staying woman, learning to be guided by my dreams and much awed by the experience." If the family had made the mistake of treating her as a trained psychologist, that was their fault and not hers. She bore no responsibility for it, she insisted; she was, if anything, emboldened by her missteps to do better. "I don't want either to repeat the experience or let it make a coward of me," she closed her letter. But it did—she withdrew from the Tuckerman family, from Jung, from the practice of analytical psychology altogether.

She would spend the next several years of her life writing about type with the same obsessive intensity as before but never pursuing the "starved, crippled, ruined" souls of her neighborhood as she had once dreamed. Perhaps she realized that there was a limit to what could be accomplished in the home, no matter how hard one might have tried to model it after the scientific or psychiatric laboratory. The personae she had prioritized for so long ("Wife; Mother; Mother-in-Law; Daughter-in-Law; Housekeeper") could not survive for long in a world where personality and type were being debated in institutions of serious, scientific study. In 1935, she decided it was time to shutter her cosmic laboratories. She wanted to see what the world had to offer Jung's theory of types—and what she could offer the world.

Part Two

CHAPTER SIX

The Science of Man

I n September 1936, several hundreds of miles away from the Briggs family home in Washington, D.C., Harvard College celebrated the three-hundred-year anniversary of its founding with a spectacular Tercentenary bash. Among the thousands of visitors who descended on Cambridge that autumn was Carl Jung, who, at the age of sixty-one, had reluctantly left his home in Küsnacht to stand in the rain at the Tercentenary Theatre and deliver an address on dreams. He would speak of certain fearful scenarios that made themselves known to people while they were sleeping: the elevator that shudders to an unexpected stop, the bottomless fall that jolts the dreamer awake, the metamorphosis of people into animals and animals into gods. The great psychotherapeutic systems of the past were religions, Jung claimed, which had little patience for the individual psyche. Religions healed people through the depersonalization of suffering. Enduring great sorrow was as important for heavenly redemption as performing good deeds or attending Sunday services. By contrast, analytic psychology cared about the individual's feelings and experiences with an intensity that was unprecedented in American society—a philosophy of emotional attentiveness that was especially pertinent to the nation's female minds. "You can't think women away or think through them," he concluded. "Feeling is the only thing applicable."

Katharine Briggs, also sixty-one years of age, had traveled a considerable distance to attend the Tercentenary bash in the hopes that she might secure a private analysis session with Jung. For a short time, she had stopped writing to him after he rebuked her for her interference in the Tuckerman family's affairs. But when she had learned about his visit to Cambridge, she had renewed her correspondence with him. "I feel as if I know you better than I have ever known anyone else, but as a human being you are not real to me," she wrote. "Your books have been my Bible for more than fifteen years, and life without what I have learned from them would be unthinkable." Theirs was a relationship that, until now, had been governed by his written word and her absolute devotion to it.

But Katharine wanted more. She wanted "a chance at proving your concrete existence," she told him. She had dreams she wanted to spread before his feet, so that he might tread upon her unconscious mind and marvel at its dim-lit visions: a recurring nightmare in which Lyman cheated on her with a woman he called his "true wife"; another in which she watched, impassive, as he had a heart attack and died at her feet; a third in which she was trapped in a boardinghouse filled with babies, each crying desperately in his crib. She had a feeling of fatedness, she told Jung, "a strong sense of being directed, of going somewhere"—a destination as yet unknown. Despite the rejection of *The Man from Zurich,* she still had an urge to write novels like her daughter once had, and the urge so possessed her that it often left her feeling empty and weak, unmoored from reality. To steady herself, she had started working on another questionnaire based on his ideas about extraverts and introverts, thinkers and feelers. It was a project she had disclosed only to her diary and to Isabel, guarding it from her husband. "It is a lonely business to keep what amounts to a religion entirely to yourself," she told Jung.

Most of all, she wanted to find a way to expand her amateur practice of personality typing, drawing on her questionnaires, her type tables, her index cards, and her unwavering commitment to the soul to spread the gospel of Jung as far and wide as she could. After the Tuckerman affair, her friends had urged her to reopen Maker's Cosmic Laboratory for psychoanalysis sessions. Her dream club now had more members than ever, more neighborhood women eager to join forces to "experiment with our dreams, assuming them for experimental purposes to be 'the word of God' about us." She took her duties as an analyst more seriously after her brush with Una Tuckerman and the devil inside her daughter. Now there was "a very neurotic woman who wants to make Jesus Christ out of me," she confided in Jung. "I appear to be her help and salvation. She has gained fifteen pounds in weight, is beginning to understand her dreams, and talks about 'the new life.' I have a lot to learn about such a relationship and I need to learn it soon." She wanted to continue to help people, but she was not sure how to proceed after she had failed her little friend Tucky.

Surely Jung had to pause and wonder at what his teacher Sigmund Freud would have identified as a full-blown case of transference: the redirection of affection, care, and even sexual desire onto the analyst. And yet his subsequent letters to Katharine betrayed nothing of the sort—this sort of thing happened to him all the time. "As I shall spend three weeks at Harvard, I'm sure to find a spare moment for consultation," he wrote back to her. And so Katharine had journeyed to Cambridge with the rest of the East Coast's students and the soldiers, the professors and the politicians, arriving on a wet fall morning just as the president of the United States, Franklin Delano Roosevelt, was finishing his welcome address to the crowd. She would note in her diary that she had remembered at that moment how much she disliked Roosevelt, an extraverted feeling type, prone to making overly emotional appeals to "human rights" over "property rights" in his New Deal legislation. A lifelong Republican, she had voted for Herbert Hoover, whom she had identified as an introverted thinker. Yet she endured the president's speech in Harvard Yard, parting the sea of men in black slicked overcoats and top hats, all of them waiting to drink in the words of her savior. She was to see him that night for a private session. For the first time, she would share everything with him.

Also in the audience for Carl Jung's lecture at the Tercentenary Theatre was Henry Murray, director of the Harvard Psychological Clinic, Jung's friend and former patient. A handsome, wealthy, and buoyant New Englander who liked to joke that he had majored in the "three R's" at Harvard—"Rum, Rowing, and Romanticism"—Murray would have felt more at home among the reveling crowds of men than Katharine. But he was plagued by certain doubts about Jung and the future practice of analytic psychology now that the ruling parties of Europe were girding themselves for yet another great war.

This war, Murray suspected, would require a different appraisal of the human psyche than what Jung and his disciples had practiced since World War I. "Because Fascism has reared its Brutal head we can attack it, & in attacking it gain strength," he wrote to his friend Lewis Mumford. But he worried about the "forward march of advertisitis," a term he coined to describe the narcissism that bedeviled psychoanalysts, encouraging them and their patients to retreat from the social and political world into the solipsism of the self. It was a quietly evil force that Murray believed was corrupting, or had corrupted, "the Emotional Integration of the whole Nation." "Advertisitis slips in the ears & eyes & runs down the nerves & eats the vitals out of the ganglia without our knowing it," he warned Mumford, weighing the growing sense of responsibility he felt that he, personally, had to figure out how psychology could save civilization from self-destruction.

His path did not cross Katharine's that morning in the autumn rain—soon, it would—but their lives had run parallel to each other's through the first half of the twentieth century. Both had grown up with earnest religious convictions that were later displaced by the discovery of Jungian psychology. Both had clung to Jung's type theory to affirm their belief that personality was a soulful, rather than a scientific, research program. Both had established strange and eccentric psychosexual relationships with Jung in the process of their typological education. Both identified themselves as introverted, intuitive, and thinking types—just like Jung.

Yet even amidst all these similarities, there were crucial differences. Whereas Katharine's labors had never fully transcended her home laboratory, Murray's work at the Harvard Psychological Clinic had become the institutional bedrock of American personality psychology by the end of the Great Depression. The infrastructure he had helped to develop just before and during World War II was unprecedented.

He had established research programs up and down the East Coast, trained dozens of students, vetted personality tests, analyzed famous people of all stripes: literary critics like Van Wyck Brooks, army officers like Ralph Eaton, novelists like Eva Goldbeck. Murray had not yet heard of Katharine Briggs or her forced-choice questionnaires, her $3'' \times 5''$ index cards, her type tables. Yet his labors would prove essential to the expulsion of personality typing from the intimate, obscure circle traced by the Myers and Briggs families into the public realms of politics, business, and higher education.

They would not have agreed on what they believed type could—or should—do once it exceeded personal considerations. For Katharine, type's public import turned on the twinned problem of salvation and social efficiency. She believed that knowing one's type could save the soul of an individual while prompting him to assume the specialized offices that would help him advance civilization. Murray had little faith that either salvation or specialization could stay the encroaching horrors of fascism or combat the solipsism that attended to political complacency. He wanted to find ways to make the personal political: to marshal the vast, often abstract scholarly conversation about what personality was and how it could be measured to help make the world a safer and more just place. His intimate knowledge of Jung led him to believe that the devotional relationships he cultivated with his patients were too self-absorbed and not amenable to the fight against advertisitis. Murray was looking for new allies equipped with new weapons to draw type into the public sphere.

Soon, his search would lead him to both the woman standing in the rain at the Tercentenary Theatre and her daughter, hard at work designing a questionnaire that would democratize type by substituting the intimacy of Jung's attentions with a deceptively impersonal language of self. Just as Murray had never heard of Briggs or Myers in 1936, Katharine and Isabel did not know Murray or his life story. Soon, they would—and soon, too, their separate missions would intersect, ushering personality testing into the modern era.

. . . .

Murray had first met Jung in 1925, two years after the release of the English translation of *Psychological Types*. At the time, Murray had just received his MD and MA in biology from Columbia University. He considered himself a scientifically minded man, skeptical of trendy nonsense like dream analysis and hypnosis. But when he read Jung's book, he was struck by a bewildered sense of admiration, a slow dawning astonishment that he had experienced only once before, when he had read the opening line of Herman Melville's *Moby-Dick*—"Call me Ishmael"—for the first time. *Psychological Types* seemed to him, as it had seemed to Katharine, like a "gratuitous answer to an unspoken prayer," a comprehensive theory of human personality that illuminated the differences and similarities among people in an idiom that was easy to grasp and even easier to believe. Reading it unhinged his confidence in his chosen profession of medicine. Perhaps, he thought, he should dedicate his life to becoming a Jungian analyst instead of a doctor. That way, he too could learn how to paint fine-grained portraits of people's souls, creating fascinating and fraught characters out of type and type pairs.

To make up his mind, he embarked on a pilgrimage. On Easter Sunday in 1925, with his beloved copy of *Moby-Dick* tucked under his arm, he set sail for Jung's home in Küsnacht. The men shook hands for the first time in Jung's office, amidst the fine old furniture and the framed pictures, the raised face of the Virgin Mary and her coven of female saints. For the next three weeks, they spent sun-glazed afternoons sailing on Lake Zurich. Jung quizzed Murray about the women in his life: his wife, Josephine Murray, and the woman he wanted to make his mistress, Christiana Morgan. Of the two, Christiana interested Jung more, not because she was all the things mistresses in fiction so often are—brilliant, beautiful, and hopelessly neurotic—but because, as an artist and lay psychoanalyst, she was also a devotee of *Psychological Types*. Murray had met her at a dinner party in New York, where she had turned to him, cigarette glowing, and asked in a low voice if he preferred Jung or Freud. He had lent her his copy of *Psychological Types,* knowing full well that to lend an unmarried woman a book was a romantic gesture, but to lend her this book was to invite a mutual contemplation of their souls. Murray asked Jung if he thought God would disapprove of the distance he could measure between Murray's desires and Christianity's moral code.

Jung had little patience for God. Murray was an introverted, intuitive, and thinking type, he said—just like himself—and for men like them, the most important thing to learn was how to disregard bourgeois ideas of right and wrong. Murray had to learn to "take [his] life in [his] own hands," he instructed. One morning, after they had docked the boat, Jung invited Murray to his home for tea so that he might meet Emma, Jung's dutiful wife and occasional stenographer, and Toni Wolff, his lover. The two women, Jung claimed, lived together in peace, as they filled two totally different roles in his life. "One could characterize these two types of women both as the 'married mothers' and the 'friends and concubines,'" he explained. The mothers took care of your home and your children. The concubines took care of your libido by inspiring new passions, both sexual and intellectual in nature. Some men repressed the desire they felt toward friends and concubines, exiling them to the realm of dreams, where they danced around one's head like Lyman's Spanish mistress. Others, like Jung, made their dreams reality and never looked back in guilt or regret. These were the easy truces that could be struck when one knew one's type.

It took only three days on Lake Zurich for Murray to diagnose Jung's "cathexis for women": his "adoration, adulation" of his female patients and the female sex more generally. Nevertheless, he took Jung's advice and decided to take his life into his own hands. He and Christiana Morgan became lovers, and together they reread Jung and Melville, Ralph Waldo Emerson and William James, and discussed how they could make Jung's language of the self the cornerstone of modern personality psychology. "To go on with what Jung has begun would be the biggest thing that could be done at the present time. Is there a bigger whale or whiter whale than the chains of the outworn attitude which fetter and hinder the spirit?" they whispered, coiled naked in the dark. In the years that Katharine Briggs spent drafting "Meet Yourself" and "Up from Barbarism" to help lead people from their primitive impulses to their enlightened selves, Murray and Morgan worked together to create a new academic discipline that would illuminate the radical freedom that resulted from knowing one's type. They would call this discipline "personology," and they would define it as "the science of men."

Personology was an ambitious, almost boundless undertaking. Its goal was to stitch together a person's entire life from all its constituent parts, much in the way the great American novelists and biographers that Katharine and Murray both admired could conjure up a character from a discrete series of expressions and gestures, thoughts and feelings. Personology accounted for everything in the objective and subjective realms: a man's observable tics, habits, and routines as well as his unconscious sexual urges; his early childhood experiences with his parents as well as his professional ambitions and work environment. It was an attempt to narrate the complicated business of existence without reducing it to anything as crude as Watson's philosophy of learned behavior or Freud's theories of sexual repression. "Personality is a temporal whole," Murray wrote in *Explorations in Personality.* "To understand a part of it one must have a sense, though vague, of the totality." Like a good novelist, the good personality theorist placed the self at the center of a story and groped through the dense thicket of social and historical circumstances to trace the story's central arc. Personology allowed the theorist to assign different stories to different kinds of types: the tale of the tortured artist, the fearless leader, the risk-taking entrepreneur, the average Joe. Instead of Katharine's personality paint box, its 2 × 4 grid populated by popular characters—the philosopher, the prophet, the explorer, the reformers—Murray offered his readers entire narrative arcs, with a clear beginning, middle, and end.

One place to tell the story of the self was at the Introvert-Extravert Club of New York, a devotional site for Jung's students and patients who, upon their return to the United States, wanted to revive the pathos of self-discovery that had characterized their time at Küsnacht. Murray had joined it almost as a joke before he had left for Küsnacht, but now he used it as a testing ground for personology's theories and techniques. He began with a Jungian questionnaire, one that was far more complicated than Katharine's—a hodgepodge of logic and problem-solving tests, pattern discoveries, and questions about intellectual preference. He administered it to thirty-eight of his friends, including journalist Walter Lippmann, poet Edward Arlington Robinson, psychiatrist Carl Binger, and New York City's police commissioner, Alfred Cohn. Once he received his medical degree, he moved his experiments to the Harvard Psychological Clinic, where, in 1928, he took over as director from Morton Prince, the founder of the American school of psychotherapy and the first psychologist to identify a case of multiple personality disorder in his 1906 book, *The Dissociation of a Personality*. Murray jointly inherited Prince's clinic with his friend Gordon Allport, who offered the first undergraduate course on personality in the United States. Together, Allport and Murray would transform his concept of personology into the institutional precursor to nearly all humanistic psychology. The clinicians who worked under him would pursue research that focused on human beings' internal characteristics—instincts, needs, styles of life—over the external factors prioritized by 1920s behaviorists, environmentalists, and stimulus-response psychologists.

Murray found his Jungian questionnaire to be as hit-or-miss as any of the questionnaires that had surfaced in the 1930s, many of them designed to identify subjects with neurotic or otherwise abnormal personalities: the Bernreuter Personality Inventory, the Thurstone Personality Schedule, the Woodworth Psychoneurotic Inventory. Murray's experiments led him to the dispiriting conclusion that all "questionnaires are always unreliable." "Subjects may intentionally misrepresent themselves," he reasoned. "They may be ashamed of what they consider their weaknesses, or they may want to ingratiate themselves with the experimenter. Or perhaps a subject has half-willfully dramatized himself as a certain kind of person, and he wants others to believe in the reality of his masquerade. But whatever the motive, the fact is he does not tell the whole truth as he knows it." Both he and Katharine had spent many years in the 1910s and 1920s designing questionnaires—he at his desk in Cambridge, she in her kitchen;

he for New York's social and scientific elite, she for the mothers of children she trained; he with a man's easy access to elite institutions, she with a woman's awareness of her limited station in life. Now he sought an alternate approach to the standardized version of the soul generated by questionnaires. "But what living personality is content to remain a psychological type: is a type, indeed, anything but a fixation, and thus to some extent an aberration?" he wondered to Mumford.

It was Christiana Morgan who helped Murray realize the alternative. In 1926, the year before Katharine Briggs first started writing to Jung, Morgan went to Küsnacht to see him. She referred to Jung with tenderness as the "Old Man," and she asked him to teach her how to reconcile her intense emotional urges—her "red hots" and "pale blues"—with her well-appointed social self. Instead of taking her out on the lake, Jung hypnotized her. Ringed in pearls and furs, her coat unbuttoned and spread out in the sun, she would sit outside Jung's study while he spoke to her of the soul and its visions, imploring her to turn inward so that she might retrieve her spirit like an oracle channeling the voices of the dead. As she entered a trance state, she began to see visions. There was a peacock riding atop the shoulders of a man ringed in gold light. There was a woman who shape-shifted into a Mithraic bull. There was Christiana herself, who did things in her visions that she would never have—could never have—done. She bathed in a river of her own blood. She stood naked before a dark-skinned man who laughed at her, a full, throaty laugh, before changing into a snake and slithering into a nearby church, up onto the cross, and around the neck of Jesus.

She described what she had seen to Jung, and he, who had already fallen a little in love with her, told her that only her visions could help Murray solve the methodological problems of personology. "Your function is to create a man," he said. "Some women create children but it is greater to create a man. If you create Murray you will have done something very fine for the world." His stark division of the world of women into opposing types—women who create children, women who create men—did not surprise or alarm her. Nor did his insistence that "a woman suffers a relationship to be and she also suffers it not to be." In the face of inevitable suffering, the noblest work a woman could do was to help a man recognize the full extent of his powers. Like the sibyls or Beatrice or any of the gracious Greek muses Jung named in *Psychological Types*, she was to serve as a medium, a lightning rod, an *inspiratrice* for male geniuses.

Murray was fascinated by how Morgan's inner self had appeared to Jung not through language but through images. They debated how to use Morgan's trance visions to help her individuate and further his career. Some years later, they were approached by Cecilia Roberts, a student of abnormal psychology at Radcliffe. She suggested reversing Jung's experiment: instead of prompting the patient to generate the images for the analytic psychologist to interpret, the psychologist could show the patient images and ask her to tell him a story based on what she saw. "Stories, like dreams, provide admirable starting points for free association," Murray wrote.

Morgan, a skilled sketch artist, drew nineteen original pictures that Murray started showing to his test subjects in a clinic. Her black-and-white images, which were based on portraits and photographs that Murray had collected from the early 1930s onward, depicted a series of mysterious, evocative, and often grotesque scenes: a man towering over the body of a woman lying in a bed, her breasts exposed, his eyes covered by the back of his arm; a woman leaning on an open door, weeping—or perhaps laughing—into her hands; a little boy slumped over a broken violin, hands pulling listlessly at his face. For each subject, Murray would hand him a picture card, allow him to examine it for twenty seconds, and then ask him to choose a proper name for the main character in the story he was about to tell. After selecting a name, most subjects would tell stories that were two hundred words or more in length, introducing a basic plot, supporting characters, and often a moral.

Murray's assumption was that the main character represented the test subject—or at least "some of the components, conscious or unconscious, of his own past or present personality"—and the plot represented "memory traces, conscious or unconscious, or some of the actual or fantasied events" that had exerted a significant influence on his development. The job of the analyst was to function as many "generations of literary critics had," Murray wrote. It was to separate the story's "grains" from its "chaff": to identify the symbols, repeated themes, and affective patterns that testified to the subject's personality. At the clinic, the practice of personality typing was just as much of a narrative practice as it had been for Katharine and Isabel at home, surrounded by their myths and their novels.

Years before Tucky had chanted "Brothers" to Katharine, using images to evoke unconscious disclosures about personality was an idea Katharine had also entertained in her cosmic laboratory of baby training. When Isabel was little, in the months after her brother Albert had died in his crib, she had invented an exercise her mother described as "a kind of picture-story-game which she enjoys hugely." She would walk over to her mother with a picture in her hand, usually an advertisement ripped from the back of an old magazine. "What is the picture-man doing?" she would ask, pointing at the man in the image, challenging her mother's imagination. "He is coming home from a big store," her mother would respond and, at her daughter's further prompting, would continue. "He has a little girl at his house— a little girl he loves very much. This little girl fell on the pavement and broke her prettiest doll. She cried and was very sad, but her father said the doll could be mended. He had just left it at the store to get a beautiful new head. And when the store people have fastened the new head on tight, they will send the doll right straight to the little girl, and she will be very happy again." Isabel was delighted, Katharine unaware of how the characters she had chosen—the sad little girl, the broken doll, the parent who tries to set things right—may have memorialized the grief she did not know how to express over her son's death. In an unanticipated reversal of roles, the little girl had played the analyst to the mother—a sign of things to come.

This kind of unconscious disclosure was precisely what Murray and Morgan had in mind when they designed what they would call the Thematic Apperception Test (TAT), with its lurid, hypnotic images. Jung, for his part, was impressed by everything the couple had accomplished. "It is astonishing how many methods you have worked out," he wrote to Murray. Murray would confess that his diligence was underwritten not just by a "certain sentimental regard for TAT," but for its co-creator, who never received full credit for her contributions. "I am anxious that the young lady be given every opportunity for refinement and for the exhibition eventually of all her potential charms and talents," he wrote, making scant mention of her intelligence, her diligence, or her self-sacrifice. For some time, it seemed like the confluence of professional practice and personal desire at the Harvard Psychological Clinic was working in everyone's favor.

. . . .

Yet now, at the Harvard Tercentenary in 1936, certain peculiarities in Jung's behavior had led Murray to grow wary of the man he had trusted with many of his secrets over the last decade. Jung was a bad flirt. He made tactless and embarrassing overtures to his female patients, many of whom became his lovers. He mocked his fellow psychologists. "*Les enfants, les petites bébés,*" he had cooed to Jean Piaget, the renowned French child psychologist, at a dinner Murray had hosted to honor the two men upon their arrival in Cambridge for the Tercentenary bash. And in the fall of 1936, with Europe teetering on the brink of war, there were unsettling rumors circulating about the company Jung kept—whispers that he had left Zurich to work as chief advisor to the German chancellor, Adolf Hitler. Murray had first heard the rumor earlier that year from Freud, who, already nursing the cancer that would kill him in 1939, was angry that Jung had received an honorary degree from Harvard instead of him.

When confronted, Jung denied ever visiting Hitler. "Whatever I touch and wherever I go I meet with this prejudice that I'm a Nazi and that I'm in close affiliation to the German government. I don't think I have paranoiac delusions about persecution," he insisted to Murray after his Tercentenary speech. He believed that jealous American psychoanalysts had doctored photos to show him standing next to Hitler's team of Nazi eugenicists. "I recently discovered that a faked photograph with my name had been sent to scientific societies years ago in Vienna. On this photo, which I possess, I'm represented as a Jew of the particularly vicious kind. Such experiences are no delusions." And yet his sense of self-importance was inflated enough that he did not deny that, had he been given the opportunity to influence Hitler, he could have steered the chancellor toward a peaceable course of action, possibly averting World War II. "Quite a number of Germans who have heard the story said they wished it were true," he wrote to Murray. "I have recently had news from Germany which confirms that all is not well in Berchtesgaden," he wrote of the town in the Bavarian Alps where Hitler made his home.

Jung's scandals distressed Murray as he stood in the rain, listening to Jung deliver the Tercentenary lecture with a mixture of irritation and disappointment. Had he encountered Katharine Briggs in the audience, he might have warned her away from her meeting with Jung, though she would not have listened. She had spent her journey from Washington, D.C., to Cambridge composing a song for him, one set to Yale University's "Boola Boola" fight song. "Dr. Jung came down from his Alpine height / And completely re-educated Yale," she wrote, perhaps as she glanced out the train window at New Haven's Union Station. "While the wise, the dumb, and the erudite / Waxed paler and yet more pale! / For they had heard great Wisdom's word / Which shook them to their boots, / When the wise, the dumb, and the erudite / Beheld their psychic roots. / Boola, Boola; Boola, Boola / Boola, Boola, Boola-Boo!"

The letter that arrived for her that evening from the Harvard College Club was written on a sheet of paper now yellow with age, its creases worn from repeated folding and unfolding as if by nervous, implacable hands. It informed her that Dr. Jung had been inundated with requests for appointments and would no longer be able to see her in Cambridge. He had, however, added a stop in New York, where he would speak in the ballroom of the Plaza Hotel. His wife, Emma, having learned of Katharine's great devotion to her husband, had urged him to make time to see her—just a brief appointment in his private room at the Ambassador Hotel on Park Avenue. Might she adjust her itinerary? Katharine agreed, and in her sleepless excitement, she stayed up all night to compose another verse, this time a song called

"They Got What They Needed to Know," set to the tune of "The Man on the Flying Trapeze": "They asked C. G. Jung if he'd come to New York / And they got him a hall and some pieces of chalk / They all came together and asked him to talk, / They got what they needed to know."

The delay was fortuitous. Before she left Cambridge, Katharine telephoned Isabel and urged her to come to New York; she wanted them to meet Jung together, she said, although she did not specify why she required her daughter's company. Perhaps she felt aged and nervous and did not trust herself in the presence of the man she had anointed her "personal God." Perhaps she wanted a witness, someone who could recount the story of their meeting in the years to come. Whatever the reason, Isabel made it clear to her mother that she was there only to indulge her whims; she cared nothing for Jung and took no interest in what he had to say. When a friend later asked what had transpired in the hotel room between Katharine and Jung, Isabel replied with indifference, "I don't know. I didn't listen."

For Katharine, it was an unforgettable day, "the day I finally met my teacher face-to-face instead of merely in a book," she wrote to Jung on a piece of stationery she pilfered from the Ambassador. She confessed to him that she had designed a type system of her own before reading *Psychological Types* and that she had burned her notes, so cowed was she by his brilliance.

"Oh, you shouldn't have done that!" he replied kindly. "You might have made a real contribution."

She was flattered, and though she had not been able to help him with her ideas, she sensed she could with her money. "I understand from our interview today that you are willing to accept contributions for the support of your work," she continued, tucking into the envelope a check for twenty-five dollars (approximately five hundred dollars today) signed in a bold, swooping hand by "Mrs. Lyman J. Briggs." "If you accept the check that I enclose, it will make me happy to feel that I have a small part in what is so wonderful to all. I wish it could be a much larger amount." She thanked him and added, almost as a polite afterthought, "My daughter thanks you as well."

The details of what happened in that hotel room, elusive though they may be, pale beside the larger implications of Katharine and Isabel's trip up north. Unencumbered by their children and husbands, plunged into the frenzied world of politicians, professors, and titans of industry, Briggs and Myers began to imagine what Jung's type theory could become—more than just the key to one woman's good marriage or successful, specialized offspring, but an indispensable tool for the systematic study of man. The home and its intimate relations, once a spur to creative thought and self-actualization, now constrained the imagination, Katharine wrote in her diary. It was time for type to alight on something—or someone—bigger, more powerful, more important to the arc of history.

As was true with Murray, Katharine's first serious attempt to make personality political would begin with World War II's most mesmerizing and infamous character: Hitler.

CHAPTER SEVEN

The Personality Is Political

n an essay that she wrote but never published in 1937 called "My Country 'Tis of Thee—The Cult of Leadership," Katharine Briggs took a faithfully Jungian approach to typing Adolf Hitler's personality. On a 3″ × 5″ index card, she labeled him an extravert (E) and an "excessive and unmitigated thinker" (T), blaming his personality for interwar Germany's abnormal "psychology of political regimentation." Hitler was a "political go-getter," she claimed, who had come to power in the 1930s by persuading intellectuals, scientists, and bureaucrats to abandon all feeling judgments and, by extension, their moral obligations to others. "The passion for planning everything and running everything according to plan was very characteristic of the old Germany where everything was efficient, organized, and the planning worked fairly well so long as it was moderated by a collective morality based upon the Christian tradition," she wrote. But when modernity had crowded out Christianity, Germany had shown the world what happened when "all the thinking is done to order by a few people, while the vast majority, made completely gang-minded and irresponsible by the loss of their traditional morality, become body cells to the brain-cells of ego inflated political go-getters." Now it was the job of the Allies to overcome Hitler and reinstate a sense for feeling in Europe.

Compare her writing to these notes, scribbled onto another 3″ × 5″ index card, which recall Henry Murray's impressions of Hitler in 1938:

Feminine comportment—wide hips, narrow shoulders.
Flabby muscles, thin spindly legs hidden by boots.

Hollow chested—voice breaking into womanly shriek.
Ladylike walk, dainty little steps—studied and bouncing.
Awkward effeminate movements, flap of his hands, limbs
    ungracefully articulated.

Hitler was a man too weak to work in the fields or enlist in the military or even learn how to ride a horse properly. Yet a man who, by 1939, had emerged as the most dangerous personality in the world. Murray spent many sleepless nights wondering how Hitler had managed to do it. Physically, he resembled a high-strung bird, with his hunched back, his skittish footing, and his dead, dusky eyes. Emotionally, Murray believed him to be totally unhinged. When things did not go his way, he threw temper tantrums, slammed doors, and locked himself in his bedroom at the Berghof, his home in the Bavarian Alps, where he would sulk until he felt well enough to plot his revenge against the person or people who had wronged him. He was more child than man; he was barely a man at all according to Murray's assessment of his "awkward effeminate movements" and his "dainty little steps."

Yet despite his apparent shortcomings, Hitler had transcended mankind. He had become a kind of demigod to the people of Germany, who had eagerly followed him into World War II and later stood by while he ordered the systematic extermination of six million European Jews. Now it was psychology's greatest challenge to tell the story of how a man endowed with such unremarkable physical and emotional attributes loomed as the most threatening political force in recent human history.

To answer this challenge became nothing short of a patriotic duty for Murray. By the time the Japanese bombed Pearl Harbor, he wanted badly to go to war. At forty, he had cut back on cigarettes and alcohol and had started rowing every morning on the Charles River, where he would watch the sun prick the clouds red and imagine taking his place on the battlefields of France. "I am planning to get my hands dirty with a clear conscience & a good vengeance," he wrote to Louis Mumford in 1942. But much to Murray's disappointment, his hands stayed clean. Neither the naval reserve nor the War Office Selection Board was interested in his services, and the Harvard Psychological Clinic was so "inoculated with pacifism," he complained to Mumford, that there was little chance of convincing the other staff psychologists to join the war effort. Imagine his delight, then, when he was approached by the Office of Strategic Services (OSS), the precursor to the Central Intelligence Agency, to assemble a type profile of Hitler for the Allied Command. He would title it "An Analysis of the Personality of Adolph [*sic*] Hitler, with Predictions of His Future Behavior and Suggestions for Dealing with Him Now and After Germany's Surrender." In what one might consider a small act of defiance, Murray never did learn how to spell Hitler's first name correctly.

Typing Hitler was an unusual project for many reasons, not the least of which was that Murray would have to assess his personality from afar. Questionnaires and TAT assessments were nonstarters. Getting close to him was out of the question, impossible even for the OSS's network of covert operatives in Germany and Eastern Europe. Like Katharine combing through the biographies of plantation owners like Henry Clay and John C. Calhoun to understand the antidemocratic vicissitudes of men, Murray would analyze Hitler by reading Konrad Heiden's *Hitler: A Biography* (1936), Hermann Rauschning's *The Voice of Destruction* (1940), and H. G. Baynes's *Germany Possessed* (1941), as well as Hitler's *My New Order* (1941), a collection of his most rousing political speeches. Like a diligent literary critic, he would conduct a careful study of the three-thousand-odd metaphors in *Mein Kampf.* He would immerse himself in classified OSS reports, which featured interviews with women who claimed to have had sexual relations with Hitler.

At the time, "An Analysis of the Personality of Adolph Hitler" was scandalizing for what it postulated about Hitler's various and contradictory sexual perversities. There was his suspected "syphilophobia"— fear of contaminated blood—which began at the age of twelve, Murray guessed, when Hitler was caught engaging in "some sexual experiment with a little girl." There was his passive homosexuality, his alleged lust for his Nazi officers. There was his habit, as described by the women the OSS had interviewed, of asking his sexual partners to squat over him and, on his command, let loose a strong stream of urine into his mouth and over his chest. At a very young age, Murray speculated, Hitler had walked in on his father having sex with his mother. Over the next thirty years, the shock and betrayal and indignity of that repressed primal scene had seeped into his political unconscious. Germany had come to represent his mother, his motherland, and Europe the father who, after World War I, had forced her to submit to his basest desires, stripping her of her autonomy, her dignity, and her self-possession. Adolf Hitler, a little boy traumatized by a sexual encounter he could not understand, would thus emerge from his adolescence as the wronged son of Germany, eager to exact his revenge on the European patriarch.

It was a wildly, perhaps irresponsibly speculative exercise, but for Murray, Hitler's psychological profile was essential to the war effort. His meteoric rise to power could not be explained in purely physical or material terms. He was neither strong nor rich nor powerful from the beginning, and so his ascendance had to involve some degree of studied self-creation, some mirage of charismatic projection that had enchanted the German people—the darkest version of Fitzgerald's "unbroken series of successful gestures." There was Hitler the man ("Insignificant, prototype of the little man," read Murray's notes), and there was Hitler the ruler, a man not equal to himself in the public eye. "People look at him & see someone else, the figure of one who might have said and done what Hitler has said and done," Murray scribbled as he pored over the OSS reports. On another 3″ × 5″ index card, he composed a list of the different Hitlers the Germans had known:

The gracious Hitler, soft, good-natured Austrian, excessively
    gentle & modest.
The possessed Hitler, speech, fury, fanatical.
The lethargic Hitler, exhausted, limp.
The sentimental Hitler, tearful, weeping over his dead canary.
The embarrassed Hitler, ill at ease in the presence of a stranger.
The soap-box Hitler, haranguing.
The expressionless Hitler, faceless.

How, Murray wondered, could one reconcile these disparate personae? Faceless, yet many faced, Hitler could simultaneously embrace and stand for the whole social body. He was the type of leader that Russian novelist Aleksandr Solzhenitsyn would later call the "Egocrat": a leader who seemed to merge with the party, the people, and the proletariat while nevertheless managing to remain distinct from them—an icon of sorts. Hitler's iconicity, Murray believed, was how he had managed, at first, to conquer so much with so little bloodshed, armed only with the promises of national glory and racial propaganda. His dark, kaleidoscopic personality had absorbed everyone, and they had, in turn, given themselves over to his vision in a moment of total identification, binding their fates and the fate of Germany to his soft, womanly body.

He had created the public image of himself, the people's Adolf Hitler, through the power of oratory. He was a master of mass-intoxicating words and crude metaphors. Destiny had cast him in the role of a "ship's captain," he shouted at his crowds. Germany, once purged of its Jewish population and its political dissents, would emerge as a "paradise" on earth. "Hitler speaking before a large audience is a man possessed, comparable to the primitive medicine man or the shaman," Murray wrote in his report. "He is the incarnation of the crowd's unspoken needs and cravings; and in this sense, he has been created, and to a large extent invented, by the people of Germany." Hitler's power was real—exceedingly, frighteningly real—but Hitler the man was a collective fiction, a node of mass transference, a public hallucination of no more substance to Murray than the monomaniacal Captain Ahab, the villain of his favorite novel, *Moby-Dick*. The two characters shared an "intangible malignity," Murray quoted from Melville, "a wild vindictiveness" that had rotted their souls before turning outward. If Ahab had directed his malice to the whale, making its white hump the sign and symbol of everything that was evil in the world, then Hitler had done the same with the Jews, the intelligentsia, the political left, the political right, the British, the French, and liberal democracy writ large. In his subconscious, Murray claimed, Hitler believed that the only way to excise his psychological demons was to give them human form. Only then could they be vanquished—annihilated from the face of the earth. "That the Jews have been a convenient symbol for the 'Devil' in Hitler and his ilk there can be no doubt," wrote Katharine in a dream study of Hitler, in which she accused him of having "no gift for metaphor."

For both Katharine and Murray, Hitler's personality offered a striking rhetorical leap from considerations of the individual self to the imposition of that self as the visionary of a new world order. "The proper interpretation of Hitler's personality is important as a step in understanding the psychology of the typical Nazi, and—since the typical Nazi exhibits a strain that has, for a long time, been prevalent among Germans—as a step in understanding the psychology of the German people," Murray explained. Like Germany, Hitler had an urge to dominate that was excessively compensatory. He wanted to be strong because he knew he was weak, "annoyingly subservient," Murray noted. He had the strongest contempt for the Jews but his appearance was said to be "very Jewish," especially when he had worn a fashionably long beard during his student days in Vienna. An advocate of mandatory fertility programs, he believed the family was the breeding ground for Aryan warriors. Yet he remained unmarried, was rumored to be either impotent or gay, and was "incapable of consummating the sexual act in a normal fashion," read the OSS reports. Hatred ran thick in his veins, emboldening his cult of brutality. But after acts of unusual cruelty, like the purges of 1934, he experienced a "feminine spell" of weeping and hysteria that Murray saw replicated in the German people's responses to the government's increasing persecution of the Jews. One man, it seemed, could wield his personality to make the world over in his image.

For both Katharine and Murray, then, the personality of Adolf Hitler had come to stand in for more properly political concerns about fascism: the centralization of authority, the rising tides of nationalism and ethnocentrism, the programs of mass deportation and genocide. In the cold light of historical retrospect, the easy slippage from the personal to the political might seem surprising. Or it might not. For even today, politics remains chained to discourses of personality in ways that are as crude as, if not cruder than, Murray's assessment of Hitler. Most people want to like their democratically elected leaders or want them to be likable or, at the very least, presentable and polite—the kind of man you could invite over for a beer, the kind of woman who might read sweet stories to your children. Sometimes it seems that we are more shocked by violations of common courtesy than we are by unfair or oppressive policies.

The politicization of personality is not wrong in any moral sense. It is simply the inevitable result of a modern democratic process that invites the people to imagine their elected officials as extensions of themselves—their representatives in a very literal sense. The body that Germans saw on display at dozens of rallies and speeches—the flabby muscles, the hollow chest, the ladylike walk—stood in not only for the nation's public preferences but for its people's private lives: their feelings of impotence, their discriminatory states of mind, the stories they had invented to explain the injustice of their place in the world.

. . . .

How do you kill an icon? How do you rob it of its aura, its immortality? Literally killing Hitler was impossible, Murray advised the OSS. His death at the hands of the Allies would only consecrate Hitler's status as a martyr for the German people. "An Analysis of the Personality of Adolph Hitler" offered a series of predictions for Hitler's future behavior—nine futures in all, arrayed from least to most likely. It was unlikely that Hitler would be imprisoned or murdered by his own troops. More likely was that Hitler would arrange to have himself killed by someone else. "This would complete the myth of the hero—death at the hand of some trusted follower," Murray reasoned. "Siegfried stabbed in the back by Hagen, Caesar by Brutus, Christ betrayed by Judas. It might increase the fanaticism of the soldiers and create a legend in conformity with the ancient pattern. If Hitler could arrange to have a Jew kill him, then he could die in the belief that his fellow countrymen would rise in their wrath and massacre every remaining Jew in Germany." For Murray, the most likely of all scenarios was that Hitler would commit suicide in some dramatic fashion, that he would retreat to his fortress at the Berghof, where he would blow himself up with dynamite, immolate himself upon a funeral pyre, shoot himself in the head with a silver bullet, or throw himself off the parapet. "This outcome, undesirable for us all, is not at all unlikely," Murray reported to the OSS.

The most desirable outcome was that Hitler would fall into the hands of the United Nations. After a show trial, during which Hitler would be pronounced mentally unbalanced, he would be removed to the psychiatric ward at Saint Elizabeths Hospital in Washington, D.C.—the same hospital where Katharine had confined her fictional characters. There he would live out the rest of his days in solitary confinement. A committee of psychiatrists would administer daily intelligence and personality tests to him, and they would film his behavior during these assessments. Murray predicated that he would rant and rave and denounce everyone, even the Germans who had fought and died for him. The most damning clips from the films would be played around the world, in theaters and on television sets, on loop if possible. They would puncture the myth of Hitler that had captivated the public imagination, and they would serve as a warning to anyone else with a will to power. This was what happened to "crack-brained fanatics who try to dominate the world," Murray wrote as he outlined the Allies' improbable revenge fantasy. The final Hitler anyone would see would be Hitler exposed, Hitler unhinged.

After some time, the clips would stop. Hitler would be left to die in his cell, alone and forgotten. "The pictures will become quite tiresome after a while and people will get bored with Hitler," Murray predicted. "Trust science to take the drama out of anything."

Trust science to take the drama out of anything. Stated as a matter of fact, it was easy for Murray to believe that this was, in fact, what the "science of man" could do: that its precise measurement of psychological causes and sober calculation of psychological effects could suppress whatever mysteries might inhere in the study of personality. Yet the drama of "An Analysis of the Personality of Adolph Hitler" was precisely the drama of personology running headlong into its own inadequacies as a predictive technique. There was no reliable way of mapping Hitler's past or present attributes—his insecurity, his sadism, his xenophobia—onto the projected behaviors of his future self. It was like plotting a very dark episode in the Choose Your Own Adventure series. Here were a series of nine future worlds, some with dead Hitlers, some with live ones. There was a world in which Hitler pointed a gun at his head and pulled the trigger. There was another in which he sat in an empty cell, waiting to become the world's most infamous film star.

Murray realized that the problem of prediction was not unique to Hitler. The predictive promise of personology—the predictive promise of all humanistic personality psychology—was deeply ingrained in its narrative ethos: if you had a clear sense of your starting point, you should be able to plot the middle and the end. "If one is willing to lean on the principle of repetition and consistency, they offer a basis for predicting the individual's behavior," he wrote. Most of his colleagues at the clinic thought very little of plucking a vector of traits from the whole of a human being and using it to propel him across an arc of psychological determinism, setting him down at some indefinite point in future time and space. In this conceptual, quasi-novelistic time machine of personality assessment, the self would maintain its integrity, coming out the other side whole and unbroken.

"An Analysis of the Personality of Adolph Hitler" brought home to Murray just how insufficient an assumption this was. "How, then, can a psychologist foretell with any degree of accuracy the outcomes of future meetings of one barely known personality with hundreds of other undesignated personalities in distant undesignated cities, villages, fields, and jungles that are seething with one knows not what potential harms and benefits?" Murray wondered. "Fortune . . . can never be eliminated from the universe of human interactions." As a Jungian, Katharine was more sanguine about the consistency of the self. In her profile of Hitler, she issued a warning to him and to all other politicians and readers: "Remember that you are a type only. Remember that the people who are running the world—or trying to—are also types." If one could determine the weaknesses of a politician's type, then one could also figure out how to make him and his empire fall.

In the months that Murray spent drafting his report, thousands of

European Jews were arrested and deported to the camps. As Hitler became increasingly erratic in his behavior, the OSS worried that German intelligence had devised counterstrategies to thwart their psychological experts. Murray, working day and night as lives hung in the balance, began to devise multiple scenarios for manipulating Hitler into the future the OSS wanted him to embrace. "Between now and the cessation of hostilities," he wrote, "the aim should be either (I) to accelerate Hitler's mental deterioration, or to drive him insane; or (II) to prevent him from insuring the perpetuation of his legend by ending his life dramatically and tragically."

The OSS could keep Hitler from committing suicide and drive him crazy in any number of ways, Murray suggested. They could airdrop hundreds of leaflets and pamphlets that warned the German people that Hitler was planning to kill himself and leave them to the mercy of the Allies. They could publish grotesque cartoons that showed Hitler rushing to his death on the Russian front. They could pay foreign newspapers to substitute the proper name "Adolf Hitler" with "False Prophet," "False Messiah," "Amateur Strategist," "Corporeal Satan," and "World Criminal No. 1." They could undermine Hitler using their own arsenal of crude metaphors.

Perhaps the most elaborate scenario Murray detailed was a fake news campaign that would trick Hitler into surrendering. It would begin with the OSS planting a report in German newspapers. Should the Allies win the war, the report would claim, all Nazi leaders would be executed except for Hitler. He would be exiled to Saint Helena, the island where Napoleon had spent his dying days, and ordered "to brood over his sins for the rest of his life." "This idea should appeal to Hitler, who greatly admires Napoleon and knows that the Napoleonic legend was fostered by the man's last years at Saint Helena," Murray wrote to the OSS. "He would imagine himself painting landscapes, writing his new Bible, and making plans for an even greater German revolution to be carried out in his name thirty years hence." Thrilled by the prospect of his genteel exile, Hitler would surrender, whereupon he would discover that there was no Saint Helena for him—only a padded cell at Saint Elizabeths Hospital.

For the remainder of the war, the OSS would use Murray's psychological assessment to wage a covert propaganda war against Hitler. They would, of course, never trick him into surrendering or institutionalize him in Saint Elizabeths. Instead, on April 29, 1945, the German Army would lay down its arms after Allied Forces swept across Germany and Soviet troops advanced into Vienna and Poland. The next day, underneath the chancellery in Berlin, Hitler would lock himself, his wife, Eva Braun, and his beloved Alsatian, Blondi, into an air-raid shelter, where he would swallow a cyanide capsule and shoot himself with a service pistol for good measure. There was no funeral pyre, no dynamite, no free fall off the ledge at the Berghof. Personology had gotten the end of the story—and maybe the beginning and the middle too—wrong.

. . . .

For Katharine Briggs, the only man more dangerous than Hitler was U.S. president Franklin Delano Roosevelt—an extravert like Hitler, but unlike Hitler a feeling type. The scrapbook she kept during the war contained no reports from the battlefields of Dunkirk or Stalingrad, no lists of saved prisoners or photos of triumphant GIs. Instead, it preserved dozens of pamphlets decrying Roosevelt's "State Socialism," emphasizing the weakness of his personality, questioning his fitness to lead the country during war. It was another issue on which Chief and his mother-in-law did not see eye to eye. "Whatever his peacetime sins, this man Roosevelt has shown that he does not intend to fight Hitler with an umbrella," he wrote in a letter to the local newspaper, an implicit rebuke to Katharine's political sensibilities, informed by her typing of the major players in the European theater of war.

As a family, the Briggses were also involved with the war effort, although not through the politicization of personality type that Katharine's unpublished writings on Hitler suggested. In 1939, Lyman, who had served as director of the Bureau of Standards for the past five years, had been asked by President Roosevelt to head the Advisory Committee on Uranium. At about the same time the United States entered the war, three of the world's leading physicists—Albert Einstein, Enrico Fermi, and Leo Szilard—had concluded that an enriched element called "uranium-235" was a fissile isotope: a material capable of sustaining a nuclear chain reaction. "This phenomenon would also lead to the construction of bombs, and it is conceivable—though much less certain—that extremely powerful bombs of a new type may thus be constructed," Einstein warned Roosevelt. "In view of this situation you may think it desirable to have some permanent contact maintained between the Administration and the group of physicists working on chain reactions in America. One possible way of achieving this might be for you to entrust with this task a person who has your confidence." The president had tapped Lyman to play liaison to the physicists while he and his advisors struggled to decide whether the U.S. government should help usher the world into the atomic age. It promised to be an era of "global neuroses," a "death haunted time," Henry Murray had predicted in 1938 of the world-altering invention of nuclear weapons.

Lyman's participation on the advisory committee was a matter of much consternation in the Briggs household. Despite her ambition to reconcile the modern social order with spirituality, Katharine feared and detested the day-to-day machinations of politics. "Nothing in the modern scene is more pitiful than the masses of people who say their prayers to 'Government,' and look to the politicians for their salvation," she wrote in her assessment of Hitler. She had no patience for Roosevelt, whose commitment to centralized planning and regimentation was matched only by Hitler's totalitarian ambitions. She was certain that Roosevelt had already made up his mind about the atomic bomb. His appointment of Lyman to the advisory committee, she told her husband, was just a ham-fisted attempt to pressure the scientific community into providing him with evidence. That way, he could justify his decision to Congress and the American people by appealing to their sensing and thinking sides—empiricism run amok.

In her diary, she dramatized the meeting between the president and her husband. "A political go-getter, a very important and powerful one perhaps, may come to a Government scientist for help," she wrote. " 'I'm preparing a political speech,' he explains, 'and I'd like you to do a bit of scientific research for me. I want you to prove that such and such is thus and so.' 'Well!' replies the scientist coldly. 'I'll be glad to investigate the matter for you, but I can't promise beforehand what will be "proved"! Perhaps such and such is not thus and so!' 'It better be!' returns the politician implying a threat to the scientist's job if his findings are not satisfactory. 'You know what I want.'" Katharine believed that Roosevelt, like Hitler, had sustained his wartime powers by persuading intellectuals, scientists, and bureaucrats to abandon their moral convictions to support his agenda.

Isabel did not share her mother's animosity toward the president; she was frightened by what the Nazis' savagery revealed about mankind's will to power. "In the darkest days of World War Two when the Germans were rolling irresistibly along and my shoulders ached with trying to hold them back and the horrible sinking feeling lived in the pit of my stomach, the thought came to me one day—I was making my bed at the time—that by letting them spoil my life that way I was helping them win," Isabel recalled to a friend years later. It was a peculiar sentiment, striking for how it mingled political sensitivity with self-absorption; the "horrible sinking feeling" that "lived in the pit of [her] stomach" was not, in any way, helping the Nazis win; their spoilage of her life was nothing compared to the lives they had stolen in the camps. She knew this, of course. She had volunteered as an aircraft spotter for the Civil Air Patrol, a nurse with the Red Cross, a secretary with a housing program for European refugee children. She had witnessed the very real toll the war had taken on families. But now she wanted to do something to help herself and to shake her fears, something more suited to her "intellectual capabilities," she told her mother, than the typical jobs assigned to women on the home front.

She was not used to reckoning with such strong feelings of despair. For her, the personal did not seem truly political: not when she gamely defended socialist revolutionaries in college; not when she acknowledged, with a smile and a shrug, the emotional labor that she performed for her husband and his fellow officers at flight camp. Until the end of the war, her experience of the world seemed buffered from anything that did not directly affect her home or her family. There was nothing of note in her "Diary of an Introvert Determined to Extravert, Write, & Have a Lot of Children" after the publication of *Give Me Death* in 1934. Life seemed to have proceeded tranquilly, if not exactly according to plan—the fame and fortune she had sought as a mystery writer had eluded her—then without any dramatic disruptions. Her children had grown into handsome, accomplished adolescents. Her husband had enjoyed a series of promotions at work. She believed she had made peace with her fate as a middle-class homemaker, even if she sometimes found it hard to distinguish between true happiness and complacency.

Every now and again, she recalled the newspaper interview she had given on type and relationships, when she had rifled through her mother's notes on feeling and thinking types, ventriloquizing her mother's passion for Jung's theories as the key to a happy marriage. Her mother, almost seventy years old and showing some signs of the dementia that would eventually claim her mind, had never landed on the right tools for bringing Jungian theory to the masses. Isabel wondered if Katharine's alignment of self-knowledge and self-mastery with spiritual conviction had hurt her cause, making it too philosophical and esoteric for the average person to grasp for any practical purpose. Now books with commanding titles like *Wake Up and Live!* (1936), *Think and Grow Rich* (1937), and *How Never to Be Tired* (1944) had hooked readers with the explicit promise that attending to the self could be useful—that it could make you richer and happier, more attractive, more productive, and more popular, but only if you were willing to change who you were. "Do you know someone you would like to change and regulate and improve?" asked Dale Carnegie in his 1936 best seller *How to Win Friends and Influence People*. "Good! That is fine. I am all in favor of it. But why not begin on yourself? From a purely selfish standpoint, that is a lot more profitable than trying to improve others—yes, and a lot less dangerous."

Isabel did not believe people should have to "change and regulate and improve" to make their lives rich and profitable. She had alighted on Jung's theory not as a personal religion but as a practical tool, first for saving marriages and, now, for safeguarding what she took to be a distinctly American way of life. With the men of the nation off fighting in Europe, more married women had started to enter the workforce, a throwback to the summer days of 1918 when Isabel, alone in her boardinghouse in Memphis, had pondered how men and women could put their "different gifts" toward different tasks. Now she wondered what she could do to stop the Germans from winning and making the world over in their image, imposing a world view that had no respect for feeling and thus no compunction about trampling on people's inalienable rights. "I made up my mind that there was no logic or justification for turning possible future unhappiness into certain present unhappiness by being afraid of it," she thought. "Do what you can to make a better world but don't throw away one day or one minute of the world you have gone."

Days after the Japanese bombed Pearl Harbor, she appropriated her mother's preliminary materials for a Jungian questionnaire to design a prototype for a test that could match people of differing gifts to different professions. Her mother's ideas about specialization had primed her for the task long ago, but it was a recent article in *Reader's Digest* on personality testing that showed her how to execute it. From reading it, she learned that there were hundreds of personality tests that promised to classify workers as normal or abnormal, so that employers could avoid assigning an overly anxious or depressive man to a high-pressure job. At the same time, there were hundreds of psychological consulting firms that had created an industry out of administering these tests—a logistical convenience, to be sure, but also a means of protecting the employers from whatever hostility might develop as a result of demoting or firing people based on the test results. But what if she could design a test that generated only positive results? It would not be a test at all but an "indicator"—a device that provided information about one's personality free from judgment or opprobrium.

She called her device "Form A" of the "Briggs-Myers Type Indicator." She insisted on placing Katharine's last name first. It seemed the right way to enshrine her deep indebtedness to her mother's life's work.

CHAPTER EIGHT

Sheep and Buck

When it came to personality testing on the East Coast, the biggest game in town was Edward N. Hay and Associates, Philadelphia's first personality consultants. The president of the company, Edward Northup Hay, was known around town for his tight toothbrush mustache and his immaculately starched shirts. He had started his career as a clerk at the First Pennsylvania Bank. A monkish worker, he had risen quietly and expertly through the ranks to become the bank's head personnel officer, a position that allowed him to grasp with sudden and great acuity the apparent randomness that inhered in hiring, firing, and promoting office workers. Salespeople, branch directors, vice presidents, even clerks like his younger self—they were responsible not for making things but for managing the various, sometimes idiosyncratic demands of customers and colleagues. There was no easy or reliable way to quantify how good they were at their jobs. The man who could master the messy intimacies of workplace human relations would emerge as the next Frederick Winslow Taylor: the man revered as the father of "scientific management," a pioneer in the study of industrial efficiency, and one of Hay's personal heroes. Only this time, the workplace revolution he would usher in would take place not on the dusty factory floors, amidst loud, hot machines and sweating workers, but in the tidy offices that looked down on them from above.

In 1943, Hay left the First Pennsylvania Bank to start Edward N. Hay and Associates, which specialized in developing workplace aptitude tests for white-collar workers, tests that quantified a worker's achievements, his intelligence, and his personality to match him to the service job that best suited his profile. The bibliography Hay amassed in just over a year was ambitious, impressive—the only one of its kind on the East Coast. For entry-level clerks, there was "A Test for Stenographic Skill," "A Finger Dexterity Test," "A Survey of Working Speed & Accuracy." For salespeople, there were tests for gregariousness and on-your-feet thinking ("The Store Personnel Test," "The Sales Situation Test"), as well as tests of supervisory attitude ("How Supervise?"), which asked candidates to indicate the desirability of company policies concerning labor unions and wage increases. For managers and mid-level executives, there was "The Personality Inventory," "The Personality Record," and the "Executive Personality Evaluation." His inventory seemed endless, all the better to please corporate clients like General Electric and Standard Oil, each of whom had pledged its loyalty to the test they were certain was better than all the rest at predicting job performance. That loyalty was unwavering—at least until the next new test came along, as Hay knew it would. His success depended on the planned obsolescence of his products.

He lived with his wife and six children in the suburbs of Swarthmore, Pennsylvania, and it was there that he met Isabel Briggs Myers, whom he initially knew only as the involved mother of one of his son's classmates. She wrote to him in January 1942, the same week that Soviet troops pushed the German army back from Moscow, the same month Hitler threatened the Jews of the world with total annihilation. She was interested, she said, in "people-sorting instruments": devices to "place the worker in the proper niche, keep him happy, and increase production." The article she had read in *Reader's Digest* had featured the popular Humm-Wadsworth Temperament Scale, a questionnaire developed in 1935 by Doncaster G. Humm, a psychologist, and Guy W. Wadsworth Jr., an industry expert. Humm and Wadsworth had derived their understanding of the different kinds of temperaments from an eclectic and decidedly unscientific reading list: the novels of Dostoyevsky and Flaubert, which they combed for descriptions of Raskolnikov's bilious, irritable, ill-tempered attitude and Emma Bovary's mercurial temperament; the notebooks of Ludwig Binswanger,

the great German theorist of melancholia; the papers of Emil Krae-
pelin, the psychiatrist who first identified schizophrenia as a mental illness. The Humm-Wadsworth Temperament Scale ranged from
1 to 5, where 1 indicated a "Normal Worker," 2 an antisocial one,
3 a manic-depressive, 4 a paranoid schizophrenic, and 5 an epileptic
(a misnomer for someone who suffered from obsessive-compulsive
disorder). In theory, the test was to be used to identify and help treat
workers or job applicants who suffered from mental illnesses; in practice, employers used it to weed out suspected union sympathizers (the
antisocial types) or communist ideologues (the manic-depressives).
Yet the reality of the test was that, while it was one of the most-talked-
about personality inventories on the market, the theory behind it a
flashy convergence of nineteenth-century literature and psychology, it
was not, strictly speaking, valid in any sense of the word.

This did not matter to Hay's clients, who trusted that he would
do the work of validation for them. But Hay was desperately short
staffed—something Isabel had learned one afternoon when Hay's
son had come home after school to study with Peter. The Humm-
Wadsworth Temperament Scale had piqued her interest, and she was
determined to learn from Hay's business of testing and typing. At
forty-four years old, she did what many people do who struggle to
reinvent themselves professionally: she offered to work for free. She
would apprentice herself to Hay so that she might learn from him the
secrets of "people sorting" for nothing more than the cost of his time,
she proposed. At the end of a year or two, she would leave to pursue
her own career in human resources. "As to where I shall eventually
work, I am content to leave that on the knees of the gods," she wrote to
him with cheerful self-assurance. But Hay was not keen on exploiting
Isabel's enthusiasm. He countered with an offer of his own. He would
pay her $1.33 an hour, four times the minimum wage in 1943, for thirty
hours a week, hours she knew she would have to herself when the
children were at school and her husband was at work.

Whatever insecurities she may have had about entering the workforce for the first time since the summer of 1918 were overshadowed
by the prospect of coming into her own as a new type of woman: a

professional. Twenty years earlier, she had witnessed firsthand how a great and terrible war could bring married women like her into the workplace in record numbers. Now it seemed history was repeating itself. From 1940 to 1945, female participation in the labor force had increased from 27 to 37 percent, which meant that six million more women woke up every morning, got dressed, kissed their husbands and children goodbye, and left home for a factory or office job. Many were uncertain about what the future would bring—after all, they had only just emerged from the domestic sphere, stepping gingerly away from endless, exhausting hours of housework and childcare, and they were not sure if they would like it. But for other women, like herself, work represented a once unimaginable freedom.

Now the workplace—and the white-collar workplace, in particular—assured women more than just a reprieve from cleaning the house and caring for the children. It also secured a space for intellectual and emotional creativity, where one could organize professional tasks and interactions according to the skills honed while performing one's domestic duties. Now was the time to put the "feminine mind" (as Katharine Briggs had referred to it) to work outside the home. Now was the time to "leverage"—a crackling new word for the interwar office worker—all those homebound habits, not just budgeting and multitasking, but managing the distinct personalities, young and old and middle-aged, who jostled one another for your time and attention. The affective labor of maintaining good household relations was, in fact, ideally suited to the managerial work of the office. A well-balanced team, reciprocal communication, high-quality leadership—these ideas were key to the efficiency of the corporation, just as they were key to the maintenance of a happy and harmonious household. And they required that professionals discover, and attempt to manage, the personalities of the people working for or around them with the lightest touch.

No one understood this better than Isabel, who prided herself on how she had used type to organize her duties as a wife and mother. While she shared none of her mother's messianic attachment to Jung or her belief in the profound and inviolable sanctity of the self, she did believe that personality assessment could initiate workers and their employers into a practical ethos of self-knowledge, one that she believed was essential to the expanding size and energy of the American workplace. "It is the fashion to say that the individual is unique," she explained in her first draft of what would become her manual of type. "He is the product of his own heredity and environment; therefore, he is different from everybody else. But the doctrine of uniqueness is not useful from a practical standpoint, unless we are prepared to make an exhaustive case study on every person whom we educate or counsel or hire. On the other hand, it is not practical to expect uniformity." What was needed was a theory that could honor the "specific personality differences in specific people" while also reducing human behavior to a "few, basic, observable differences." What was also needed was a way of instrumentalizing that theory—of making it both useful and accessible.

Her primary concerns with personality testing were practicality and profitability. When Hay asked her to start by validating the Humm-Wadsworth Temperament Scale, she told him that she found the test not just scientifically invalid but useless as well. An avid reader of management theorist Elton Mayo's articles on human relations, which stressed the primacy of employee morale to job performance, she knew that the most effective way to increase worker productivity was not to peg workers as normal, antisocial, or manic-depressive. Rather, it was for management to make every worker feel as if he was needed somewhere, doing something, no matter how unglamorous the task; to increase the attention they paid to the psychic lives of their employees. The idea was not to accept work as a grim reality—the proverbial grind—but to set up the ideological conditions under which one would bind oneself to it freely and gladly, as a point of pride and a source of self-validation. As Katharine had written in one of her child-rearing articles, "We often say of young people who are slow about getting down to the business of becoming adult, that they have not found themselves yet. We mean that they have not yet found any worldly adult occupation congenial enough to enable them to <u>lose themselves</u> in it." To find oneself only to lose that self in work—this was the impulse that shaped the history of type as it passed from Katharine's to Isabel's hands.

As the world lurched toward the bloodiest and most barbaric days of World War II, she began working for Hay and, unbeknownst to him, working on her type indicator.

. . . .

By the time Isabel started validating the Humm-Wadsworth Temperament Scale for Hay in January 1942, the German authorities had started to deport Jews from the Lodz ghetto to the Chelmno concentration camp; "people sorting" had taken on a darker, deadlier meaning after the rise of European fascism. Yet despite her mother's fascination with Hitler's personality type, and despite her father's intimate involvement in the development of the atomic bomb, the war influenced Isabel only insofar as it convinced her to turn away from the psychology of the abnormal and the depraved, to retreat from the unsavoriness of politics. The kind of type system she sought to design would assert the importance of returning to a state of normalcy and happiness after terrible suffering and hardship, a state where the most important and pressing things in life were doing one's job well and without complaining, getting along with one's colleagues, respecting one's boss, loving one's family. For Isabel, nothing could be further from the unspeakable horrors she had learned were taking place across the ocean.

Many social psychologists vehemently disagreed. Writing in the same years as Isabel, the German social theorist Theodor Adorno, who had fled to the United States upon the Nazis' assumption of power, would make the connection between type and fascist ideology explicit in *The Authoritarian Personality* (1950). Perhaps the most famous sociological study of the midcentury, *The Authoritarian Personality* offered a blistering critique of the typological work Hay and Isabel did and its relationship to Hitler's ethnocentric fascism. "The critique of psychological types expresses a truly humane impulse," Adorno wrote. It was "directed against that kind of subsumption of individuals against pre-established classes which has been consummated in Nazi

Germany, where the labeling of live human beings, independent of their specific qualities, resulted in decisions about their life and death. The desire to construct types was itself indicative of the potentially fascist character," Adorno argued. No matter what system of type one used—the Humm-Wadsworth Temperament Scale, the Bernreuter Personality Inventory, various schema of ethnic or racial or national categorization—the impulse to categorize people gestured to a basic rigidity of thought, an anti-humanist, anti-enlightenment propensity for flattening individuals into predetermined classes so that they could be managed and manipulated with greater ease.

For Adorno, type and its people-sorting instruments had not created this state of affairs. They were merely a symptom of a more invasive psychological disease: social modernity. The rise of industrial capitalism and the division of people into classes—owners versus workers, white collar versus blue collar—had left an indelible imprint on the souls of men and women, stamping certain predictable ways of thinking and feeling onto their psyches. Those who believed in the sanctity of the individual had been conditioned to do so by their class positions. If one worked a managerial job, the kind of job that stressed creativity and gumption and thinking "outside the box," one would be more inclined to consider oneself a freethinking, free-acting human being. A factory worker, a mechanic, or a deliveryman had not been initiated into this language of self-actualization because he had no profitable use for it. "There is reason to look for psychological types because the world in which we live is typed and 'produces' different 'types' of persons," Adorno wrote. "The critique of typology should not neglect the fact that large numbers of people are no longer, or rather never were, 'individuals' in the sense of traditional nineteenth-century philosophy." Most people did not enjoy real freedom of action or true individuation. The concept of the individual was an "ideological veil," Adorno insisted—a romantic capitalist fiction in a society committed to categorizing and dividing people while pretending to safeguard their souls.

Yet Adorno was eager to acknowledge that not all typologies served as devices for dividing the world into "sheep and buck." Some of them had "hit upon something," he speculated—a hazy kind of truth about the self. Not all forms of assessment proceeded by pathologizing personality, by dividing human beings into those who were "normal" and those who were not, as the Humm-Wadsworth did. Some typological systems offered individuals more than just passive membership in a predetermined psychological class. They armed the populace with a clarifying language of self-awareness, a language capable of fighting widespread political and social manipulation where it began—in the minds of the people. Within such ideal typological systems, the very idea of having a self emerged as a weapon of mass resistance, undoing the impulse to type—and thus to control—from within. Adorno was hard at work designing a questionnaire that identified prefascistic tendencies, and he believed that his test, which he would later call the "F scale," was the premier example of such a typological system.

Although she was not interested in critiquing industrial modernity, and although she never would have used the language of self-determination with the same critical verve Adorno did, Isabel would nevertheless have claimed an equally exalted place for the personality indicator she had started experimenting with in 1943. For one thing, her indicator did not originate in the modern corporation, even if that was to be its first resting place. Ever the devoted child, she had launched her design of the indicator just as her mother had launched her cosmic laboratory of baby training: in the comfort and safety of her home. With the same deck of 3″ × 5″ index cards and the same card file that Katharine had once used to chronicle Lyman's dreams of dark Spanish girls and embarrassing pecks, she proceeded by typing every member of her family. At the top of each card, she wrote the name of the family member and, under that, what she believed to be their Jungian type and their type's most salient characteristics. She called herself the family's "type watcher," a panoptic position she claimed to have occupied for all the years she watched her children grow and her husband flourish but was ready to take seriously only now. The more carefully she watched her family's interactions, the more she became convinced that type was no longer just one among many theories for explaining differences in observed human behavior or expressed preferences. It was a fact of nature.

She started by pitting herself and her mother, two feeling types (or so she believed—she did not appreciate her mother's rational side), against her husband and father, two thinkers. She wrote down everything she believed distinguished the feelers from the thinkers—her mother had once dubbed them "fish" and "canaries"—taking care not to judge one as better than or preferable to the other. They were simply different. The feelers made decisions based on what was important to them; the thinkers made decisions based on what was logical. The feelers wanted their decisions to reflect their values of compassion and fairness; the thinkers wanted their decisions to be uncontaminated by personal sentiment or wishes. The feelers were the guardians of personal relationships, the "cheering section" for others; the thinkers were scientists, more at home with the impersonal objects of the world—the laws of mechanics, electronics, or chemistry. The feelers were generally women; the thinkers, men. "There are a lot more women who prefer feeling than there are women who prefer thinking," Isabel asserted after evaluating her immediate family. As President Roosevelt called the idle engine of the American economy to action, urging business owners and employers to subordinate their interest in profit to the greater good of the nation, she recalled her mother's disdain for the president and his extraverted feeling politics. "When we gave suffrage to women we rather violently increased the number of feeling-types in the electorate," she added. "I think if you wanted to go back and check this trend in legislation since then there may be some laws because of that."

The more type characteristics she accumulated on her 3″ × 5″ cards, the more she began to get a sense for each type's concrete preferences. Now the challenge was to ascertain what kinds of questions would lead a test taker to reveal these preferences. She wanted to be loyal to Jung, but Jung's soulful theory of type pairs was too complicated for her purposes. "If I ask complicated questions, no one could answer them," she told a friend. "I'll have to find little, inconsequential everyday things in everyday life that people can answer." She proceeded to simplify his characterizations of the different types in *Psychological Types* through an intimate process of trial and error: she, an introverted intuitive feeling type, would write an item and ask Chief, whom she decreed an introverted sensing thinking type, to answer it.

"*Are you inclined (a) to value sentiment above logic; or (b) logic above sentiment?*" she would ask her husband. "*Would you rather work under a boss (or teacher) who was (a) good-natured but often inconsistent; or (b) sharp-tongued but always logical?*"

When his answer surprised her, she would ask him why he had chosen the answer he did. "I thought you would make the other choice," she would insist, puzzled.

"If you wanted me to pick (a) instead of (b)," he would respond, "you would have had to phrase it differently. You didn't phrase the question the way you really meant it." He found her language clumsy and imprecise. The writing and revision of her questionnaire items were everywhere inflected by his criticism, some of it constructive, some of it less so. As a thinker, he was not much of a compliment giver—she estimated that he might have given her five or six in the three decades they had been married—but she believed the devotion of his leisure time to her work on the indicator was compliment enough.

Her daughter, Ann, was easy to type—she was an introverted intuitive feeling type like her mother—but her son, Peter, proved more difficult. She identified him as an extraverted intuitive feeling type, and the opposite on every dimension from Chief. Father and son had loud and endless squabbles over schoolwork and responsibility, and she tried to explain to her husband that the most important thing for an extraverted intuitive feeler was the freedom to do what he wanted. She gleaned this from a conversation she had with Peter about his distaste for his high school algebra class. "Why do I have to learn these things now?" he asked his mother when he struggled to solve for x and y one day after school. "When I come to a place where I want to learn them, I will learn them then." Isabel explained to him that sometimes one had to endure "humdrum, mundane, repetitious, routine things" as an "investment in future freedom." "If you escape the necessary things now, you condemn yourself to a much less interesting life later," she told her son. Later, on his 3″ × 5″ card, she would write, "A feeling type is likely to have a sort of selective blindness. You hate to look at the things that speak against the things you value, against the things you are emotionally committed to wanting to do. But there is no use living temporarily in a fool's paradise . . . if there is some big, black consequence standing in the way that you haven't had the nerve to look at and deal with."

To Peter and Ann, Isabel presented the first version of her questionnaire—"Form A" as she tentatively labeled it—as a kind of "game," a series of pleasurable and provocative questions to answer among friends, laughing at what you might discover about one another. The earliest version of the type indicator seemed custom-made for helping teenagers discover their true selves without taking the process very seriously, the kind of frivolous quiz one might have discovered on the final page of a glossy midcentury magazine (or, today, on the internet). *"Are such emotional 'ups and downs' as you may feel: (a) very marked; (b) rather moderate?"* *"In school, do you prefer subjects made up of: (a) facts to be remembered (geography, history, civics, biology); (b) general principles to be applied (grammar, math, physics)?"* She encouraged them to show the indicator to their friends and to Peter's girlfriend, Kathy, to go to them armed with their own set of 3″ × 5″ cards and document how well their expressed preferences aligned with the results of the test items she had designed.

Ann's high school class was where Isabel found her first cross section of type "data," Ann and three of her girlfriends: two intuitives, two feelers. "One of them was the editor of the high school magazine and my daughter was the editor of the yearbook and the third became the editor of the *Phoenix*"—Swarthmore's student newspaper—"and the fourth one had the gift but not the energy to do anything that was evident," Isabel recalled. She had the girls over to her house and administered Form A, encouraging them to talk about their dreams, their schemes about what they might do after high school. As they spoke, she made each of them a 3″ × 5″ type card and used their chatter to populate it. She took the cards to Peter and Ann's high school principal, and once she had explained to him how the type indicator could be useful for streamlining course selection and anticipating disciplinary problems, she persuaded him to let her administer the indicator to all students in the seventh, eighth, ninth, and tenth grades. She also, astonishingly, persuaded him to give her copies of all the students' permanent records and their IQ tests, without their consent or their parents' knowledge.

To evaluate her first cross section of test subjects, Isabel mapped answers to the questionnaire onto a set of initials she had derived from Jung's writings: introversion (I) and extraversion (E); intuition (also I in the initial versions of the test) and sensing (S); and feeling (F) and thinking (T). To Jung's original scheme, she added a fourth category: the judging (J) function and the perceptive (P) function, which Katharine had once claimed as an implicit, yet unexplored, aspect of Jung's type theory. "Every time you use your mind for any purpose whatever you perform either an act of <u>perception</u> (becoming aware of something) or an act of <u>judgment</u> (coming to a conclusion about something)," she wrote. A person identified as judging if she lived in an orderly and disciplined way, "aiming to regulate life and control it," she wrote. By contrast, a perceiving person would "live in a flexible, receptive, spontaneous way, aiming to understand life and to adapt to it." Her mother's J/P distinction was key to understanding the entirety of type development, as it helped differentiate between a person's "dominant" and "auxiliary" functions, the "captain of their ship" and the "first mate," as she described the pair. If a person was a perceiving type (P), she preferred to take in information, and her dominant function was whichever one of the two perceptive functions she preferred: sensing (S) or intuition (I). If a person was a judging type (J), he preferred to make decisions, and his dominant function was whichever of the two judging functions he preferred: thinking (T) or feeling (F). She believed that J/P "served admirably" as the final dichotomy in her type system, rounding out Jung's triumvirate.

When Peter and Ann left for college the next year, she would ward off loneliness by spending long nights with her type indicator, adding and subtracting questionnaire items until she felt ready to deem it Form B. She was proud of what she had accomplished, Chief less so. Her husband, once so progressive in his advocacy of women's work, began to complain that she was neglecting him and her housework. And for what? Her aged mother's religious obsession? On one "disastrous occasion" that stayed with her for the rest of her life, he referred to her sarcastically as "Mrs. Executive," mocking her entrepreneurial ambitions. Once or twice he suggested that a divorce might be prudent.

But Jung's typologies had given her a language by which she could dismiss his demands as the product of irreconcilable, yet still manageable, psychological differences. "I said to myself when Chief"—a thinking type—"says anything like that it is entirely different . . . from what it would have meant if I had said it," she explained to a friend. If Isabel had said it as a feeling type, it would have meant something. But Chief, her "thinking husband," had simply got into the habit of introducing it as an observation—that perhaps a divorce made sense. "I just don't have to bother about it," she concluded, feigning detachment.

But to Katharine she expressed her concern that if mother and daughter had developed their type system before she met Chief, she would never have married him. She was an IIFP. He was an ISTJ. Like the fish and the canary of Katharine's fable, they had nothing in common, she observed. Her feelings determined what mattered to her; she was "tractable," she noted, while he was stubborn. The only thing they shared was an indifference to the opinions of others, a classic introvert trait and one that seemed sufficiently romantic in one's twenties, when one still had the luxury to poke fun at authority figures and wax poetic about revolution. At the time, she had thought that would be enough.

By the end of 1943, she had a product, one compelling enough to quiet Chief's grumblings. Now the greater source of resistance was her mother. Like Isabel's marriage to Chief, and like her career as a mystery novelist, the type indicator irritated Katharine, even though she was credited as its primary creator. She condemned her daughter's uncritical embrace of testing, writing in her diary that nowhere was the psychology of extraversion and introversion "more superficial" than "in the 'scientific' tests based upon such definitions—tests quite generally accepted by academic psychologists as 'scientific' instruments of 'scientific' measurement upon which to base 'scientific' work!" (With a pen and dark ink, she drew lines through the scare quotes around 'scientific' and reprimanded herself in the margins: "Don't be sarcastic.") She reminded Isabel that she had not needed a questionnaire to validate what she had seen so clearly with her trained eye: Peter's extraversion and Ann's introversion. She had typed them when they were barely a year and a half old, and the results of her assessment were no different from the results of her daughter's questionnaire. The expertise she brought to her role as a type watcher was a point of pride, and even though she had once encouraged amateurs like herself to outfit their personality paint box, she did not understand why Isabel felt compelled to democratize type in its shallowest, silliest form. "I have already given you a questionnaire for the testing of your own integration which might be modified to meet the needs of those who have not yet questioned their type faiths," she wrote to her daughter. "We might ask: Exactly what sits upon your throne of God giving you your sense of security? For what do you sacrifice easily and labor diligently?" These questions had no easy answers. "It is not a questionnaire to be dashingly filled in, 'Yes or No'!" she chided her daughter when she learned about the indicator's forced choice design.

Isabel's unwillingness to listen to her mother was as ideological as it was personal. For Katharine, the language of type had offered itself up as a "personal religion" as William James had once described it: an experience of belief that did not need any external validation, scientific or otherwise. For Isabel, it represented something entirely different. Type was a vocation, a calling: a task bound to a higher purpose, but one nevertheless rooted in the professional codes and conducts of industrial modernity. What the Church called "revelation," she called "intuitive perception," she explained to Peter as she continued to revise the type indicator. This was her way of moving from particular cases—the personalities of her son and daughter, her husband and mother—to general theories. For revelation to be valuable, it had to be useful and demonstrable to the world at large, not just to one woman sitting at her kitchen table, conducting imaginary conversations with her idol. Isabel's writing betrayed none of the reverence for Jung or for the self that her mother had once entertained. She was all business from the start—Mrs. Executive, indeed.

. . . .

To understand what the Myers-Briggs Type Indicator is today, you must first understand what it was when Isabel debuted it to Hay on July 1, 1943. Imagine her in his office, wearing her favorite dress—nylon blue with little pink flowers on it—ready to make her case for why her homegrown tool should be added to his suite of products. Although her career as a writer of mystery novels had ended with little fanfare after *Give Me Death,* she told him, one mystery had continued to preoccupy her: the problem of the intelligent division of labor. For her mother, the most important division of labor in the world had been the divide between feminine and masculine labor; those who performed housework and those who performed office work; the feelers and the thinkers. Yet with the end of World War II and the explosion of the labor force, she and Hay both knew that this division no longer dominated conversations about work. What was needed was a test for all the new men and women in the workplace that did not punish them for their perceived vulnerabilities but convinced them and their employees that they had none—only a set of interests and preferences that were better suited to some jobs over others. What was needed, too, was a person who possessed "enough detective instinct" to "enjoy following up whatever clues" such a test might unearth.

She was that person, she told Hay, and the story of type she wanted to tell him was more riveting than any detective story she could have conjured. It was a love story—a story of matches made if not in heaven than under the auspices of personality science. "The more you know about what a man is like, the more effectively you can work with him or under him, or assign him to the right job," she wrote to Hay. "You find out eventually, of course, by trial and error, where his strengths and weaknesses lie, how things strike him, which matters are in his field, and which are not. But that is a time-consuming and sometimes painful process, like trying on all the shoes in a shoe store to find a fit. If men came like shoes, with the most vital data as to size and style marked outside the box, many a cramping misfit could be avoided."

Here was a fairy tale with a perfectly modern twist—the glass slipper screened, scrutinized, and labeled before it ever touched Cinderella's foot; the employer restless to find the right match; the whole thing an example of the same romantic capitalist pursuit that Adorno had denounced. "The most logical answer" to the painful problem of employee misfit, Isabel proposed, "lies in the work of Dr. Carl G. Jung of Zurich" and his "four basic 'functions' of the mind: E/I, S/I, T/F, J/P. (She did not tell him that she had added J and P to Jung's original schematic.) An individual's preferences for each function could "be picked out by a questionnaire-form-Type-Indicator," a 117-question multiple-choice test in which respondents answered questions by picking from one of two options. Once the answers were scored by hand, the test subject would be presented with her "personality pattern" in the form of a simple four-letter acronym. There were sixteen possible combinations in all—sixteen possible types looking to lose themselves in the best jobs available to them. Enchanted by her story's "theoretical rationale," Hay agreed to use and distribute the indicator, believing that it would make a "tremendous mark on industry, the schools, and vocational guidance."

To read the first published version of the questionnaire, now called Form C, is to realize how hard Isabel worked to distance it from tests of psychological judgment like the Humm-Wadsworth. The questions were preceded by a cover sheet with instructions that were folksy, fun, and comforting. They stressed the naturalness of what was no doubt a highly unnatural exercise in self-interrogation. "This is not, strictly speaking, a test at all, for it has no time limits and no right or wrong answers," the instructions reassured the anxious reader, speaking in a mother's soothing voice. "For the best results, answer easily and naturally, as though talking to your family. Don't bother about keeping your answers consistent. Consistency doesn't matter. And don't worry about how you will come out. You may belong to any one of a number of different types, and"—the rest of the sentence was bolded to profound effect—"**each type has its own special advantages.**" There was no suggestion of separating normal workers from antisocial or neurotic ones. There was only a glimpse into a future corporate utopia in which everyone would find the right job to perform—from each according to his ability to each company according to its need.

The questions in Form C dated themselves in quaint, almost charming, ways. Their idiom was squarely the idiom of 1940s suburban mythology, with its corner stores and its social clubs and its afternoon card games. Question 61 asked the test taker, "*Are you generally: (a) a 'good mixer'; or (b) rather reserved in company?*" Question 66 followed, "*Do you: (a) very much enjoy stopping at soda fountains; or (b) usually prefer to use your money for other things?*" Question 108 offered a scenario that was impossible to imagine taking place outside of a sleepy suburb: "*When the fire engine goes by, are you: (a) tempted to follow it and see the fire; or (b) more inclined to keep on with what you are doing?*"

Dated too were the separate answer sheets Isabel designed for "Men & Boys" and "Women & Girls." The latter was not available when the indicator was first published, and there was no great rush to produce it. It was assumed that nearly all the initial test takers would be men. "Quite a few questions prove to be effective only for one sex," Isabel wrote to Hay. Questions that assessed the test subject's preference for thinking and feeling could not yet account for women's biological tendencies to feel everything more acutely than men, whose "natural offices of thinking" admitted little emotion. The persistent psychological gap between the sexes, first asserted by Katharine in her writings on "the feminine mind" and later adopted by Isabel in her design of the indicator, loomed largest in the institution of marriage, which reinforced a man's anti-feeling tendencies. A man, Isabel observed in a study she did for Hay, "thinks it is obvious when he marries a woman he has demonstrated once and for all that he esteems her above all other women, and that when he works hard and provides for her he is demonstrating day by day a fundamental concern for her well-being (it would probably be a little sentimental to refer to it as happiness), and that therefore it is superfluous to mention either fact. So he doesn't. He only mentions what he considers worthy of note—the respects in which she departs from the ideal, and respects in which their well-being (hers as often as his) would be greater if she would do differently from the way she naturally does. There is no nourishment in any of this for her feelings, and she reacts accordingly, and that gives him no nourishment for his feelings and makes him less and less likely to express his softer side."

What to make of the distinction Isabel drew between a woman's "well-being" and her "happiness"? Was her dismissal of sentimentality a veiled confession about the state of her own marriage? After all, she was one of the women she described; ever since she had met Chief, he had judged her value to him by her ability to withstand all the "uncomplimentary criticism" he could "mass against her," as he had once written to her mother. In time, however, his criticisms had grown, had accumulated, and now his disapproval had overrun their lives with the same sordidness as the dishes she no longer washed, the clothes she no longer laundered. Was the story of the thinker and the feeler—the fish and the canary—the story of her life? The lack of appreciation, the resentment, the slow desiccation of feeling? Was this the fate of married men and women everywhere? If she could not reconcile the two types, she reasoned, they would have to go their separate ways. And so they did—she separated men and women into two separate answer sheets.

Once she had her questionnaire and her answer sheets, she and Hay started setting her prices. In 1943, the cost of a Briggs-Myers test booklet was fifty cents. An answer sheet cost five. For an additional five cents, you could receive a personality "profile card" that visualized your type through a game of connect the dots, zigzagging from one type dimension to the next. And for three dollars—the most expensive offering on Hay's list of paraphernalia—you could purchase *Type as the Index to Personality,* a seventy-two-page booklet that Isabel had written to introduce newcomers to Jung's terms and theories. She did not charge anything for the detailed answer sheet that accompanied each test, which provided the test taker with a cheerful summary of his personality profile. Each type was brought to life with a list of adjectives ("realistic" or "idealistic," "individualist" or "cooperative"),

Extraversion, he will use it in the outer world, upon people and things and situations, working matters out in action.

(E)I
If he prefers to use his favorite function for—

Introversion, he will use it inside his head, upon concepts and ideas, working matters out by considering and reflecting.

Sense-perception (the 5 senses), he will tend to be realistic, practical, fun-loving, observant, and good at remembering and working with facts.

S(I)
If he prefers to take things in by means of—

Intuitive-perception, he will tend to value imagination, inspirations and possibilities, and will be good at new ideas, projects and problem-solving.

Thinking-judgment, he will tend to analyze, weigh the facts, and "think" that impersonal logic is a surer guide than human likes and dislikes.

(T)F
If he prefers to make decisions by means of—

Feeling-judgment, he will tend to sympathize, weigh the personal values, and "feel" that human likes and dislikes are more important than logic.

Judging function, (either T or F) he will live in a planned, decided, orderly way, aiming to regulate life and control it.

(J)P
If he prefers to deal with the world with a—
(Shows extravert's 1st, introvert's 2nd function)

Perceptive function, (either S or I) he will live in a flexible, receptive, spontaneous way, aiming to understand life and adapt to it.

Original rubric for the Briggs-Myers Type Indicator, circa 1943

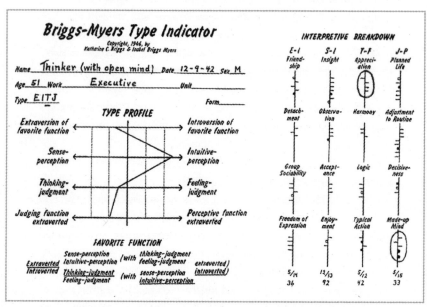

Original type profile for the Briggs-Myers Type Indicator, circa 1943

nicknames (ISTJs were the "Superdependables," EITJs the "Standard Executives," ESTPs the "adaptable realists," EITPs the "enthusiastic innovators"), and glowing descriptions of the type's virtues.

Her type descriptions for all sixteen types were based on a combination of her observations of her family and her instincts, a mixture of the "empirical and the theoretical," she called it. "The process of putting those together made me think of pulling cotton out of a cotton picker," she would later recall. "Have you seen cotton put up in a long, long roll coiled inside of a cylinder and just a little bit of it sticks out and you get hold of a little bit and you pull and it comes and it comes and it comes? You pull it out of your unconscious treasury that way." Once the test taker had received his results, all Isabel asked was that he read his personality profile with a pencil in hand and cross out whichever descriptors did not fit well or write down any characteristics she might have missed. "Above all things," she instructed, "it would be valuable to know which kinds of work (or which parts of your work) you particularly enjoy and which you definitely do not care for."

With the war entering its final year, Isabel had everything she needed to launch her product: her questionnaire, her answer sheets, her personality profiles, her user's manual. These pieces of paper were the culmination of the penetrating and sometimes painful analyses she and her mother had performed on the people they loved in order to grasp their souls. Now all she had to do was wait for someone to take her test.

To her surprise, her inaugural client was not one of the corporate giants that routinely retained Hay's services: General Electric, Standard Oil, Bell Telephone. They would come a year or two later. The request for the first set of test booklets and answer sheets came from an address in Washington, D.C., an organization that she may have heard rumors of through her father's classified work with the atomic bomb: the Office of Strategic Services. Its team of wartime psychologists, led by the former director of the Harvard Psychological Clinic, none other than Henry Murray, were interested in matching covert operatives to the secret missions best suited to their personalities. It was all a very hush-hush operation, Isabel was told, and, as if to signal her discretion, she listed the OSS in her client roster as the "Murray Corporation." It is unclear if she knew exactly what they used the test for, or that her desire to help stop the Germans came true, albeit not in the way she had imagined.

CHAPTER NINE

A Perfect Spy

S ometime in the fall or winter of 1943—the precise date remains classified—Henry Murray helped the U.S. government lease a large and lovely country estate on a hundred-acre tract of farmland one mile outside the township of Fairfax, Virginia. Every Friday around five-thirty p.m., the residents of Fairfax would watch as a canvas-covered army truck sped through town and up to the entrance to the estate, where it waited for military guards to open the gates so it could continue up the dirt drive and over the hidden brook that cut across the property. It stopped in front of the house, and out stepped thirty men and women, all dressed head to toe in foliage green. They were escorted into the house and later glimpsed wandering around the property, diving into bushes or leaping across the brook or guarding an innocuous-looking pile of rocks.

Rumor had it that the estate—the old Willard family place, as it was known around town—was now an army asylum, a place where soldiers who had suffered terrible atrocities during the war were sent by the government to heal. The residents of Fairfax warned one another about its inhabitants, who, it was whispered, had come back from Europe as starved, crippled, damaged souls, as air raid survivors and torture victims, Nazi sympathizers and communists. The rumors persisted long enough that they became the truth, this despite the fact that no one could recall who had said what to whom. To everyone's relief, the inhabitants of the house never ventured into town and the townspeople never got too close to the house's gates.

But the country estate in Fairfax was not a government asylum. It was the headquarters of Station S, the nation's first personality assessment center for covert operatives—a special project organized and funded by the Office of Strategic Services. A precursor to the Central Intelligence Agency, the OSS owed its existence to William "Wild Bill" Donovan, a bright-eyed, bull-nosed army major and lawyer whom friends described as an irrepressible patriot, a man determined to meet the U.S. government's every espionage and counterespionage need no matter the inconvenience or cost. In 1942, when the agency first opened, its tasks were often overambitious and haphazard. They ranged from the banal and quasi-secretarial work of intelligence gathering— assembling research reports, conducting geographic surveys—to far more exciting fare. Donovan's agents intercepted and decoded Axis communications, spied on key players in the European theater of war, aided and trained resistance groups in Eastern Europe, and launched massive propaganda campaigns to "disintegrate the morale of enemy troops"—the kind of psychological campaign Murray had once proposed to discredit Hitler.

Station S was just one of the OSS's many special projects, and the asylum was a cover story that Donovan and his bureaucrats had planted for local consumption, trusting the townspeople to embroider it with all the embellishments of a gothic novel. Had they known the true identities of the people who moved in and out of S under the cover of army canvas—the president of a major American bank, a prominent French ballet dancer, a pro football player, a Japanese mathematician, the soon-to-be-infamous spy Jane Foster—they might not have wanted to keep their distance. These minor celebrities were among the 5,391 people who would be subject to dozens of personality tests and live-action assessments to figure out which OSS job, if any, was best suited to their abilities: paratrooper, resistance leader, saboteur, spy, liaison pilot, pigeoneer. They would learn how to use their self-knowledge to practice the artful manipulation of their personalities, how to wear the many masks, both literal and figurative, that could help them infiltrate resistance groups, gain access to classified information, and take down puppet governments. By the end of the war, S would offer a blueprint for many other institutions—corporations, colleges, churches, hospitals—that wished to use personality assessment to bring their operations into the modern era, wedding the tools of self-discovery to techniques of manipulation and social control.

Among the tools that S would introduce to the American psychological community was the Briggs-Myers Type Indicator, which Murray's graduate student, Donald MacKinnon, had purchased from Hay and Associates in 1944 with the guarantee that it would help the OSS match recruits to the jobs that were right for them. For Isabel, her first clients made it possible for her to claim that the indicator had played some role in the war effort, however small and unobtrusive and (as she would later conclude) disappointing that role was to be. "It was evident that we weren't going to win the war with it," she insisted to a friend, but one could hear in her insistence the veiled hope that her creation would, in fact, find a way to leave its mark on the annals of history. After all, what could be more important to winning the war than matching Allied spies to the operations that best suited their types? Who better to take down the Nazis than the introverted sensing (IS) type, the type of many "army officers," she claimed in the first version of her manual, whose "complete, realistic, practical respect for the facts" and "outer calm" made him the perfect intelligence agent?

What she did not know was that Murray was woefully underprepared for the task when he and his colleagues first arrived at S with the type indicator in hand. Murray had recruited a seven-person team of clinical psychiatrists, sociologists, anthropologists, and psychologists of various persuasions—Freudian, Jungian, Watsonian, even an animal psychologist—to help him with his assessment duties. Yet no one on the team had any sense for what a saboteur or a pigeoneer did, let alone how to predict whether any individual candidate or type was well suited to these jobs. They had no idea what the political or cultural conditions were on the bases where the OSS had operatives stationed. The information they received from their contacts overseas was scanty, unreliable. Murray confessed that all his ideas about spies and spying came from novels he had read: W. Somerset Maugham's *Ashenden, or The British Agent,* Helen MacInnes's *Assignment in Brittany,* the thrillers of E. Phillips Oppenheim, the cloak-and-dagger heroes of legend. But the shadow and sheen of fiction would quickly be dulled by the very practical questions Murray found himself asking when he had to decide whether to send a man into the field, possibly to his death.

The first recruit his team assessed (code name: Bud) was a man who was to be air-dropped into Western Europe, where he would slink from city to city uncovering the identities of secret Nazi operatives. "Will he be able to govern his anxiety up there in the plane as the moment for the drop approaches?" Murray wondered as he observed Bud eating his meals, jogging outdoors, and answering interview questions. "Will he get along with the British? How about the French? Will he find isolation tolerable? Can he hold his liquor?" The second recruit (code name: Roy) was to assume command of an intelligence bureau in Calcutta. The questions Murray asked of him were entirely different from those he had asked of Bud. "How will this man tolerate the monsoon season? The prickly heat? Athlete's foot?" he wondered as he watched Roy pass Bud the salt during lunch. "How often will he frequent the nightclubs and flirt with the girls? Will he treat the Hindus with respect?" As the recruits piled up and as the missions Washington proposed became increasingly complicated and increasingly heterogeneous, the questions Murray found himself asking multiplied. How strong and well armed were the resistance groups in France? What could an operator expect when he touched down in Yugoslavia or Greece? Could one trust the Chinese to cooperate with American agents? How susceptible were healthy midwestern boys to the Burmese strain of malaria? Would the stubborn-looking heavyset recruit in the corner appeal to a band of Albanian guerrillas? None of these questions presented obvious answers or even obvious ways of finding an answer. "No matter how substantial are the advances of scientific psychology, the best series of predictions of *individual* careers—apperception operating as it does—will involve the play of experienced intuitions, the clinical hunch, products of unconsciously perceived and integrated symptomatic signs," Murray wrote.

"The assessment of men . . . is the scientific art of arriving at sufficient conclusions from insufficient data."

Time was of the essence, but the war had caught everyone unprepared. Murray could not afford to engage in long theoretical discussions of personality or to adjudicate the inevitable squabbles that would arise between the Freudians and the Jungians, the biologists and the behaviorists. "Beliefs in themselves are of negligible import" he told his team. They could not bring in different teams of analysts to assess the Americans, the French, and the Japanese recruits, carefully calibrating their interviews and tests to reflect cross-cultural and linguistic differences. Nor could they interview each recruit separately, sifting through the thousands of applicants to find the one uniquely suited to the job. More important than in-depth psychological analyses were the psychological "facts, acts, and gadgets" that S's team could design to generate quick, clean answers to the questions that would keep men like Bud and Roy alive in the field. What was needed was a generic profile of the perfect spy, no matter his task, location, or language, and a battery of tests that could measure each of S's recruits against this ideal.

It was easier to define the perfect spy by what he was not than what he was. Above all, Murray wanted to avoid men who were "stupid, apathetic, sullen, resentful, arrogant, or insulting" in their dealings with others, either members of the Allied units or foreign nationals. "To this must be added the irreparable damage that can be done by one who blabs," Murray stressed. The primary objective of the assessment program was a reduction in the "sloths, irritants, bad actors, and free talkers" who might jeopardize the nation's security. Its secondary objective was to find men—some introverted sensing types, some not—who matched the seven criteria that the team agreed were essential to the effective performance of any OSS job overseas:

Motivation for Assignment: war morale, interest in proposed job.
Energy and Initiative: activity level, zest, effort, initiative.
Effective Intelligence: ability to select strategic goals . . . ; quick practical thought . . .

Emotional Stability: ability to govern disturbing emotions, steadiness and endurance under pressure, snafu tolerance, freedom from neurotic tendencies.

Social Relations: ability to get along well with other people, good will, team play, tact, freedom from disturbing prejudices, freedom from annoying traits.

Leadership: social initiative, ability to evoke cooperation . . .

Security: ability to keep secrets; caution, discretion, ability to bluff and to mislead.

For especially high stakes missions, they added another three criteria:

Physical Ability: agility, daring, ruggedness, stamina.

Observing and Reporting: ability to observe and to remember accurately significant facts . . .

Propaganda Skills: ability to apperceive the psychological vulnerabilities of the enemy; to devise subversive techniques of one sort or another; to speak, write, or draw persuasively.

This was the ordered disorder that took place behind the scenes at S as Murray prepared to greet his assessment subjects as the sun set over the old Willard place. "We would never know certainly whether we had been an asset or a liability to the OSS," Murray wrote in his chronicle of his work at S. For his subjects, it would be a different experience altogether.

. . . .

Say that you aspire to be the perfect spy. Say you have been told by a government recruiter that soon you will be sent to the countryside to attend a three-day assessment school. He does not specify what you will do at this school. He tells you only that you must go incognito; you must leave behind all letters, books, and photographs, all monogrammed shirts, towels, and handkerchiefs—anything embroidered with your initials. No one at the school will know your name and you will know nothing about the people you meet there. You will be instructed to pick a new name for yourself, the name by which they will address you. The recruiter tells you these precautions are necessary for your safety and the safety of "the organization."

On the day of your departure, you report to the Schools and Training Headquarters on the corner of Twenty-fourth and F Streets in Washington, D.C. There, inside an unmarked and abandoned brick schoolhouse, you take off all your clothes and destroy any identifying insignia on your underwear and undershirt. You are issued two pairs of army fatigues, your uniform for the next three days. Once dressed, you are ushered into a room with twenty-nine others dressed just like you. You are told to wait and to be quiet. Every so often, someone who cannot bear the silence makes a joke that cracks the air, hangs with unease, and disappears. At five o'clock a sergeant comes in and calls roll. He shouts your name—your new name—and you pause to consider it before responding, "Yes, sir!" You step into a canvas-covered army truck, which will drive for fifteen miles until it arrives at a place the sergeant refers to as "S." You will never learn what "S" stands for. All you know is that it, whatever it is, has stripped you and your fellow travelers of your social selves—your names, addresses, professions, ranks, all the tangible things you had once appealed to as proof of your existence and your place in the world, all the things that allowed others to recognize you in turn.

Upon your arrival at S, you are surprised by the beauty of the estate and the openness of the fields surrounding it. You had expected to be taken some place dirty, disorderly. You are surprised, too, by the congeniality of the director and his assistant. He gives a short, warm welcoming speech. "Our job," he explains, "is to seek to discover your special skills, unique abilities, and individual talents in order that they may be put to the fullest use in this organization . . . Our job here [is] to see that square pegs are not put in round holes." Over the next three days, you will be subject to dozens of assessments. You will fill out a personal history questionnaire and a health questionnaire, which asks you to list your height and weight and to describe any recurring nightmares you may have. You will take an IQ test, a vocabulary test, a reading comprehension test, a test of cultural sensitivity, and a memorization test, in which you will be given a hand-drawn map to study for eight minutes, after which you will be quizzed on the locations of lakes, railroads, and airfields. You will be asked to complete sentences like "The main driving force in my life is _____" or "I feel scared when _____." You will be instructed to swing on a rope, to climb a wall, to walk a catwalk, to ford a river, to play a game of baseball. You will find out from a test called the Briggs-Myers Type Indicator whether you are an EITJ (the "Standard Executive," "strong in initiative and creative impulse") or an ISTP (the "Superdependable," "analytic and impersonal"). All of this will determine which missions, if any, are best suited to your individual talents.

But first you must complete a more theatrical task, one that will test your ability to bluff. You must create a new persona to outfit the self you have stripped bare. The director instructs you to develop, maintain, and spread a cover story, one that takes your new name as its point of origin and weaves a life story around it. There are certain minimum requirements. You must claim to have been born in someplace other than where you were born. You must pretend to have been educated in institutions other than the ones in which you were educated. You must pretend to engage in work other than the work you are engaged in, and you must pretend that you live somewhere other than where you live. The horizon of self-creation is endless. You are giddy with possibility—or perhaps frozen with dread. But the director, sensing your excitement or your unease, cautions against straying too far from your personal experiences. "It might be unwise for you to claim to be a medical doctor if you know nothing about medicine," he says. "Similarly, it might be very unwise for you to claim Chicago as your place of residence if you have never been there and know nothing about it." A certain level of fluency with your new persona is essential. Members of the staff, the director warns you, will try to trap you into breaking your cover. You must exercise constant vigilance.

Immediately after he delivers his instructions, the staff distributes a personal history questionnaire. You are instructed to fill it out as your "true self."

"Go ahead!" the director says. "Be yourself!" He assures you that this is not a trap, but you are wary. Which version of yourself do they really want you to be?

So distracted are you by your doubts that you do not realize the assessment has already begun, long before your pencil ever makes a mark on the questionnaire. The staff has been watching you since you first stepped out of the truck. Since they have access to none of the exterior cues commonly used in judging personality—the cut and condition of your suit, the pattern of your tie, the crease of your hat, the shine of your shoe—they have taken great pains to assess your self-comportment. They have noted whether you jumped down from the truck, agile and boyish, eager to introduce yourself to the officers who greeted you, or whether you measured your steps, hesitating or halting as you approached the front door. They have paid special attention to how you spoke your new name. Did you look the welcoming officer in the eye and state it with confidence? Did you speak it slowly and softly, shaping the lie in your mouth for the first time? Did you forget the name you had chosen, stuttering something incomprehensible and scramble to cover your mistake? They have observed the ease with which you donned your fatigues, whether the anonymity of your outfit was a source of reassurance or shame. They have watched you react to the director's instructions, noting who leaned forward, impatient to match wits with the staff, and who slumped back, affecting the hard-boiled pose of the high school rebel.

Absent the public markers of your personality, the external traces of it—the contortion of your face, the angle of your gestures, the tone of your voice—remain intact and visible. To be a good spy is to learn how to erase these deeper traces of the self. It is to learn how to perform new and unfamiliar ways of being in the world, and it is to perform them with such an air of grace that one is tempted to forget that it is a performance at all. To be a perfect spy is to convince yourself that it is not, in fact, possible to disentangle the notion of a "true self" from the many performances of the self that one must enact—the observations, manipulations, defenses, and avoidances with which one navigates other personalities in the world. To be a perfect spy is to learn how to be a saboteur, spy, pilot, or pigeoneer, but most of all, a patriot.

. . . .

For Murray, the perfect spy was as self-contradictory as the Egocrat, a master of tailoring his personality to suit whatever circumstances were thrust upon him. He was not the glamorous "man of mystery," at least not in the deep, psychoanalytic sense that Jung, Murray, or Katharine would have interpreted the term, so much as he was a perpetual character actor. Like the intelligence agents in W. Somerset Maugham's short stories, Murray's perfect spy was as comfortable impersonating a Greek shipping magnate as he was infiltrating an Italian street gang or performing the subversive duties of a Russian revolutionary. Yet while the Egocrat used his personality to make the state over in his perverse and often unstable image, the perfect spy was a staunch defender of the status quo, a protector of the government's interests. He was fundamentally conservative in the deployment of his personality, even if it was constantly shifting. At the basis of the spy's personality was a loyal traitor.

As the first organization to use the Briggs-Myers Type Indicator, the OSS was also among the first to recognize that its notion of the "true self"—the "fact of one's nature," as Isabel had called it in her early manuals—was useful only under certain conditions. In the high-stress interpersonal scenarios of sneaking, bluffing, and secret keeping that Murray took to be the spy's métier, other models of self-making seemed more appropriate. The spy's dexterity could not be measured through pen and paper questionnaires alone. What was needed was a theory that could accommodate the capriciousness of spying, one that embraced Murray's metaphorical presupposition that any OSS scheme took place "in a theater" of make-believe and improvisation and, as such, needed good actors to ensure its success. What was needed too was a new set of testing procedures, one that could assemble a squadron of "theatrical deceivers." This at least was the recommendation Murray issued in his OSS debrief at the end of 1944. Then he turned the whole operation over to his protégé, Donald MacKinnon, who would not only lead the charge at Station S but also would help introduce the Briggs-Myers Type Indicator to other fields after the war.

What models of the self were best suited to S's search for "theatrical deceivers"? For MacKinnon's contemporary and occasional correspondent, sociologist Erving Goffman, the best way to make sense of any social interaction, from an intimate handshake to a large military exercise, was to envision it as an extended series of performances in which everyone, more or less self-consciously, played a role. To be a person in the world was to measure the distance between your forms of expression and the impression they made on your audience: the man whose hand you shook, the sergeant who watched you march. They, in turn, would try to ascertain the impression their expressions made on you—the strength of their grip, the tone of their voice—and so life would proceed as a series of performances and counter-performances, with adjustments made along the way to ensure that one's performance was, in fact, creating the impression to which one aspired. This was not acting, not in any deliberate or directed sense of the word, but Goffman's theory did involve a certain degree of flexibility, of self-making and unmaking, that questionnaires like the type indicator precluded in their assessment of the "true self" and its innate preferences.

While the first day of assessment at S was overrun by pen and paper tests, the second day commenced by preparing the recruits for an evening exercise called "Improvisations": a series of theatrical situations, tailored to each candidate's cover story, that tested his or her ability to play an assigned role, a role that asked him to manage a tricky interpersonal situation. "We are not interested in your ability as an actor. As a matter of fact, acting usually shows up very badly here," MacKinnon would insist to his test subjects. "What we are interested in is how effective you can be in the role in which you are placed." Drawing the same subtle distinction between conscious acting and unconscious performance that Goffman did, MacKinnon urged the recruits not to think of themselves as in "character." They were not to give studied speeches or affect elaborate mannerisms, for this would defeat the purpose of the exercise. If each man was totally absorbed in his role, if he believed in it and inhabited it with every fiber of his being, then he was more likely to reveal something about his true personality.

The scenarios in which the recruits were placed ranged from the mundane to the harrowing: a workplace conflict, a marital spat, a military exercise. In all cases, the staff assigned each subject a role they did not believe he could fulfill successfully based on his personal history, a role that would generate a good deal of tension, anxiety, and embarrassment, thereby short-circuiting each man's ability to reflect on and alter his natural pattern of behavior. Consider the following examples from one assessment session:

1) Mr. F. of this organization has been working as an administrative assistant for about two months. He feels he has been doing a good job. His superior, Mr. G., however, is so dissatisfied with the work of his assistant that he decides to call him into his office. The scene enacted is the conversation between Mr. F. and Mr. G.

2) E., the leader of a guerrilla band, must order F., one of his men, to undertake what is likely to be a suicide mission. He does not feel that he can go himself because he will be needed to command the rest of his men. F. feels that the proposed mission is not likely to succeed and that he should be saved for something for which he is better qualified. He goes to E. to protest. The scene is this meeting between E. and F.

If, in a group of fifteen recruits, one played Mr. F. and the other played Mr. G., then the thirteen remaining men would play the role of the audience, watching the scenario unfold, cheering or jeering as they saw fit. (Of course, their responses as audience members were likewise recorded and preserved in their case files.) The scenario they watched varied based on the type of men whom the staff had assigned to play each role. If Mr. G., the disappointed manager, was played by a man the staff had identified as an extravert with exhibitionist tendencies—someone who felt the need for recognition and prestige, someone who sought to elevate his self-esteem by displaying his talents in front of an audience—then this man would make every effort to outdo himself and his partner. He might play the part of the magnanimous boss, clapping Mr. F. on the back, handing him a scotch, asking with mock concern if everything was all right at home, encouraging him to share his concerns. Or he might play the part of the tyrant, scolding his assistant, insulting him, even dismissing him from his employ before Mr. F. could issue a word of greeting, believing this demonstration of unbridled confidence to be the right tactic for "passing" the exercise. If E., the leader of the guerrilla band, was played by a man who was an introvert, a man who knew that the pattern natural to him would convey a bad impression, then he might resort to "ham acting," stuttering, lisping, or tripping over his own feet to draw laughter from the crowd. Or he might try so hard to alter his tics and habits that the result would be a stilted and wooden performance, like watching a child's after-school play. Whatever the case, the Improvisations revealed more than any pen and paper test about the subjects' true selves.

Sometimes the man tapped to play a role was so annoyed by the frivolity of the exercise that he would grow angry. Murray recalled the case of one test subject, an able and ambitious young army officer whom the staff suspected of having a very low tolerance for criticism. In the scenario that the staff designed for him, he was asked to assume the role of a famous actor X. opposite another test subject—a "very cool, smooth-talking fellow," Murray noted—playing the part of the drama critic who had panned the actor's last performance. In inhabiting X., the subject "displayed a great deal of genuine anger, stormed at the 'critic,' and finally pretended to shoot him," Murray recorded. When the audience expressed their horror at the shooting, he grew bitter and defensive. He stormed off to drink; it was not unusual for the staff to give the subjects the key to the liquor cabinet as a test of their self-control. When he came back, stone-cold drunk and on the verge of becoming violently ill, he shouted at the staff, condemning the whole exercise and the whole weekend as a waste of his time. Here was a discovery even more alarming than a man's tendency to blab or annoy his superior officers: a man's tendency to become bullying and punitive, to resort to acts of terrible violence when things did not go his way.

To identify who among the candidates might have violent and possibly authoritarian personalities, Murray and MacKinnon devised the "Murder Mystery" game. On the final day of testing at S, MacKinnon would assemble the recruits and, with an air of great solemnity, distribute copies of that day's *Fairfield Chronicle,* a fake newspaper. The headlines announced the discovery of a dead body on the road to S, the body of a Mrs. J. W. Weeks, whose death the Fairfield district attorney had ruled a suicide. As the recruits crowded around the paper, the staff, who had recently gone to town to pick up supplies, began to talk about rumors they had heard in the Fairfield general store that Mrs. Weeks's death was not what it appeared to be. There was something sinister about it, they said, something having to do with the people at S. One staff member, known to the recruits as "Sid," said he had more important information to share. At that point, MacKinnon would cut Sid off—he would bark something like "Stop talking nonsense" or "Back to work now"—and, moving to the periphery of the group, he would watch to see if the recruits would rise to the challenge of interrogating him.

When the recruits started to play the game by asking Sid questions, his answers improvised on a pulpy script that Murray and MacKinnon had drafted for him.

RECRUIT A [*he speaks in a gentle, tentative tone*]: Hey, Sid, can we talk to you a minute?

SID: Certainly, fellows, I've got a stop watch here and can time you . . .

RECRUIT A [*mumbling the question*]: Do you know Weeks?

SID: Do I know weeks? . . . You bet I do. Fifty-two of them and each one has seven days.

RECRUIT A [*impatient now*]: No, no, J. W. Weeks. The dead lady's husband?

SID [*shaking head "No"*]: Yes. Yes. Maybe. No. Yes.

RECRUIT B [*jumps in, frustrated by Recruit A's unassertiveness*]:
  Were you in town today?

SID: Yes.

RECRUIT B: Did you hear anything about a [*pauses for dramatic effect*] murder?

SID: A m-u-r-d-e-r?

RECRUIT B [*patient now*]: Yes.

SID: Draw up chairs, fellows, and I'll tell you a story that's positively guaranteed to grow hair on a billiard ball.

To Murray and MacKinnon, it did not matter if the recruits discovered who Mrs. Weeks's murderer was (a German spy named Kirsch who had a long scar on his cheek) or why he had killed her (she was an OSS operative). The point was to see how the recruits adjusted their interrogation techniques when confronted with Sid's impossible chatter. Many laughed at his wisecracks and deflections. Others played along with him, beating back his puns with wordplay of their own. But some grew angry with Sid and tried to persuade others to take him down to the basement interrogation room, which was dark and bare and well insulated against noise. There an otherwise timid GI began to snarl at Sid, threatening to hit him if he did not give straightforward answers to his questions. Another recruit—an introverted and intuitive shy guy—slapped Sid every time he made a joke. Murray and MacKinnon noted how many of their test subjects took advantage of these games of make-believe to assert their unchecked power as authority figures, to harm others in ways their personality profiles had not anticipated. In the spies' games of make-believe, the line between self-discovery and self-creation began to blur until, for some people, it faded into violence.

"S was a society like a ship's crew organized by a temporary necessity which separated them from the rest of the world," Murray wrote in his OSS debrief. It was more than a place where tests and situations were administered to men. It was where they lived, ate, and slept, competed with one another and played games; it was where some rose to the top and some crashed to the bottom of a mysterious hierarchy. It was a place of pure anonymity, which, paradoxically, was the only way, Murray claimed, "to see the person whole and to see him real." Sometimes, reality was terrifying.

. . . .

Murray and MacKinnon's Improvisations anticipated, by several decades, Stanley Milgram's 1961 experiments on the conflict between obedience to authority and personal conscience, in which volunteers, playing the role of a "teacher," were directed to administer increasingly powerful shocks to a screaming "learner" when he answered questions incorrectly, and Philip Zimbardo's 1971 Stanford prison experiment, in which college students assigned to play the role of prison guards abused and tortured college students assigned to play the role of prisoners. More immediately, Station S's role-play resonated with critical theorist and German émigré Theodor Adorno's theories of fascism, which he was developing at the same time Murray and MacKinnon were watching their test subjects scream and slap and pretend to shoot one another in the basement of the Willard estate.

In his collection of prose *Minima Moralia: Reflections on a Damaged Life,* Adorno would recall Hitler's speeches: the drums beating, the torches burning, the madness in the air that led the German people to their "half-knowing self-surrender to perdition." Adorno had escaped, first to England, then to New York, and finally to California, where he waited for the war to end and tried to figure out what the purpose of social theory should be after Auschwitz. The conditions of his exile in the United States, the horrors of the Holocaust, had made it impossible for him to think about how people should live a good life now that the mirror of philosophy had shattered into a million pieces. What was possible was the more pessimistic task of thinking about evil—and not just thinking about it, but designing methods to ferret it out of an apparently democratic society. This way, he hoped, what had happened in Germany could never happen anywhere else in the world. "The splinter in your eye is the best magnifying-glass," he wrote, turning his gaze, cracked but still discerning, to the future of fascism.

As the war came to its end, Adorno joined forces with Berkeley psychologists R. Nevitt Sanford, Else Frenkel-Brunswik, and Daniel Levinson in a joint mission, funded by the American Jewish Committee, to investigate the cognitive and behavioral dimensions of fascism. The book that resulted, *The Authoritarian Personality,* offered its readers a sketch of the "potentially fascistic individual": a person whose psychological makeup made him susceptible to antidemocratic propaganda, even if he never engaged in any violent behavior. In contrast to a personologist like Murray, Adorno and his team were interested not in the singularity of Hitler but in the audience members who had been seduced by Nazi ideology—those prone to the same prejudice, hostility, and irrationality to which Hitler gave voice. "The task of fascist propaganda . . . ," the authors wrote, "is rendered easier to the degree that antidemocratic potentials already exist in the great mass of people." The Nazis were effective insofar as they were able to "activate every ounce" of the German people's antidemocratic potential while stamping out the "slightest spark of rebellion."

It was not enough to expose one fascistic leader as a babbling madman to prevent the rise of fascism elsewhere, when fascism was an extension of industrial modernity. The hierarchical division of society into classes meant that the marks of social repression were impressed onto the soul long before a demagogic leader ever opened his mouth to speak. The only solution, Adorno believed, was to eliminate the static, biologized understanding of type and substitute a thoroughly self-reflexive test of personality. What the postwar world needed, then, was not a test of selfhood that divided people into normal and abnormal types but a "critical typology": one whose major dichotomy lay "in the question of whether a person is standardized himself and thinks in a standardized way, or whether he is truly 'individualized' and opposes standardization in the sphere of human experience." The trick was to design a test of type that would, paradoxically, undo the impulse to think typologically.

From both a theoretical and a practical point of view, the problem was how to predict any individual's potential for fascistic behavior—not his explicit preferences, not his past actions, but the latent desires that could push someone to behave like a fascist at some unspecified point in the future. Adorno and his team began by drafting what they called the "F scale," a questionnaire that asked its respondents to indicate how strongly they agreed or disagreed with each of its forty-four items. Each item proceeded from Adorno's belief that fascistic leaders preyed on men who lacked critical acuity, men who were conventional, obsequious, respectful of middle-class values, eager to glorify and submit to authority. ("*Obedience and respect for authority are the most important virtues children should learn,*" read one item.) The uncritical mind was predisposed to superstition and stereotype and distrusted imaginative thought. ("*The business man and the manufacturer are much more important to society than the artist and the professor,*" read another.) It was invigorated by hostility, seduced by paranoia, and overly concerned with sexual "goings-on." ("*The sexual orgies of the old Greeks and Romans are nursery school stuff compared to some of the goings-on in this country today, even in circles where people might least expect it.*") By systematizing their study of evil, Adorno and his team believed they could identify it in its nascent psychological forms before it could mature into a terrible political phenomenon.

The *Authoritarian Personality* argued that fascistic tendencies did not always emerge in the most obvious ways. To validate the F scale, Adorno and R. Nevitt Sanford interviewed two college men, code names "Mack" and "Larry." Mack, who exhibited a strong inclination to authoritarian thinking, broadcast his contempt for any person or institution he deemed weak: Franklin Delano Roosevelt, the New Deal, the civil service, and all minorities. He believed that homosexuals, sex criminals, political dissidents, and anyone who did not demonstrate "undying love" for his or her parents should be regarded as a deviant and punished by the state. But the most striking aspect of his personality was his cynicism. Of all the items in the questionnaire, he expressed the strongest agreement with the item that read: "*Human nature being what it is, there will always be war and conflict.*"

By contrast, Larry was soft and accommodating, a self-proclaimed "philosopher" who devoted considerable attention to his feelings and the feelings of others. He expressed no desire to blame or punish anyone for anything—not the Great Depression, not the First World War, not the Second. He believed that all men were created equal. And in contrast to Mack's cynicism, Larry displayed a "naïve optimism and friendliness toward the world." He was a man of hope—a man who, Adorno believed, could give others hope that the critical, individualized self could be resurrected in the wake of European fascism.

Yet such hope, as Adorno and his coauthors noted in the conclusion to *The Authoritarian Personality*, required altering the total organization of industrial society, not the psychological makeup of the Macks who constituted it. "People are continuously molded from above because they must be molded if the over-all economic pattern is to be maintained, and the amount of energy that goes into this process bears a direct relation to the amount of potential, residing within the people, for moving in a different direction," they wrote. What the history of type after World War II would reveal was not just the maintenance of the economic pattern that Adorno and his coauthors bemoaned but its intensification. Type would continue its creeping spread through all the institutional organs of postwar America: the corporation, the college, the hospital, the psychological laboratory. It may not have helped the United States win the war, as Isabel lamented in 1944, but it had established a formidable barracks in the heart of American industry.

CHAPTER TEN

People's Capitalism

During her seven years as a part-time employee at Hay and Associates, Isabel earned $1,108: $504 from her hourly wage and $514 from sales of the type indicator from 1943 to 1950. Aside from her first contract with "the Murray Company," her accounts had started small: $1.20 from the Dry Dock Savings Bank in New York for two test booklets and four answer sheets; $0.80 from W. Tomlinson, a publishing house in Philadelphia, for one test booklet to be shared among six employees. For the sales manager of the Old Reading Brewery in Reading, Pennsylvania, she evaluated just one man for a job as a traveling beer salesman. His name was Mr. Moe and the indicator revealed him to be an EIFP: an extraverted, intuitive, feeling, and perceptive type. "Mr. Moe's Briggs-Myers Type Indicator would indicate that this man, although he has a great deal of imagination and initiative for organizing new projects, may leave some of his jobs half done," she dictated to Hay's assistant. "He would have to have a very sincere concern for your organization before he could be depended on to carry out many of his projects. It appears on the surface that he would not be quite the type of man you want for a Reading area salesman and still not have the self-discipline required to be a good driver salesman." She concluded that any further evaluation of Mr. Moe would have been a waste of both her time and the brewery's money.

With her profits, she liked to play the stock market. She owned shares in General Motors, Phelps Dodge, Philadelphia Life Insurance, and United Carbon—good solid American stocks that she bought and sold and sometimes donated to Swarthmore's alumnae fund in prudent amounts of five, ten, or twenty-five dollars. She did not always trust her instincts; she had been burned badly during the Depression, losing almost all of her book prize money. "Maybe I should sell GM on the technical rally, which I think has happened," she wrote to her mother in February 1954. "Trouble is, I sold Phelps Dodge the same time you did, on the decline in the spring, and am still feeling bruised about it, and inclined to experiment on this 'getting out of the market' with my own funds." She sold GM at 50¼ and instantly regretted it, and she regretted regretting it, for her regret seemed a testament to her uncertainty. "Maybe I am just chicken-hearted," she worried. But her confidence soon rebounded. "The important thing is to <u>learn</u>. At the moment we are very well off with our investment funds. If we can just do the wise and prudent thing with 'em."

Isabel was learning more than just how to game the market; she was learning how to manage the wellsprings of feeling—disappointment, desire, glee, insecurity, regret—that came with being a capitalist, a proud and partial owner of the corporations that once made America great. In 1955, her brokerage firm of Walston, Hoffman, & Goodman, the largest in the country, advised its clients of an impending "Eisenhower bull market," spurred by the election of a pro-business Republican president who foretold the rise of a "people's capitalism": capitalism of, by, and for the people, the happy prelude to a society in which workers with employee pension plans and savings accounts shared in the spoils of industrial productivity. Everybody could be a capitalist, a self-satisfied fat cat—this was the gleaming promissory note that Eisenhower and Theodore Repplier, president of the Advertising Council, wanted to sell American workers besieged by Cold War propaganda and the communists' demands for total political, economic, and social revolution led by the proletariat. People's capitalism was "as American as apple pie," Repplier boasted, and its benefits transcended the financial realm. American workers could enjoy more leisure time. They could find the money to attend ballgames and renovate their houses. They could learn to love their jobs, since they would have the "*complete* freedom," Repplier insisted, "to work where they wished, to invest, to start a business." When, on the eve of her thirty-year college reunion, Isabel filled out her Swarthmore College alumni questionnaire, she no longer listed her present title and position as "housewife and mother" as she had in previous years. Now that she had left Hay's employ, she identified herself as the "owner of Briggs-Myers Type Research," headquartered in the basement of her gabled colonial at 321 Dickson Avenue, Swarthmore, Pennsylvania. One could sense in the bold strokes of her hand pride and, perhaps more important, love for the business of type.

The pervasive belief that liking or even loving one's job could function as a powerful liberating force had a history that was intimately tied to how the Briggs-Myers Type Indicator ensnared the American workplace after Isabel debuted it to Hay during World War II. According to sociologist William H. Whyte's 1956 best seller, *The Organization Man*, 60 percent of American corporations were using personality tests in 1956, not only to screen potential employees but also to "check up on people" already employed by the company—to ensure that their employees were content and carefree and still believed in the inherent goodness of work. "Once the man's superiors would have had to thresh this out among themselves; now they can check with the psychologists to find out what the tests say," Whyte wrote sardonically. For him, the tests represented the controlling voice of the organization and its principles. "Let [us] ponder well what the questions are really driving at," Whyte invited his reader. "Indicate whether you agree, disagree, or are uncertain: [6] I am going to Hell. [7] I often get pink spots all over. [8] The sex act is repulsive. [9] I like strong-minded women. [10] Strange voices speak to me. [11] My father is a tyrant." One could project from the very phrasing of such questions the company's collective vision of the types of people they valued.

But personality tests spoke for more than just the individual company; they represented an entire emergent culture of white-collar work. By the mid-1950s, at companies like General Electric, Standard Oil, Bell Telephone, the Washington Gas Light Company, the Pennsylvania Company, and the National Bureau of Statistics, the language of type had helped give rise to a new spirit of capitalism: one in which the worker would be matched to the job that was divinely right for him: the job that would permit him to do his best and most creative work, afford him the greatest sense of personal satisfaction, endear him to his bosses and colleagues, and thus encourage him to lodge his sense of self ever deeper into his nine-to-five occupation. The mass testing of personality was partially responsible for the birth of the liberal-humanist figure that Whyte dubbed "the organization man": the worker who had "left home, spiritually as well as physically, to take the vows of organization life," believing that work could make him whole. The organization men were the "mind and soul" of the post–World War II workplace, prophets of a secular faith in the goodness of rationalized, hierarchical labor. They were nice, normal, hardworking individuals. More important, they were loyal subjects—the type of employee a manager today might describe as a "good team player." They had heard the voice of the organization, echoing loud and clear in the tests they had taken, and they had answered it with a promise of their own: on our backs the fortunes of corporate America will rise and fall.

As a devoted organization woman, Isabel would find her fortunes rising along with the fortunes of people's capitalism and white-collar work in the 1950s, just as her mother's prospects would dwindle. Katharine was not made for this new world order. At eighty years old, she had grown white and frail and forgetful to a degree that frightened Isabel and Lyman. In the family photos that they asked her to pose for at Isabel's birthday and her grandchildren's college graduations, Katharine lingered outside the frame, staring back at her daughter and her grandchildren with vacant, unbelieving eyes.

Despite the progressive severity of her dementia, Katharine could never forget Jung. Years after their meeting in the hotel room in New York, she encouraged Isabel to send him a letter informing him of their achievements in type theory. "The function types are so important that people ought to take them into account in every field—education, vocational choice, marriage, human relations," Isabel insisted to Jung. "My mother and I waited eighteen years for somebody to do something about it, and then decided to do it ourselves, having brought my family up on type in the meantime and found it invaluable for our mutual understanding and happiness." With her letter, she enclosed a copy of the Form C questionnaire. She asked if Jung might be available for a meeting the next time she and her husband visited their son, Peter, who was now studying at Oxford as a Rhodes Scholar.

Jung, who was recovering from a tedious illness at the time, had his secretary respond warmly but with none of the vigor he had directed at Katharine in the 1920s. "As you have given the matter a great deal of thought I think you have done so much in this direction that I'm hardly capable of criticizing it or even knowing better," he wrote. "For quite a long time I haven't done any work along that line at all, because other things have taken the foreground of my interests. But I should say that for future development of Type-Theory your Type-Indicator will prove to be of great help." That was his final act of correspondence with either mother or daughter. Shortly thereafter, he died, as now seems fitting, never knowing that his name would forever be linked to Briggs, Myers, and their strange creation.

. . . .

From the end of World War II to the beginning of the arms race in the early 1950s, news of the Briggs-Myers Type Indicator thundered through Pennsylvania, New York, and Washington, D.C., loudly championed by happy clients in positions of influence. As Chief and her neighbors built bomb shelters and their children practiced attack drills in school, Isabel picked up accounts, and these accounts began to double, even triple, in size. She took on large orders from colleges, government bureaus, and major pharmaceutical companies; from her alma mater of Swarthmore; from her father's longtime employer, the National Bureau of Standards; from the First National Bank of Boston, Bell Telephone, and the Roane-Anderson Company—a subcontractor for atomic weapons that her father had introduced her to through his contacts on the Manhattan Project. She was not shy about asking for help or using her family's connections. Never one to miss out on an opportunity for self-promotion, Hay wrote to his client list on her behalf, taking credit for the indicator's success despite his apparent lack of familiarity with its origins or the theory behind it. "The test is based on Jung's Psychological Type-Mind," he told one client. "It was developed by Mrs. Isabel Briggs Myers out of an experience she had with me in 1942. I have used it in my consulting work quite a little."

By the mid-1950s, her clients were the largest utilities and insurance companies in the United States. They regularly spent upwards of fifty dollars a year on test booklets and answer sheets. The Home Life Insurance Company in New York purchased it twice: first, to determine whether a job applicant would make for a successful life insurance salesman; then, to calculate whether a life insurance applicant should pay a larger premium on his insurance. (According to Isabel's summary of her results, extraverted intuitive types—EITPs and EIFPs—were more likely to exhibit risk-taking behavior.) General Electric asked Isabel to type their highest-ranking executives to develop a theory about the contributions of a man's type to his managerial success. "Under all the shifting problems that cross an executive's desk lie three basic necessities," she wrote.

1. He must decide.
2. He must be right.
3. He must convince certain key people of his rightness.

Deciding came easiest to the J's, the judging types, but since deciding was only one component of executive success, only 50 percent of General Electric's executives tested as J's. The others were P's, the perceptive types, who were better at considering other people's viewpoints, "more inclined to stop, look and listen." The introverted thinker (ISTP or IITP) was more likely to "arrive at the profoundest decisions," while the extraverted feeler (ESFJ or EIFJ) was more likely to convince others that he was right through free and tactful communication. She decided that there was no perfect executive type. "No type is <u>naturally endowed</u> with everything that would be useful for the necessary decision, the necessary analysis, and the necessary communication," she wrote. Instead the different types of executives had different strengths. Her job now was to help them overcome their weaknesses, their "inferior type functions."

She prescribed these executives drills. The feeling types had to do logic exercises, in which they practiced inserting hard facts and dollar figures into their memoranda. The thinking types had to write out "formulas" for criticism, in which they prefaced harsh remarks with "little chunks of sympathy or appreciation." Isabel asked the executives to note the differences between the following (a) and (b) statements.

a. "I think you're all wrong about Jones—"
b. "I see why you feel that way, but I think you're probably wrong about Jones."

a. "Of course Bates lost the position. He should never have—"
b. "Tough on Bates to lose the position. He should never have—"

a. "That coat doesn't fit across the shoulders."
b. "That's a becoming color on you. Too bad it doesn't fit across the shoulders. Spoils the effect."

"Nine times out of ten," she advised her executive clients, "the thinker . . . does think it's tough on Bates to lose the position, even though he brought it entirely on himself. He does think the coat is a becoming color, though he can't condone the fit. He could just as well mention these mitigating circumstances. But he does not think it worth the trouble." Yet from the standpoint of good human relations—and overtasked human relations departments—it was well worth the trouble. It prevented people from fighting executives on both minor and major points of difference; it made subordinates feel respected and appreciated even when they were being reprimanded or, in the case of the hypothetical Bates, dismissed from their jobs. And, finally, it gave the executive a profound sense of self-satisfaction. "His own too-little-used feeling will be happier too," Isabel concluded.

It seemed only natural that she should expand her business from testing to counseling—after all, what good was the point of knowing one's type if one did not use that knowledge for any real profit? Her strongest conceptual ally was a client Hay introduced her to named Oliver Arthur Ohmann, assistant to the vice president of the Standard Oil Company and head of its industrial relations department. Ohmann was also one of the first management theorists to formulate the now ubiquitous and overdetermined idea of a "work-life balance," although this meant something very different to him from what it does to workers today. What Ohmann saw when he cast his eyes upon Standard Oil's managers and workers, and upon the working class in general, was the spiritual impoverishment of the human psyche. "Our economy has been abundantly productive, our standard of living is at an all-time peak, and yet we are a tense, frustrated, and insecure people full of hostilities and anxieties," he lamented in the *Harvard Business Review*. The problem was not "the division of the spoils as organized labor would have us believe," Ohmann assured his readers, lest they think he was sympathetic to union leaders or socialists. Rather, it was something endemic to the idea of what it meant to work, something that affected everyone from the highest executive to the lowest oil rigger. "Is our industrial discontent not in fact the expression of a hunger for a work life that has meaning in terms of higher and more enduring spiritual values?" he asked. "How can we preserve the wholeness of the personality if we are expected to worship God on Sundays and holidays and mammon on Mondays through Fridays?" The conflict between work and life was not a matter of simple time allocation. It required preserving one's spiritual and psychological integrity across the domains of labor and leisure, the workplace and the home.

Ohmann was on a quest to find a new religion to address the old capitalist problem of alienated labor: the estrangement of the worker's psyche from the act of production. It was a quest that he undertook not because he felt it was right in any moral or ethical sense, but because, as an executive, he felt he had no other choice if his company was to thrive. The Briggs-Myers Type Indicator, which Ohmann first purchased from Hay in 1949 to sort Standard Oil's workers, offered him the perfect solution to preserving the "wholeness of the personality"—

a way of introducing people to their true selves and convincing them the work they were doing was a natural extension of how God had created them. The fact that it might also help enhance productivity seemed, to Ohmann, the ideal marriage of "higher and more enduring spiritual values" to the realities of corporate work. In its primordial form, the idea of "work-life balance" was a bargain struck between God and mammon, brokered in large part by the Briggs-Myers Type Indicator, Ohmann told Hay and Isabel.

Despite the prescience of Ohmann's vision—it must have reminded her of her mother's mystical talk of type—Isabel did not share his sense of spiritual charity when it came to type. The benefits of knowing one's type did not accrue to all workers equally. If a corporation mainly employed unskilled laborers, she dissuaded them from spending too much money evaluating their workers, stripping them of the assumed benefits of self-knowledge. "The type differences show principally in the more intelligent and highly developed half of the population," she explained to Hay, echoing a similar rationale to the one her mother had articulated many years ago to separate the world into its "primitive" and "enlightened" psychological classes. From her experience, executives revealed an extraordinarily high degree of type development by "every criterion we have," she wrote to Hay. They outstripped every group of workers she had sampled except some top research scientists from the National Bureau of Standards—the government organization where her father, approaching eighty, and now her son, fresh off his Rhodes Scholarship, worked. By contrast, manufacturers, mechanics, and other blue-collar workers demonstrated the weakest type development.

Of course, there existed no controlled study, no real evidence, to validate Isabel's belief in the inverse relationship between intelligence and the strength of one's type preferences. But as was the case for the 1940s' most famous test, the intelligence quotient (IQ) test, evidence mattered less than the indicator's ability to justify as "natural" or "normal" the division that already existed in the world, a world in which the wealthier, whiter, and more upwardly mobile were found to be more self-aware than everyone else. It did not occur to anyone, even

Isabel, as unusual that the strongest preferences were always expressed by successful, self-assured men with ready access to power, whether in the form of cold hard cash or institutional authority.

Often it was these successful men who paid her to manage the personnel dilemmas they found unsavory or tedious. Hiring, firing, promotion, and attrition were all easier to talk about when employees were veiled by the abstract, pseudoscientific language of type. "The expectation that an employee placed in a job suitable to his type will do the job better, like it better, and stay with it longer" would help mount "a double-barreled attack upon turnover," Isabel hypothesized with militant certainty. Proof of her hypothesis arrived, resounding and clear, in the form of 550 test subjects from the Washington Gas Light Company, where she had first administered the indicator in 1946. Since then, 223 men had quit or been fired, 296 were still with the company, and 31 were still with the company but had "reprimands or other unfavorable items on their records." Of the ones who had stayed and thrived, most were in "type-favored jobs," Isabel concluded: introverts in accounting and clerical work, extraverts in meter reading and mechanical jobs. Again, there existed no controlled study, no real evidence to validate Isabel's observations. "The attempted validation proceedings died of malnutrition," she wrote to Hay. Yet based on her recommendations, the company's personnel department began shuffling its workers around, placing them in jobs based on their Briggs-Myers type or firing them if they could not find the right match.

Every so often, a bank or hospital would ask her to evaluate its female workers—typists, nurses—to determine the relationship between personality type and a woman's "excellence" on the job. Sometimes the theory she thought she knew so well caught her off guard. The best nurses, she was surprised to learn, were introverts. Indeed, the correlation between introversion and job performance was perfect, which she found strange but did not dwell on at any great length. It was not the only suspicious result she faced. Sometimes subjects whom she tested and retested seem to change type overnight; thinkers became feelers, judgers became perceivers. The technical term for it was "enantiodromia," she learned from rereading Jung—a "going over to the opposite" in which one of the preferences a person did not express ascended to a "much more honored place" in the psyche. Her inability to validate the indicator—to show that it produced consistent results for test subjects over time—had a theoretical basis in Jungian psychology, she reassured Hay.

She illustrated it to him with the following story. An unnamed woman, a secretary to whom Isabel had administered the indicator, had demonstrated a strong preference for intuition (I) and thinking (T) the first time she had taken it. But the second time, she emerged as a sensing (S) and feeling (F) type—a violation of the indicator's assumption that type never changed. Either she had faked her original results, Isabel speculated, or simply learning the language of type had prompted her to undergo a dramatic, possibly violent psychological conversion in her unconscious mind. Isabel decided to interview her to determine which it was.

She showed up on the secretary's doorstep unannounced late one Sunday night, and like her mother used to do with her father, she pulled out a $3'' \times 5''$ index card and asked the woman to share any dreams she might have had as of late. She waited for the woman to speak, and suddenly, as if she had entered a trance, there was, she later reported, a sudden uprush from her test subject's unconscious of "a great many symbols and metaphors." She told Isabel that she had had a dream in which she had purchased a run-down house to renovate and, while standing outside of it, had encountered "a colored woman to whom one could talk to exactly as equals." "Members of the dark and inferior race are standard symbols for the suppressed and considered-inferior parts of one's own psyche," Isabel explained to Hay—the same explanation Katharine had once provided to both Isabel and Mary Tuckerman for their interracial dreams. The fact that the woman could be treated as an equal despite her skin color seemed to Isabel a sign: the test subject was ready to treat the inferior parts of her psyche (her sensing and feeling functions) as equal to its superior parts (its intuitive and thinking functions).

The analysis of her test subject's dream gave Isabel some pause. This was not because of the racist premises of her allegory—it had been a very long time since she had had any keen feeling for equality or justice—but because she knew she had to find a way to reconcile the woman's inconsistency with her indicator. She was hopeful, she told Hay, that this act of crossing over meant that the indicator did more than just passively reflect the true self; it provoked the emergence of a better self from within the mind's cocoon of uncertainty and self-hatred, preserving modes of perception (like sensing) and judgment (like feeling) that society had debased as inefficient, weak, or feminine. "The revelation, the discovery, is a discovery of value in the undervalued, in the part of her psyche which she and others have undervalued," Isabel concluded. Her interpretation of dreams represented a striking extension of her mother's racialized imagination, now preserved by the indicator across the generations.

. . . .

Could the woman have falsified her type? Could she have cheated on a test with no apparently right or wrong answers? William H. Whyte's *The Organization Man* concludes with a famous appendix titled "How to Cheat on Personality Tests," which encourages test subjects to do just that. Its tone is ruthless, pragmatic, and deeply funny, provided one shares Whyte's belief that the more a test insists that it is "for the individual"—that it promotes objective self-discovery, that it "encourage[s] difference, not conformity"—the more it masks the "total integration of the individual" within the organization's social ethos. "As in all applications of scientism," Whyte argues, "it is society's values that are enshrined. The tests, essentially, are loyalty tests, or rather, tests of potential loyalty. Neither in the questions nor in the evaluation of them are the tests neutral; they are loaded with values, organization values, and the result is a set of yardsticks that reward the conformist, the pedestrian, the unimaginative—at the expense of the exceptional individual without whom no society, organization or otherwise, can flourish."

For this reason, Whyte encourages applicants, exceptional or otherwise, not only to cheat, but to cheat in the most strategic way possible. If asked to take a personality test as part of a job application, one should not aim for self-discovery or honesty. One's goal should be to project the essence of complete and total mediocrity. "The important thing to recognize is that you don't win a good score: you avoid a bad one," Whyte writes. "What a bad score would be depends upon the particular profile the company in question intends to measure you against, and this varies according to companies and according to the type of work. Your score is usually rendered in terms of your per-centile rating—that is, how you answer the questions in relation to how other people have answered them." "Your safety," he warns, "lies in getting a score somewhere between the 40th and 60th percentiles, which is to say, you should try to answer as if you were like everybody else is supposed to be."

Of course, it was not so easy to know what everyone else in any given company was supposed to be like. Presumably, there were some differences, however indiscernible, between the men who worked at General Electric and the men who worked at Standard Oil. One could, however, make certain assumptions based on the familiar figure of the organization man, whom Whyte described as entirely nondescript. Organization men were conservative, affable, and bland, with no thought in their collective head but to work hard and to work dutifully alongside others; the spotless and respectable characters dissected just one year earlier by the novelist Sloan Wilson in his best-selling novel *The Man in the Gray Flannel Suit*. Whyte encouraged all test takers to memorize the following dictums to provide the most "conventional, run-of-the-mill, pedestrian" answers to any given question.

a) I loved my father and my mother, but my father a little bit more.
b) I like things pretty well the way they are.
c) I never worry much about anything.
d) I don't care for books or music much.
e) I love my wife and children.
f) I don't let them get in the way of company work.

The comedy of Whyte's list is, at first, the comedy of the person who seems to have no personality—the futility of trying to extrapolate anything from such flat, noncommittal proclamations as "I like things pretty well the way they are" or "I don't care for books or music much." At the same time, it is the comedy (or tragedy) of a nonpersonality or impersonality constituted entirely by an exaggerated devotion to one's employer, a devotion that outpaces love for one's wife and children, a devotion that yields a studied indifference to reading books and listening to music—solitary and imaginative pursuits (classic introvert characteristics, according to the Briggs-Myers Type Indicator) that threaten to undercut the incessant sociability on which the organization man's personality relies. At heart, though, the comedy of the list is the comedy inherent to faking a personality—any personality, even one characterized by its excessive blandness. To commit these dictums to memory, to recite them as one sits with pencil poised over answer sheet, is to replace the self with a kind of awkward, unhinged machine—a "cheerful robot" in the words of sociologist C. Wright Mills, or one of Adorno's protofascist workers.

Even tests like the Briggs-Myers Type Indicator, which claimed to have no correct answers, had to be navigated with great caution. "While it is true that in these 'inventory' types of tests there is not a right or wrong answer to any *one* question, cumulatively you can get yourself into a lot of trouble if you are not wary," Whyte cautioned. It did not matter if you answered question 61 ("*Are you generally (a) a 'good mixer'; or (b) rather quiet and reserved in company?*") by admitting that you liked to keep to yourself at parties. But there was sure to be trouble if you answered too many similar questions the same way, like question 4 ("*At social gatherings do you (a) try to corner somebody you like to talk to; or (b) mix with the group?*") or question 24 ("*When you have to meet strangers, do you more often regard it as (a) pleasant, or at least an easy, matter; or (b) something that takes considerable effort to carry through successfully?*"). No one wanted to hire a wallflower.

The trick, then, was not to answer naturally or to be yourself as the instructions for the Briggs-Myers Type Indicator encouraged. Rather, Whyte advised his reader to forge a test-taking persona to "mediate yourself a score as near the norm as possible without departing too far from your own true self." You were to take the test "in character," he instructed, and you were to "stay in character"—to remain firm, unwavering, and consistent in your answers, just like Murray's OSS spies. The character you created was to be a hybrid of your "own true self," the values of the test maker (so far as you could discern them), and the profile of the job you wanted. From the lowliest clerk to the president of the company, each position had an ideal personality profile. "To be considered a potential executive, you will probably do best when you emphasize economic motivation the most; aesthetic and religious, the least," Whyte wrote. "If you were trying out for the research department, you might wish to say that you think Sir [Isaac] Newton helped mankind more than Shakespeare and thereby increase your ratings for theoretical leanings. Were you trying out for a public relations job, however, you might wish to vote for Shakespeare, for a somewhat higher aesthetic score would not be amiss in this case."

Whyte's irony was, at every turn, opposed to Isabel's earnestness. She never doubted that people were telling the truth when she administered the indicator to them, even when they knew their employers would make promotion and firing decisions based on their type preferences, even when their types changed after they had dodged the executioner's axe. Nor did she ever entertain the idea that the values enshrined in the indicator's questions were anything but her values, as she had inherited them from her mother and Jung. The test spoke in her voice, modulated by the voices of her husband and children. She did not boast of its objectivity or its empiricism but of its capacity to prompt easy, intimate, and useful self-revelations. "The point of it is that they are such simple everyday unthreatening, unloaded questions," she wrote. "They are much easier to answer than soul searching ones would be and they are not important in themselves. They get answered one way by people at one end of the preference spectrum and another way by the others."

As her confidence in the indicator increased, so too did its reach. Her cross section of test subjects had expanded considerably since she had typed Ann and her three girlfriends around the kitchen table.

After exhausting Peter's and Ann's high school classmates and Hay's client list, she asked her father, who was on the board of George Washington University's medical school, to help her persuade the school's dean, Dr. John Parks, to let her administer the indicator to his medical students. "Medicine was a case where it was very important to have people, the right people, in the right place," she reasoned—more literally a matter of life or death than the sorting of people in the corporate realm. At the meeting her father had organized with the dean, she presented the type indicator as a multipurpose sorting tool, useful not only for determining admissions decisions but for predicting a student's performance in medical school, his willingness to practice in a small or rural community, his choice of specialty, and his clinical competence. Excited by the possibility of streamlining admissions, the dean invited her to campus to type his students. As she collected their answer sheets, she realized she could make her study even bigger, even broader.

With Chief as her chauffeur, they spent the summers of 1952 and 1953 "tackling other medical schools," traversing America on a series of long, frenzied road trips, pleading Isabel's case at Western Reserve, Howard University, the College of Medical Evangelists, the state universities of New Mexico, Utah, Tennessee, Oregon, California, New York, and Pennsylvania. By the end of 1954, she had typed medical students at forty-two medical schools across the United States. "Type Indicator goes swimmingly," she wrote to her mother from the road. It was pleasant, energizing work—a kind of second honeymoon with its little routines and rituals, made possible by the fact that the children were finally out of the house. Every morning, after she and Chief would wake up in a roadside motel somewhere in between cities, they would check that the answer sheets they had collected were where they had hidden them the night before—under the back seat of the car. Satisfied, they would embark for their next target. On Sundays, they would linger a little longer, sleeping in or seeking out the nearest diner to treat themselves to breakfast. It was a weekly date that cost them thirty cents, or, as one could imagine Isabel converting it, six Briggs-Myers answer sheets.

Her assessment of medical students was the first large-scale study she undertook, drawing in 5,355 medical students from forty-five schools; 5,355 answer keys that Isabel scored by hand, sometimes sitting at her desk at Hay's office, sometimes with her feet on the dashboard of her car. This was the first time she had aspired to make sweeping changes to an entire profession rather than shuffling around one or two people in a company. Her study revealed that intuitive (I) types offered "the most impressive credentials for admission on the whole, because the kind of perception they relied on made a crucial difference in MCAT scores"—their semiconscious gut reactions to multiple-choice questions gave them a clear advantage on a test that one had to complete in limited time. But sensing (S) types, who had less impressive MCAT scores, tended to perform better in school and on tests of clinical competency. While the intuitive types sought out more lucrative specialties, the sensing types tended to practice primary-care medicine in smaller, more rural communities. Did the admission of candidates based purely on their MCAT scores, rather than on a combination of their MCAT scores and types, serve the real purpose of medical schools? Or was it a mistake?

"Studies with the indicator suggest that it is a mistake," Isabel concluded in a letter she later addressed to the American Medical Association (AMA). She encouraged them to issue new guidelines for medical school admissions: to eliminate timed test taking and to stack admissions committees with more sensing types. That way, like could recognize like. "These are needed to help ease the shortage of physicians in primary patient care and in the smaller communities," she wrote, and, as the greatest subsection of her data came from Howard University's school of medicine, she added, "And they are needed in justice to the sensing types, of whatever race."

As she widened her horizons from individuals to institutions, she realized that what she needed was legitimacy: access to the professional credentials that would make organizations like the AMA and its doctors take her seriously. "One medical student was quite outraged that we could think that such trivia would have anything to do with what kind of a doctor he would make," she reported. Deliverance came from an old friend: Donald MacKinnon, who, along with Henry Murray, had purchased the indicator for Station S back in 1944. Now he was a professor at the University of California, Berkeley, and he was interested in using the indicator in a series of studies he was conducting on higher education and creative people: writers, artists, architects. He invited her to California to witness for herself the success of type's journey from east to west.

CHAPTER ELEVEN

The House-Party Approach to Testing

I t was an unseasonably cool day in August 1949 when a local construction firm picked up the Sigma Phi Epsilon house at 2395 Piedmont Avenue in Berkeley, California, and put it down less than half a mile away in a vacant lot at 2240 Piedmont. There it was to serve as the headquarters for IPAR—Berkeley's new Institute of Personality Assessment and Research. The move, which cost the university $34,500, was not altogether successful. As the building crawled down Piedmont Avenue, the stucco cracked, the plaster buckled and peeled, and when the house finally came to rest on its new foundations, the moldings collapsed into the street. But when the institute's director, Dr. Donald MacKinnon, stepped through the dust and around the debris to open the door to 2240 for the first time, he believed he could see the future of personality testing with greater clarity than ever before.

It was a bright future, aglow with stars and celebrities. To catch a glimpse of the people who MacKinnon and his staff ushered through the door of 2240 was to catch a glimpse of fame, fortune, and creative genius. Creativity was what interested MacKinnon the most. He had spent the last two years at OSS Station S matching spies to the missions that best suited their personalities, but now he wanted to do something even more exceptional. He wanted to plumb the depths of individuals who possessed a singularly imaginative and inimitable vision of reality, those who could divine, amidst the anger and anxiety of the nuclear threat, the possibility of restoring love, harmony, happiness, and beauty to the world. He believed it was the creative types who would save the world from the fascistic group-think that Adorno had warned against in *The Authoritarian Personality*. To this end, MacKinnon proposed what he called a "living-in assessment." He would invite small groups of academics, writers, painters, architects, and industry executives to the Bay Area, where they would share a house for a long weekend while undergoing a series of personality assessments, therapy sessions, and friendly games. "The assessment of well-monitored individuals under conditions of living together and competing with each other creates a situation of optimal stress and strain for the study of personality," MacKinnon wrote. He wanted to find out what happened when the most brilliant people in America stopped being polite and started getting real.

In a sense, the institute was one of America's earliest incursions into reality programming. What today's reality television shows flaunt as their "special living environments"—the mansions, the hotel suites, the desert islands—was for MacKinnon the ideal experimental setup. Life in the fraternity house was the closest he and his staff could get to total psychological access; a rare chance to see people act and react to each other in real time, absent whatever inhibitions might seize a patient on a therapist's couch or a test taker in a quiet room. Not everyone he asked to live in 2240 shared his enthusiasm. "I contribute this reaction to your study of personality," wrote Katherine Anne Porter, Pulitzer Prize–winning author, in her response to the suggestion that she fly to Oakland for a long weekend of evaluation. "You may study this question you have in mind, by the methods you seem to be using, until we begin to commute to the moon, and you will never learn anything more about it than poor good doctor Kinsey—and a nice man, too!—learned about sex." Even those who agreed to participate in MacKinnon's experiment expressed their skepticism about his study of personality. "Let's don't say personality, it is such a cheapened word," begged Truman Capote. Upon his arrival at 2240 in 1957, he would confess to the psychologist who interviewed him, "I've lost interest in myself as a personality."

In Capote's reluctance to utter even the word, we can catch echoes of a grievance about personality that had, by the late 1950s, become a common refrain in American culture. Now that typing people had emerged as a routine procedure for matching workers to jobs, the concept of personality came with a price attached to it—the salary from a steady job, the possibility of a promotion. Individual personalities had congealed and hardened into commodities, and, as Capote quite rightly intuited, cheap commodities at that. Now human beings were traded on what social theorist Erich Fromm called the "personality market" of the corporate workplace. "Success depends largely on how well a person sells himself on the market, how well he gets his personality across, how nice a 'package' he is; whether he is 'cheerful,' 'sound,' 'aggressive,' 'reliable,' 'ambitious,'" Fromm wrote. The romantic idea of personality as a singular set of character traits, the sanctity of the individual—these seemed like flickering images from a dimly remembered past now that people had been eclipsed by types.

No one knew this better than MacKinnon, the first person to purchase the Briggs-Myers Type Indicator from Hay and Associates and use it to streamline psychological warfare during World War II. While one could not undo the psychological effects of industrial modernity, he and his staff were determined to resurrect certain nineteenth-century ideas about the individual self as a bulwark against the horrors of recent history. Many members of IPAR's research team were familiar with the hardships of war and the devastation of the camps. There was Sigmund and Anna Freud's old student, Erik Erikson, who had escaped the Nazi occupation of Vienna to make his reputation in the United States as a brilliant child psychoanalyst. There was Harrison Gough, a brash air force officer, a compulsive designer of pen-and-pencil questionnaires. There was a young research assistant named Francis Xavier Barron, a romantic name for a romantic man, a poet who ran with the hippies and the beatniks and would occasionally disappear to Cuernavaca with his friend Timothy Leary to eat mushrooms and expand his consciousness. There was one female researcher, Ravenna Helson—the only member of the institute still alive today and the only one who went unnamed in research reports, identified simply as "the young woman." There was R. Nevitt Sanford, one of Adorno's coauthors on *The Authoritarian Personality*. They were all here—the émigré, the veteran, the poet, the woman, the anti-fascist—and in their shared commitment to the resurrection of the true self, they presented a cross section of America as it barreled headlong into the Cold War.

They were not alone in their endeavor. To establish the institute, Berkeley had received sizable grants from the Rockefeller Foundation, which believed that the emergent field of social psychology and its interest in the spiritual well-being of mankind would serve as an antidote to the barbarism of the Holocaust. Now was the time for the Western world to re-create the conditions for the "optimum performance of human beings as civilized creatures," claimed Alan Gregg, the head of the Rockefeller Foundation's Medical Sciences Division and one of the early supporters of IPAR. Like Isabel Briggs Myers, whom MacKinnon first invited to Berkeley in the mid-1950s to consult on what he called his "house-party" approach to testing, Gregg believed that personality psychology had preoccupied itself with the "cult of the abnormal" for far too long. It was time to set aside the study of neurotics and fascists to "identify the personality characteristics which made for a successful and happy adjustment to modern industrial society," he insisted. When he handed over the first installment of money to MacKinnon, he, like many others in the field, believed that IPAR was at the forefront of a new phase in personality testing's life cycle, propelled by the desire to make "the catastrophe of . . . personality," as poet Frank O'Hara deemed it, "beautiful again, / and interesting, and modern."

. . . .

The journey of type from east to west started in May 1945, when the German High Command surrendered to the Allied Forces. MacKinnon, who had taken over as director of OSS Station S from Henry Murray earlier that year, would take another two months to leave his secret tract of farmland in Virginia. There were case files to be sealed, spies to be debriefed, interrogation rooms to be dismantled. And there was the matter of an intriguing offer from Robert Sproul, president of the University of California, Berkeley. Sproul wanted to know if MacKinnon would consider coming to Berkeley to establish an institute of personality assessment, in the hopes that MacKinnon could use the tests he had designed or discovered at S to make college and graduate school admissions more effective—an urgent problem given the staggering rise in applications after the passage of the GI Bill. "A measure of the acuteness of the problem of selection in the Medical School alone is seen in the fact that although there are each year approximately 3,000 applicants for admission, only 75 can be admitted," MacKinnon noted. How could the school ensure it was admitting the seventy-five people whose personalities were best suited to being a doctor?

Today we tend to think of the admissions process as a game, or more accurately, a system that can be gamed given the proper resources and training. Gaining access to higher education is a competitive activity, and like all competitive activities, it follows a set of rules that determine success and failure, rules that come inscribed in SAT prep books and anthologies of the best college essays, rules that are more or less or not at all legible depending on one's place in the world. But in 1947, when MacKinnon first stepped foot onto the Berkeley campus, there was still a certain idealism to the admissions process, an earnest commitment to the fantasy that some people simply deserved to be doctors or lawyers or college graduates and that figuring out who those people were would, on the whole, make life better for everyone. This was the dawn of the age of intellectual meritocracy in higher education, and with it came a new language and a set of tools for measuring the human characteristics that were previously thought to be unmeasurable. "Integrity, responsibility, warmth, charm, independence, courage, initiative, and a capacity for leadership"—for one dean of admissions, this list of descriptors covered all the "outstanding qualities of character and personality" in applicants. MacKinnon's job was to put together a suite of personality tests, among them the Briggs-Myers Type Indicator, that could distinguish desirable students from undesirable ones, the successful from the slovenly.

Lurking behind the dean's list of accolades was an even more seductive fantasy about personality and the admissions process. Given the proper tools of assessment, any applicant could become completely knowable to the admissions committee—so much so that one needed never look him in the eye or converse with him to grasp, with absolute clarity and confidence, the workings of his inner life. One could conjure up an entire person from his test results alone, imposing flesh and blood onto what was once a mere silhouette. This Rorschachian act of projection was as fantastical as it was familiar to MacKinnon from his work at Station S. But the university officials at Berkeley believed they were selecting people for something far more daunting—the rest of their lives as members of the professional elite. And if, as many people believed, a college degree was the key to the American Dream, then personality testing was the gatekeeper to the promised land.

Before Truman Capote, before Katherine Anne Porter, before the writers and architects and other creative types, there were the graduate students—the institute's first guinea pigs. Throughout the spring of 1950, they arrived in groups of ten, sixteen groups in all. Each group occupied the former Sigma Phi Epsilon house from 4:30 p.m. on Friday until Sunday afternoon for what MacKinnon called a long "week-end party." They counted in their ranks chemists, economists, historians, physicists, political scientists, and zoologists, but no minorities or women. "We did not take any Oriental students, of whom there were several, feeling that since they came from a different type of background, they would require special consideration," MacKinnon explained in his research briefing. As for women, he could admit only that "the problem of the successful woman in what remain largely male professions has not been much discussed by us"—an "unconscious omission," he claimed, on the part of his staff. Black-and-white photographs of the first test subjects confirm that life inside 2240 did not look all that dissimilar from life inside the fraternity house it had once been. Here was a group of elite white men handpicked to "participate in games and other competitions and collaborations, engage in social conversations, and submit to organized interviews." Here were young men who, over the course of three days, would settle into an uncomfortable intimacy, sleeping one atop the other on a large sleeping porch fitted with ten wooden bunks.

Yet inside the IPAR "fishbowl," as MacKinnon prettily referred to it, there was far greater surveillance than the fraternity house. Before the weekend began, the staff asked each student's faculty advisor to fill out a personality questionnaire that assessed the student's "promise in professional work," his "originality of vision and freshness of thought," and his "general psychological soundness." MacKinnon and his staff already knew who was considered a personality with "High" potential and who was considered a "Low." They believed they knew which bright young man might one day discover a new law of the universe, which shaggy-haired slouch could barely keep up with his assignments. The goal of the next two days was to map the Highs and the Lows onto a consistent set of personality traits: the "personality package," to echo Fromm, that would enjoy the highest return in the personality market of college admissions. The IPAR staff could then create tests that would identify the personality characteristics of the Highs, allowing admissions officers to admit the Highs and weed out the Lows from the applicant pool.

Picture the scene inside 2240 on a Friday evening. There are cocktails and light conversation—it is important to the staff that the boys get a little loose, a little more honest—and after several rounds of drinks, the testing begins in earnest. First is the Adjective Checklist. From a list of 248 adjectives, each student must check the ones that best describe his personality. Is he "conscientious," "deliberate," "industrious," and "unaffected," as so many Highs proclaim themselves to be? Or is he "adventurous," "bossy," "careless," "commonplace," "disorderly," "dull," "emotional," and "spunky"—the preferred adjectives of the Lows? The students cannot linger for too long on any given word. Like all the tests, this one is strictly timed. After fifteen minutes, the checklists are whisked away and staff members distribute the IPAR questionnaire, the brainchild of Harrison Gough. It consists of declaratory statements, each of which must be marked as true or false. "*I have to admit that I don't believe women in my field make very good wives or mothers*"—true or false? "*In temperament I resemble my mother more than my father*"—true or false? Next is dinner, where the members of the staff pretend to eat while transcribing the boys' conversations on a preselected topic of discussion.

"Who are the greatest ten people of the last fifty years?" one staff member asks the boy sitting next to him.

"What would you do if your faculty advisor stopped showing up to his classes?" asks another staffer. He looks at the boy across the table for an answer, and when he is silent, prompts him. "Would you report him to the dean? Or would you keep quiet and give his lectures for him?"

Wherever one turns, there are tests. There are tests as a prelude to bedtime: a test to appraise social status, a sentence-completion test, Murray's Thematic Apperception Test (TAT), each of its black-and-white images projected onto the wall of 2240's special Dark Room, where the boys huddle together on the floor, scribbling stories they can barely make out. There are tests beginning at nine a.m. on Saturday that continue into the early hours of Sunday morning: Adorno's F scale to determine prefascist tendencies, a test of masculine and feminine qualities, a test of humor, and, of course, the Briggs-Myers Type Indicator. All told, there are more than twenty tests, one after the other, an endless procession of pictures, patterns, and fill-in-the-blanks swimming before the boys' eyes. To relieve the testing fatigue, there are games of charades, which the staff watches from a distance, using a 1 to 5 scale to rate each student on the ingenuity of his hand signals, the imaginativeness of his body language. There is a midnight raid on the icebox. It is not scored, at least not explicitly. But like everything else that takes place in 2240, it is observed and recorded for posterity.

Despite the innovativeness of IPAR's methods, there was something eerily retrograde about the house-party approach to testing. At the turn of the eighteenth century, the English philosopher Jeremy Bentham introduced the Western world to the idea of the Panopticon, or the "inspection house." Its purpose was precisely that: to keep people under inspection at all times or, seeing as this was literally impossible, to make people feel as if they were under inspection at all times. Prisons, factories, madhouses, hospitals, schools—all these institutions could, in principle, accommodate the dense and impenetrable atmosphere of surveillance that Bentham imagined. Writing nearly two hundred years later, Michel Foucault, the great French theorist of social control, would describe the Panopticon in ruthlessly scientific terms as a "laboratory of power." It was a "privileged place for experiments on men"—experiments so intense, so exhaustive in nature that they possessed "the ability to penetrate into men's behavior." By this, Foucault meant something quite astonishing: the inspection house was not just a space of observation but a system that, through its observational techniques, imposed a particular language of self-understanding on its subjects. Through the specter of constant vigilance, the incarcerated would learn to think of themselves as prisoners; schoolchildren would come to see themselves as disciples; and the boys at 2240 would understand themselves as coherent and classifiable types.

In other words, MacKinnon's goldfish bowl was never as innocuous as its games and icebox raids and good-natured roughhousing made it out to be. Picture again the scene inside 2240 on a Friday evening, only this time imagine it from the point of view of the test taker: a young student selected by his faculty advisor to participate in a psychological study about which he knows nothing. For two days, he is moved from one room to the next, taking test after test, reflecting on who he is. With every flick of his answer sheet, he considers and reconsiders himself, trying on the different vocabularies of personality that the institute has placed before him. *Am I too cold or too emotional? Deliberate or disorderly? An introvert or an extravert?* When a questionnaire like the Briggs-Myers Type Indicator forces him to pick between two options, he takes it at its word that such character traits are mutually exclusive, that he must embody one or the other. On the rare occasion when he is not taking tests, he is discussing his personality with others. Words like "introvert" and "extravert" roll off his tongue with the eagerness of a stranger who speaks, for the first time yet fluently, in a foreign language. The more tests he takes, the more he talks to other test takers, the more the idea of his individual self takes on an invisible heft and weight, becoming as incontrovertibly real to him as the wooden bunks on the sleeping porch. He inhabits it, and it, in turn, inhabits him.

"Everything is grist for the assessment mill," proclaimed MacKinnon in the 1952 IPAR annual report. It was true enough of the daily movements of the students at 2240. But it had also become true in a broader, more historically uncanny sense. By the time Isabel Briggs Myers boarded her flight to Oakland, MacKinnon had airlifted the type indicator out of the East Coast corporation and into the golden land, where it had started to gain a following among his staff and students. Now the assessment mill was churning faster and stronger than ever before, fueled not only by the new geographic reach of personality testing but by the design of new tests in response to the findings of old ones. Whereas IPAR had once limited itself to designing tests for Berkeley's admissions office, now it began to expand its offerings: first to local high schools, then to local businesses, and then to the California prison system, which enlisted MacKinnon and Gough to help design tests that would assign guards to whichever prison—minimum, moderate, or maximum security—best suited their personalities. Harrison Gough, who would invent more than thirty tests before he left to found his own testing company in the 1970s (Consulting Psychologists Press, soon-to-be publisher of Isabel's indicator), believed that maximizing the scale and specificity of testing would one day help "forecast what a person will say and do under defined conditions."

Looking back, one begins to suspect that the relentless production of new tests, each one rich with new techniques of inspection and classification, was far more valuable than whatever social or psychological insights these tests generated. Every year, IPAR debuted a new test or two or three, and every year, each new test had to be tested and retested and altered until it became, in effect, a different new test, which also had to be tested and retested and altered, until there were dozens of tests in circulation. This was an ever-expanding vortex of testing whose epicenter, at least on the West Coast, was IPAR. The initial motivation behind it all—the restoration of the individual self to modern psychology—had been eclipsed by the institute's promise to Berkeley that it would design a more efficient and utilitarian admissions process.

Yet the benefits for happiness and productivity remained elusive in theory and in practice. When it came time for MacKinnon and his staff to prepare their findings to submit to the university, they could say very little about the personality profiles of people well adjusted to modern industrial society. Successful students, MacKinnon observed, moved "at a slower tempo" and demonstrated "a sense of calm," "poise," and "social responsibility," while unsuccessful ones showed "considerably more instability, irritating others." But what was one to do with an observation like this? When pressed, MacKinnon suggested that the only way forward was to design more tests, one of which might someday—maybe—get at the psychic constitution of the happy individual.

. . . .

When, on August 2, 1955, Nikita Khrushchev promised the world that the Soviet Union would launch a satellite into space in the next year, IPAR's preoccupation with well-adjusted personality types evaporated like the contrails of the first rocket. Neither individual happiness nor a bourgeois professional order would help the United States rise faster or higher than the Soviet Union, at least not according to John Gardner, president of the Carnegie Corporation and President Lyndon Johnson's secretary of health, education, and welfare. For Gardner, America's secret weapon was its "creative spark," and it had to be "nourished—or at least, not smothered—in our young people." In the suburbs of Moscow, scientists and engineers labored and cracked under pressure from the political leadership, but in the United States, Gardner claimed, creative genius would know no such constraints. In the United States, there would emerge a totally autonomous yet maximally productive creative class: a cadre of young inventors, entrepreneurs, and artists whose unshackled brilliance would forever confirm the superiority of liberal individualism over state control. "We cannot believe that bound minds will ever be as resourceful as free ones, or that diabolical ingenuity will ever match creative vision, courageous planning, and bold pioneering," affirmed the San Francisco *Argonaut* in December 1955. Left to its own devices, American-bred creativity would burn bright, setting the world, and then the sky, on fire.

Yet to think of America as it was in the 1950s is not to think of free minds and creative sparks. "These are the fifties, you know. The disgusting, posturing fifties," Hannah Arendt observed, the decade in which the stench of political paranoia was accented by cheap gasoline and apple pie. These were the years in which Berkeley's President Sproul ordered every faculty member to sign an anti-communist oath and saw two of IPAR's key staff members, Erik Erikson and R. Nevitt Sanford, resign in protest. Research into the self was booming in higher education, but the same institutions that sponsored this research were also fighting hard to suppress the typical traits of the creative individual: conviction, complexity, nonconformity. Their ascendance would have to wait until the 1960s, when, after the election of John F. Kennedy and the arrival of the Beatles, after the Vietnam protests and the Freedom Rides, Dr. Timothy Leary, once a promising graduate student at IPAR, would urge a gathering of thirty thousand hippies in Golden Gate Park to "turn on, tune in, drop out"—to commit to "mobility, choice, and change," to embrace "one's singularity" in the world.

In retrospect it is easy to see that we have absorbed a distinctly mythic view of the 1950s and 1960s, one in which conformity and creativity do battle across a vast cultural divide. Yet this was hardly the case in California, where type and temperament were everywhere entwined, and never so intimately as in the figure of Francis Xavier Barron—Leary's good friend and IPAR's creativity expert. The staff joked that Barron looked the part of the poet, with his windswept hair and his craggy, pensive face. He talked and joked like a poet too, writing ironic and existentially grave test questions for inclusion in Gough's questionnaires. "*Life is devastating in its poignancy for me much of the time*"—true or false? "*I feel chilled to the depths of my soul*"—true or false? But he also believed that creativity had to serve a utilitarian political purpose, especially now that mankind's mutually assured destruction was a new fact of life. "As a species," he wrote, "we are at such a point of historical no return that it behooves us to muster all our powers, in the name of the Creator if necessary, to meet consciously the problems that our own evolution has set for us . . . Put creativity to work!"

We have, most of us, a certain image of the creative person. We have heard rumors of his eccentricities, his tics, and we have accepted, as a general rule, the idea that there exists some necessary trade-off between genius and grace. Insomnia and alcoholism, infidelity, rage—these all seem like small prices to pay for cultural advancement, for the composition of symphonies and the writing of novels. No one was more committed to this idea than Barron, whose theory of the creative person elevated the romantic fantasy of creativity from a bad stereotype to a pseudoscientific theory. "The creative person," he wrote, "appears to be distinguished by two fundamental traits: (1) the capacity of his brain to record and retain and have at ready call the experiences of his life-history, and (2) the relative absence of repression and suppression as mechanisms for the control of impulse." He—and Barron's creative person was always a man—was highly alert and adaptable, a "problem solver" who deployed his superior powers of concentration to express what ordinary people tended to repress: the hyperaggression and sexual mania that Barron called "the life of impulse."

Whether the creative person was born or made, Barron could not say. But this was the question that, from the perspective of higher education policy in the late 1950s and early 1960s, required an immediate answer if the self, the state, and the society were to be defended from the Soviet threat. "Better Testing Sought for Creative Students" advertised a press bulletin from the California Teachers Association. In a cover article called "The Cold War: The Creative Task," *Time* described creativity as the most powerful weapon in America's arsenal and urged parents and teachers to cultivate creative thinking in their children from an early age. "Can we teach people to be creative?" Gardner wondered. The question was not a hypothetical one. He ordered the Carnegie Corporation to give IPAR $150,000 in 1956 to find an answer through a new study of creative types—fiction writers, architects, mathematicians, and entrepreneurs—directed by Barron, the most creative member of the staff, at least by his own standards.

If you happened to be walking past 2240 on January 24, 1958, you might have seen one of Barron's first test subjects. He was a man short of stature and slight of build, with thinning hair and horn-rimmed glasses; a man with a slightly puckered mouth and, as the staff would note in his case file, "a most thorough-going baby talk." This man was Truman Capote, an EIFP, the staff would deduce. At thirty-three years old, he was already one of the most virtuosic writers in America— "the most perfect writer of my generation," proclaimed Norman Mailer, another of Barron's test subjects—and thus a perfect specimen for Barron's study of creative types. Capote was also openly gay and famous for his soft falsetto voice, his large and busy hands. At first, many members of the staff were disturbed by what they referred to as his "peculiarities." "The impression of both child and woman is so striking in his manner, that one senses in oneself and in his other listeners at first an embarrassed surprise, and then a protective feeling that urges one to seek quickly for the things one can respect behind this façade," wrote John W. Perry, the psychologist charged with taking Capote's personal history—the first order of business on the morning he arrived at 2240.

After his history was complete, Capote would undergo nearly a dozen assessments. From ten to eleven a.m., he would kneel on the floor of a study room littered with tiles and piece together a mosaic out of his favorite colors—red, black, green, and yellow. "Since the colors were basic, thought it best to do a sort of Mondrian," he explained to the nervous PhD student assigned to record his progress. At eleven a.m., he descended into the Dark Room to take the Tartan Test, which involved picking his favorite Scottish clan tartan from a series of nine tartans projected onto the wall. At noon, he would lay his hands over MacKinnon's, and together they would drift across a Ouija board. The house was old, the floors creaked terribly, but 2240 was not haunted. The Ouija board staged a basic test of suggestibility, designed to see if the slightest movements of the researcher's hands would compel the test subject to respond in kind.

Capote was so good-natured, so undefensive in the face of all this psychological prodding that the staff soon felt ashamed of their first impressions and sought to make amends. He was a shameless name-dropper, and they thrilled to stories of his famous and tragic and beautiful friends. "One felt that this world of literati and actors and actresses was his own particular element," read one note in his file. "With Tennessee Williams I've been friends for years—we always skate on the edge of bitchiness with one another," he confided to Barron. "I don't think writers can really be friends." With very little prompting from the staff, he talked for hours about what he called his "emotional problems." He had a compulsive desire for fame, which he believed originated with his mother, a jealous alcoholic, and his father, a bright, charlatan lawyer who abandoned the family when Capote was three, leaving him in the care of his three aunts, two of whom were lesbians. As a teenager, he had had prophetic dreams. The first one was when he was nineteen and at a writers' conference where Robert Frost was presiding. "I was upstairs, slightly ill with the flu," he relayed. "In the dream I was in the auditorium, and Robert Frost was talking about me, and got to shouting, and it became a nightmare. Later I went to the auditorium, and because of a crick in my neck was unable to rise on a certain occasion or raise my head: he misinterpreted this as intentional, slammed his book, and threw it at me in rage." The staff concluded that he had sought celebrity to escape his insecure, unloving home and that he had tended to his private wounds by making himself over as a thoroughly public presence—a "personality" in the most glamorous sense of the word.

When Capote was done for the day, he would board a bus and retire to the nearby Claremont Hotel. (Most of the writers refused to stay in the fraternity house.) His room was adjacent to the rooms of the other writers Barron had invited for that week: poet Howard Baker (IITJ), short story writer Jessamyn West (IIFJ), Pulitzer Prize–winning novelist MacKinlay Kantor (EIFP), and literary critic Ken-

neth Burke (IITJ). The next day, all the writers would return to 2240
to participate in a group storytelling contest in which each would take
turns constructing "a character or personality"—"a person of any age,
sex, or calling in life," explained Dr. Robert Knapp, the psychologist
who led the exercise—and "evolve some kind of intrigue or plot" that
would draw each of the writers' characters together in "human actions
or human complications." Most of the writers, reluctant to claim the
story as their own, crafted minor, unobtrusive characters, but Capote
was eager to supply the group with its protagonist and its plot. His
character was a seventeen-year-old girl named Anna Bouchari, the
daughter of a waitress in a small town. "Only she's changed her name
to Anne Benson," he explained. "She wants to be a model and go to
live in New York and she reads fashion magazines and movie magazines all the time and actually she is quite naïve really. She leads a
most sophisticated life and tells everyone she is 23. She is being kept in
an apartment by a gentleman and she has several gentleman friends."
She was a predecessor to Capote's most famous fictional character:
Holly Golightly of Breakfast at Tiffany's, which would appear later that
year in Harper's. But IPAR was where she made her debut as Anna
Bouchari/Anne Benson, who was about to run off with a poor but
decent man named Tom. "That's the beginning of the plot and my
character," Capote announced.

Capote's self-assurance caused a good deal of conflict. Kenneth
Burke, diagnosed by his staff psychologist as a man in possession of
a "severe" and "anxious" mind, was not amused by Capote's "boy-
wonder affectations" or his hijacking of the plot with Anna Bouchari.
"Mr. Burke not only did not fall for this but felt called upon to combat
it in a sort of hidden way," the staff noted. As Knapp urged the writers to continue adding to the story, Capote and Burke started arguing
about the direction the story should take. "There took place a first
class combat of one-upmanship," read Knapp's file, "in which Mr.
Burke would utter more and more profound observations about the
nature of man and art, in the manner of a weighty scholar, while Mr.
Capote would dance around these points with amusing little observations from the world of stage and screen." The members of the staff,

all of whom were by that point very protective of Capote, concluded that Burke "suffered from feelings of social inferiority, against which he reacted by being 'snooty.'" The exercise ended with hurt feelings all around.

In Capote, Barron found all the confirmation he needed for his profile of the creative type. "The apparently effortless verbalization of a very rich fantasy life was delivered, for the most part, with the overt nonchalance of a virtuoso," read Capote's file. His dreams were vivid and colorful—a sign that his unconscious strained against repression, Barron claimed. He was judged to be "aesthetically sophisticated," "more at ease with irreality than reality." He "felt little tension to resolve aesthetic incongruities." Most important of all, he had a sufficiently agonized backstory. He came from a family of drunks and deviants. He had struggled in the many ways a person could struggle, and these struggles had provided him with the raw material he needed to transform his private experiences into a luminous world of make-believe.

"Relentless, restless, and flighty." "Doubtful and distrustful of love." "Actuated by a sense of destiny." Barron's conclusions about the creative type would echo through his assessments of Kenneth Burke, Kenneth Rexroth, Norman Mailer, and MacKinlay Kantor, sanctifying the idea of the male artist as a romantic, tortured, and fatalistic soul. The Carnegie Corporation was quick to point out that his study was plagued by problems of experimental design. The sample was too small. There existed no control group of "noncreative" writers against which to compare the creative writers' assessments, a flaw Barron tried to correct by inviting advertising copywriters and staff writers for *Reader's Digest* to 2240 for a weekend of assessments. Yet whatever the methodological shortcomings of the study may have been, its characterization of the creative type endured as part of the mythology of the American artist.

Over the next several years at IPAR, the men would come and go. Few, if any, would notice the woman who lurked in the background of their tests: the woman in the Dark Room who turned the lights on and off; the woman who cleaned up the mosaic tiles after they had left them scattered on the floor; the woman who sat at the dinner table, waiting, watching, but never participating with the same ease as the male research fellows and psychologists. Like Isabel Briggs Myers, this woman, a recent transplant from the East Coast whose name was never consistent across IPAR documents—sometimes "Mrs. Nelson," other times "Mrs. R. Helson"—was impatient for the day when research into personality would matter to her and to the women of her generation. In 1962, the year that Isabel visited IPAR for the second time, she made her bid for the relevance of women to IPAR's research program.

. . . .

The new psychology professor at Smith College, Ravenna Helson, was thirty-one years old and, upon receiving the results of a recent gynecological exam, knew she was running out of time to have children. In 1954, she was considered an "elderly prima gravida"—an old first-time mother—and her doctor, a strict Catholic, urged her to have as many children as she could in the next five years. That night, Ravenna had a dream in which she opened the top drawer of a wooden dresser and found a baby sleeping inside. That settled matters. Her husband, Henry, a mathematics professor, had received a job offer from Berkeley, and although there was no position for Ravenna there, she took the baby in a dresser as a sign that this was the right time to set her work aside and devote her energies to becoming a mother. "So that's what I did," she would recall. The first baby arrived in 1956, the second in 1958. To her surprise, there was a third in 1960. Yet even after giving birth to three children in four years, she never could commit to what that baby in the drawer had represented: a career stashed away amidst musty linens and retired baby clothes, a life devoted to housework and childcare.

When Ravenna first arrived at 2240 to interview for a position as a research assistant, her oldest son was an infant and she was several months pregnant with her second child. Don MacKinnon showed her into his office, and if he noticed her condition, he did not comment on it. She would remember him as a shy, self-effacing man, the kind who was easily cowed by his wife, Mamie, a woman Ravenna decreed too domineering for her own good. Don was tightfisted, but Ravenna had expected as much. He was from Maine and, as she had learned since moving away from her hometown of Austin, Texas, people from both coasts were stingier with their time and money than southerners. The institute had only two telephones, one in his office and one for his secretary. There were no computers to score the tests they administered, only one nimble woman who came in once a week to score them all by hand. Don told Ravenna that a woman was cheaper than a computer. Yet he did not hesitate to hire Ravenna or to offer her several months of paid maternity leave—a startling act of generosity. "Don thought a very important part of creativity was the environment around you," Ravenna said. "He knew that if he made it possible for me to get paid, I would work harder for him."

In the early years of her job, she helped Barron with the writers' assessments. To Frank O'Connor, the gentle Irish writer of short stories, she administered the Street Gestalt Test, a visual exercise in which she showed O'Connor a series of black blotches and asked him to group them together to create a recognizable image. She tested the seventy-four-year-old physician and poet William Carlos Williams on his perception of verticality. Together, they entered the Dark Room, where a single line of light, thirty centimeters long and one centimeter wide, flickered at an oblique angle. In his crisp and pleasant voice, Williams instructed Ravenna to rotate the line—first left, then right, then left again—until he believed it was perfectly straight. Later she spoke to him about the pains of childbirth. "Here is a great woman / on her side in the bed. / She is sick, / perhaps vomiting, / perhaps laboring / to give birth to / a tenth child," wrote Williams in his poem "Complaint," which Ravenna had read before his arrival at the institute. His hands trembled as he listened to her complaints—he had recently had a stroke. But she felt he was eager to receive the story of her suffering. "With him one soon finds oneself thinking, this is a truly loving man," she noted in his file.

It was not long before Ravenna tired of her role as Barron's assistant. She found him to be too possessive of the writers, scolding anyone who questioned their behavior or their brilliance. She wanted a study of her own, something that reflected her experiences with creativity. On Tuesdays, she would hire a babysitter, kiss her son goodbye—"He looked so glum when I left," she remembered—and arrive at 2240 for the week's business lunch, expecting to talk about the mysteries of the human psyche. Instead, Harrison Gough, overconfident as always, wanted to assess how good her memory was, quizzing her on the capitals of all fifty states or the names of the ballrooms of the best hotels in San Francisco. The rest of the staff was friendly, but no one asked for her opinions and no one shared her ideas. One night, when she came home from work, Henry warned her that anything a wife did to show that she was serious about her "creative drive," as he referred to it, made it harder for a husband to feel the importance of his. She remembered his words when a friend telephoned her from the University of California, Davis, to ask her to accept a full-time faculty position in the psychology department. She picked up the phone with one hand, while the other pressed down on one of her babies—she could not remember which one—who was wriggling out of a diaper change and soiling her hands, her clothes. She did not see how she could accept the job.

At Smith, Ravenna had read French feminist Simone de Beauvoir's book *The Second Sex* and she found herself impressed by Beauvoir's diagnosis of the problem of women's creativity. Physically and emotionally burdened by childcare and housework, women sought the expressive outlets of art and literature so they would not go mad with resentment. "But the very circumstances that orient the woman toward creation also constitute obstacles she will often be unable to overcome," wrote Beauvoir. "When she decides to paint or write . . . [her] paintings and essays will be treated as 'ladies' work.' " When she first read those words, Ravenna had entertained only an abstract connection to the women's movement; France was an ocean away, and in the 1950s, it was too early for such ideas to take hold in the United States. But now, as Ravenna contemplated her positions at the institute and at home in the 1960s, Beauvoir's ideas came back to her with full force. When MacKinnon suggested that she begin studying creativity in women, she accepted out of a sense of self-interest.

Almost fifteen minutes south of Berkeley on an uncommonly green stretch of land in the Oakland foothills is Mills College, the first women's college west of the Rocky Mountains. It was founded in 1871 by Cyrus and Susan Mills, two Christian missionaries who had returned from a trip to the Hawaiian Islands to find themselves in the newly established state of California, where there were no opportunities for women to pursue higher education. There was, however, a Young Ladies' Seminary, which the Millses purchased for five thousand dollars and founded the school that would bear their name. It was a place of firsts: the first laboratory school west of the Mississippi; the first women's college to offer a computer science major in the 1950s; and, in February 1958, the source of the institute's first group of women test subjects.

There were thirty members of the Class of 1958 whom Ravenna invited to the institute for a daylong creativity assessment; a welcome change, she thought, to have thirty women in the house. But she found herself disappointed by the consistency of the futures the women imagined for themselves: a life dedicated to caring for their husbands and children—four children on average—and very little thought for their own self-advancement. In October, she repeated her assessments with the Class of 1960 before realizing that the tests Barron, Gough, and MacKinnon had designed revealed nothing about what the fates of these women would be once their teenage dreams became adult realities, once they had left school, married, had their four children, entered middle age, and grown old.

She bided her time and, ten years later, when the women in the study turned thirty, she tracked them down, making her way to Texas oil plants and New York advertising firms, to graduate school classrooms and immaculate suburban homes to administer the same tests she had given them when they had entered college. She discovered that the women who were married and had children now scored lower on tests of creativity and higher on tests of "femininity": a measure of sympathy combined with fearfulness, dependence, and vulnerability. The women who had remained single or had separated from their husbands reported feeling bad about themselves. She tested the group again fifteen years later, when the women had all turned forty-five, and found that many of them—single or married, with or without children—felt a nagging doubt about the directions their lives had taken.

Their story was Ravenna's story too. Her forties had started pleasantly enough with a birthday trip to Ireland, where MacKinnon had sent her to assess the creative potential of Irish entrepreneurs. For the first time, she and Henry had left the children in California so that the two of them could walk the fields of the Irish countryside hand in hand. One morning, when it was still dark outside, they lit candles and descended into the stony ruins at Newgrange, where there stood a temple to the sun god. They made their way through a long inner passage, their fingers tracing the ancient markings in the stone walls, and entered the central shrine. There Ravenna watched as a beam of light, a missive from the sun god, pierced a small slit in the roof of the chamber and, with each passing minute, widened and spread, until the entire room was bathed in the glow of the rising sun. Something inside her broke—her heart, she thought, or maybe just her tolerance. She remembered the refrain of a popular song she had heard sung in the streets of Dublin: "One day, we'll be neat and clean and well-advised / Won't the English be surprised?" For the first time, she felt enraged by her subservience to Henry and to the men at the institute. It was a vestige of colonial life, she thought: imperious, exploitative, and no longer endurable.

She did what any sensible woman would do. She fell in love with not one but two men. The first was a poet whom she met at a party later that night. She had lost Henry in the crowd, but she did not care. She and the poet talked for hours, a conversation that, in her memory, had no discernible shape or direction, only the thrum of desire. The second was one of the businessmen she was supposed to assess, a coarse fellow who approached her one brisk morning when she was sitting alone, wearing a tight knit suit with an Irish sweater over it.

"That's a beautiful sweater," he said. "I'm sure what's underneath is just as beautiful." His words made her dizzy, moved her to "the final stages of desire"—the most powerful orgasm she had ever had, she recalled. That night in her dreams, she was visited by a man with a beak and feathers: the sun god whose temple she and Henry had explored earlier that week. He warned her she was to be burned at the stake if she did not return to her children and her work, the two sources of her creativity. Like Katharine Briggs, Ravenna was a committed Jungian when it came to dream analysis. She took the dream as a sign that her psyche was disintegrating under the influence of false gods: anger, lust, self-effacement. She had to go back to California, back to her work at the institute, to recommit to her true self.

For Ravenna, the dream was also an allegory for the situation that many of her Mills subjects found themselves in as they approached midlife. One of Ravenna's favorite test subjects, a funny and frank woman named Sheila Ballantyne, had written a best-selling novel called *Norma Jean the Termite Queen,* and it seemed to Ravenna that Norma Jean, a highly educated housewife approaching a total nervous breakdown, was a patron saint for all the women she had ever known or studied. "On applications, Norma Jean has referred to herself variously as: Housewife, Homemaker (mentally adding 'Creative'), and Mother," Ballantyne's novel began. "Of course these terms do not belong under the heading Occupation; they never did because they do not adequately describe what you do. Doctor, teacher—these terms are descriptive; they carry an imprint that fixes readily in the mind and graphically illustrates the nature of the work done. Housewife? We all know how sloppy that one is." When Ravenna interviewed Sheila Ballantyne and her classmates on their fifty-third birthdays, she was happy to discover that most of them worked part-time now that their children were grown. They scored higher on personality measures of confidence, assertiveness, and independence. Their scores on creativity and cognitive ability were the highest they had ever been. They reported a newfound sense of happiness.

Ravenna never met Isabel Briggs Myers when she came to visit the institute in 1954 or 1962. She had used the Briggs-Myers Type Indicator on the Mills women, but she had assumed, in an act of reflexive sexism, that its creators were men, for men were the only test creators she had known. Had she known of Isabel, she would have invited her to meet the Mills women who resided in San Francisco and Oakland. She would have liked to confirm, to them and Isabel and herself, that, as women, none of them were alone in their pursuit of a creative life, even if they did not match Barron's description of the creative type. But Isabel did not linger long enough for any kind of encounter. Issuing her apologies to MacKinnon, she told him she had business back east at another esteemed center of personality testing: the Educational Testing Service—her new home institution, the source of a new set of trials for the type indicator.

CHAPTER TWELVE

That Horrible Woman

The first national conference on personality measurement, which was held at the Princeton headquarters of the Educational Testing Service (ETS) in October 1960, was a call for America's rival schools of personality research to assemble in peace. In attendance was a familiar cast of characters from the East Coast and the West, philosophers and practitioners alike. There was Donald MacKinnon, representing the "house-party" approach to personality assessment that he had originated at OSS Station S and refined at IPAR. There was his Station S partner, Henry Murray, invited to speak on behalf of projective tests like the TAT, which groped after the unconscious in the inner world of fantasy and narrative. There was Silvan Tomkins, ETS fellow and founder of affect theory: the study of the nine hardwired, genetically transmitted emotional responses— joy, excitement, surprise, rage, disgust, distaste, distress, fear, and shame—that he believed existed in all human personalities. Further from the pure theorists was a team of physiology researchers, who seemed to read in every bodily motion, from the slightest tilt of one's chin to the most exaggerated wave of one's hand, a veiled psychological desire. There was Henry Chauncey, president and founder of ETS, who, despite the incommensurability of all these methods and all these men, was determined to bring them together to advance the science of the self. Finally, there was the woman whom the ETS staff described as Chauncey's "pet project": sixty-three-year-old Isabel Briggs Myers. To her face, they addressed her with apparent disdain as "Mrs. Myers." In their letters to one another, they called her "the little old lady in tennis shoes" or, more to the point, "that horrible woman."

Like many of the turns her life had taken, the story of how Chauncey and Isabel met was a matter of precise historical timing. Chauncey was a former Harvard dean who, in 1943, had inaugurated the era of large-scale cognitive testing in the United States, administering the first modern version of the Scholastic Aptitude Test (SAT) to three hundred thousand army and navy reserve officers while they were waiting to do battle against the Germans. By the 1960s, when the SAT was well established in the college admissions process, Chauncey's interest had turned to instruments of mass personality testing as a complement to cognitive testing. He was heartened by how researchers like MacKinnon and Murray had turned away from the "domain of the abnormal" to the "science of the normal man" in the wake of World War II. "The development of tests in the personality area may in the long run make possible an increase in the adjustment and happiness of people," he wrote to his friend and collaborator Dael Wolfe, director of the Commission of Human Resources, a new government agency founded to identify and cultivate whatever specialized human talents might help the cultural advancement of the United States during the Cold War. "I am inclined to think," he added, "that the knowledge gained in the research leading to the development of tests will help in understanding and dealing with people, particularly with the methods of bringing up children and educating youth." But Chauncey worried that personality research was already beginning to fracture and specialize into "cliques" and that each clique would follow "its own lead until it has built up a semi-private nomenclature and body of doctrine (as has happened in the past: N.B. Freud, Adler, Rorschach, Murray)." The worst possible fate for personality research was for its "genius" researchers to become independent "specialists," devoting themselves to ideas that were "currently glamorous" within their academic silos instead of working together to "develop the ideas that would be glamorous 5 or 10 years hence."

To combat the problem of intellectual dispersal, Chauncey proposed the creation of a new Personality Research Center (PRC) housed within ETS that would validate different approaches to personality assessment, picking the most scientifically credible tests to publish for mass consumption. His experience with the SAT during World War II had shown him just how fast research could move when "attacked on an organized, programmatic basis." Just as his militant ambition had once "stimulated unprecedented progress of cognitive tests, so we may hope and believe it will accelerate progress on the non-cognitive," he wrote in his proposal for the center, which featured on its board of advisors MacKinnon and Murray, along with respected academic psychologists like David McClelland, Katharine McBride, and Gardner Murphy, president of the American Psychological Association. It was Murphy who supplied Chauncey with the initial idea for how PRC should work. "I envisage a day when PRC would have several high-level double-headed monsters whose job it would be to roam the country picking up good ideas and hypotheses," he joked at a board meeting. "These would then be turned over to a complex machinery capable of validating all hypotheses."

Chauncey would spend the years leading up to the conference doing precisely what Murphy had suggested, acting as a kind of traveling salesman, only in reverse. He would search far and wide for homegrown instruments of personality assessment and invite their creators to ETS, where his team of statisticians, psychometricians, and psychologists would vet their amateur designs and methods with the necessary scientific rigor. At any given moment in the 1960s, ETS had dozens of tests queued up for validation: Harrison Gough's California Psychological Inventory (CPI), which Gough had designed at IPAR and was now trying to publish through ETS; Silvan Tomkins's Picture Assessment Test (PAT), which measured the test taker's affect by instructing him to describe figures with faces drawn as happy, sad, or angry, and which Tomkins later disavowed as pure nonsense; the Guilford-Zimmerman Temperament Survey (GZTS), which measured ten dimensions of personality: general activity, restraint, ascendance, sociability, emotional stability, objectivity, friendliness, thoughtfulness, personal relations, and masculinity vs. femininity. By sifting these tests and others, Chauncey believed that ETS would find one that would do for personality assessment what the SAT had done for cognitive testing, a test that would reconstitute basic practices of child-rearing and education, usher in a new and more democratic process for access to jobs and government offices, and of course, turn a tidy profit for the ETS board of directors.

The October 1960 conference was held on the same day that images of Vice President Richard Nixon debating Senator John F. Kennedy flickered onto millions of American television screens. It was one of the first presidential debates to be broadcast live, a personality contest for the ages: Nixon, waxy and weak from a recent illness, facing off against the handsome future president. It was also a fitting occasion for Chauncey to debut the personality inventory for which he had the highest hopes: the Myers-Briggs Type Indicator, better known by its acronym, "MBTI." He had persuaded Isabel to switch the last names of mother and daughter when an ETS staffer had observed that the most popular tests were always referred to using initials, and that, as things stood, the Briggs-Myers Type Indicator could too easily find itself the "BM" type indicator—a scatological implication they would just as well avoid.

The name change was just one of the many alterations the test had undergone since it had arrived at ETS. Chauncey's statisticians had been testing and refining the indicator for three years, writing new questions, discarding old ones, recalibrating answer keys, breaking the questionnaire up and cobbling it back together so that it might meet ETS's standards for scientific validity. Now, after three major rounds of revision based on test results from more than twenty thousand subjects, the staff believed that the indicator was ready to face the scrutiny of America's best researchers and theorists, even though some of them, like Donald MacKinnon, had already been using it for many years in its original form.

Standing next to Chauncey as he described the virtues of the MBTI, its indebtedness to Jungian theory, and its sixteen distinct personality types were three men—two ETS staffers and MacKinnon—and Isabel. She had been a late addition to the conference, invited almost as an afterthought by Chauncey, a dutiful kindness, her name scribbled in pencil on the program ETS handed out to its participants. When the time came for her to speak, she skipped from MacKinnon's side to the podium, as she tended to do when she was excited. "Yes, she actually skipped," one staffer would marvel. "To see a woman in her mid-sixties skip with long, magnificent leaps, into one's office was like discovering the eighth wonder of the world." She addressed the crowd, her ashen hair heaped atop her head, her eyes squinting from behind cat-eyed glasses, her voice thick with the love of a creator for her invention. She knew what many of the men in the room thought of her—she had known for years—but she did not care. After years of hiding, first behind Hay, then MacKinnon, and finally Chauncey, it was her turn to step to the front of the room.

. . . .

When, in February 1956, Henry Chauncey first heard rumors of the Briggs-Myers Type Indicator from a friend in Washington, D.C., he drafted a memo to his staff titled "Reasons Why the MBTI Seems Promising." (Even before Isabel started working with him, Chauncey changed the intuiting function's abbreviation from *I* to *N* to distinguish it from introversion, giving the type scheme its contemporary appearance.) In it, he enumerated why ETS ought to pursue it as a possible candidate for the institution's flagship personality test:

- It is based on theories of Jung which have many adherents among leading psychologists and have well stood the test of thirty years.
- The theory is basically simple, but appears to be fundamental and of relevance.
- The theory is concerned with normal individuals rather than psychological abnormalities.
- The types that are the result of classification of several factors do not make invidious distinctions. Each type has its place and usefulness. Each type has its strengths and weaknesses.

· The types resulting from the test seem to be useful in relation to the <u>kind of work that a person undertakes</u>, as in predicting occupational achievement.
· The test itself is <u>well constructed</u> and has been in the process of development and study for fifteen years.

Chauncey's list, which stressed the test's populist appeal ("The theory is basically simple," "Each type has its place and usefulness") over its scientific validity, was sure to alienate ETS's psychometricians even before they met the test's creator. When Chauncey invited Isabel to present her work to his all-male staff in the winter of 1957, neither she nor he could have anticipated the ridicule that would await her upon her arrival in Princeton. She came with her hair up, her glasses on, and one sleeve rolled up, wearing a sling from a recent operation she had undergone to remove a suspicious lump in her arm—an early sign of the metastatic cancer that was to kill her over two decades later. The invitation from ETS was "just manna from heaven," she told a friend. "I thought it dropped from the skies." The staff looked her up and looked her down. She was wearing her blue nylon dress, dotted with pink flowers, and awkward but functional shoes. After determining her age (somewhere in the midfifties, they guessed) and hearing about her various occupations (mystery writer, housewife, inventor, entrepreneur), they could not bring themselves even to feign enthusiasm for her ideas.

She was unperturbed by the coolness of their reception. The second-guessing of her abilities was nothing new to her. The only man whose opinion mattered was Chauncey, for he controlled ETS's research agenda and its purse strings. With the same breathless, thrilling voice she had once deployed when she spoke about the secret to a good mystery novel or the key to a successful marriage, she enthralled Chauncey with the story of how she and Katharine had dedicated their lives to adapting Jung's type theory; how their calling had overridden all other personal and professional goals; how, like a modern-day Lewis and Clark, she and her family had traversed the United States to spread the gospel of type. Whatever she lacked in statistical training or theoretical rigor, she made up for with the ardency of her storytelling. Her mission was sacrosanct.

Just as Katharine had once contrived myths to teach Isabel about the natural world, now she told Chauncey the story of type by invoking the myth of platonic human relationships. At her instruction, he began to speak of the sixteen types "as if they were sixteen different biological species," he wrote in a memo to his staff. There seemed to exist a natural affinity between two people of the same type, much as there might exist a natural affinity between two frivolous and swooping songbirds or two industrious monkeys, happily picking fleas from each other's backs. "Each type gets along best with members of its own or closely related types," Chauncey noted. "This follows theoretically from the existence of a natural and realistic basis for empathy between persons who structure their roles similarly and employ the same functions." According to data that Isabel had given him from the Swarthmore families she had typed in the 1940s, "the most common situation in a series of married couples was similarity on the E-I, S-N, T-F Indices, and dissimilarity on the J-P index." If the indicator could generate such simple yet forceful insights about the psychological foundations of domestic harmony, it might have even more to say about workplace harmony or political harmony, Chauncey thought. Should the same or similar types be assigned to work together? Could the indicator help predict how two types would handle an office dispute or even a high-stakes political crisis?

"Just by chance we might happen to come up with something pretty good," Chauncey concluded after his many meetings with Isabel over the years. He judged himself to be "favorably impressed with the reasoning she has done in setting up some of the patterns which she described" among the friends and family members she had typed on her 3″ × 5″ index cards. "She seems to be insightful," he reasoned. Yet there was reason to hesitate. "The danger is that the small sample of items which she uses, sometimes only a single item as a partial basis for determining a pattern, may be too flimsy. It may turn out that we will need to lengthen and strengthen the test if we are to accomplish some of the objectives which Mrs. Myers feels she can accomplish by the Indicator as it stands."

Lengthening and strengthening the test—Form C had ballooned to 250-item Form D by the time Isabel arrived at ETS—was no easy undertaking. It required ETS to set up a new Office for Special Tests whose sole purpose was to validate the indicator through the application of state-of-the-art statistical methods, to temper Isabel's passionate outpourings, her anecdotes about friends and family with social scientific evidence. Indeed, ETS was the first institution in which the quasi-mythical language of type would collide with the formalized language and methodology of statistics, a mathematical discipline that had penetrated American industry and politics with aggression in the 1930s and then, amidst the global upheavals of the 1940s, had undergone a quiet but radical transformation with the invention of the computer. Like the army, the navy, the air force, and the United States Census Bureau, ETS owned an RCA 501 transistor computer, "the world's most advanced electronic data processing system," according to its sales brochure. It was an intimidating machine, one that resembled a church organ, with a keyboard painted after a Mondrian city grid and four racks of processors, which, when hooked together by a large cable, created a phalanx of 17,000 transistors. The RCA 501 made it possible to score tests at an inhuman rate—one test every nine seconds in 1958, the year the computer first arrived at ETS. It also allowed ETS's statisticians to write programs that could perform basic statistical analyses across large samples of test subjects: the calculation of means and modes, correlations and causations, the determination of significance.

But the computer was more than just a convenient time- and labor-saving device. It was an indispensable technology given the new scale of Isabel's and ETS's operations. In just the first few years of their partnership, the indicator swept the country from east to west and back again with a frenetic, vital energy. ETS's list of early adopters included not only Hay's corporate clients and MacKinnon's creative types but also the Protestant Episcopal Church in the United States of

America, which had given Form C to seventy-two women applying to serve as directors of religious education for the church's national council; the Palo Alto Public School District, which had tested two thousand students to help select participants for its gifted child program; Brown University, which had administered the indicator to all 950 members of its 1958 class; and the California State Department of Corrections, which had used the indicator to divide the inmates at their Vacaville prison into low- and high-risk populations. Through the early 1960s, ETS planned to check the validity of each individual item Isabel had written by testing and retesting teenagers across the country: 200 at the California Institute of Technology, 300 at Amherst College, 900 at Rensselaer Polytechnic Institute, 900 at Rutgers, and 2,200 eleventh- and twelfth-grade students across twenty-three high schools in Massachusetts—schools that would "sacrifice their students for the cause of test validation," Isabel reported with excitement.

Gone were the days when Isabel would sell one, two, or three test booklets to the local brewery, scraping in a couple of dollars here and there. Gone were the nights spent hunched over her Monroe calculator, the hand-crank adding machine she kept in her living room next to the moldering stacks of answer keys she had accumulated over the previous decade. Gone too was the haphazard, if intimate, research program that had defined the indicator's early days. For Isabel, the typing of friends and family members had proceeded without controlling for any of the confounding variables that would differentiate introversion and extraversion, sensing and intuiting, thinking and feeling, judging and perceiving, from the other factors that determined an individual's personality: age, gender, economic status, education, political orientation. "Neither of these authors has had formal training in psychology, and consequently little of the very extensive evidence they have developed on the instrument is in a form for immediate assimilation by psychologists generally," Chauncey warned his staff as he prepared them to start work on the indicator. "Indeed, many of the ideas employed are so different from what psychologists are accustomed to that it has sometimes been difficult to keep from rejecting the whole approach without first examining it closely enough."

Those who worshipped at the altar of facts and figures, of t-tests and p-values, had little patience for Isabel's kitchen table experiments, the imprecise, if enthusiastic, attempts at validation that had accompanied Forms A, B, C, and D. ("I sometimes kind of shook in my shoes with the old [versions] because the scores would be coming out on the basis of so few questions," she later recalled.) Although Isabel had taught herself some basic statistics when she was working for Hay during the war, the ETS staff dismissed her autodidacticism with quiet contempt. Her sense of enterprise seemed an affront to their hard-won institutional authority; they took her ambitions personally. "Mrs. Myers was not trained in psychometrics," wrote Junius "Jay" Davis, who, in his role as Chauncey's assistant, had been tasked with ensuring that Isabel and the ETS staff maintained some degree of peaceful coexistence. "She was simply a very bright lady with a lot of enthusiasm and the belief, validated by her experience, that she could do absolutely anything she wanted to." His passive-aggressive tone was echoed by his fellow ETS staffers, who complained that Chauncey had pressured his psychometricians into "proving the preconceived and popular but naïve notions of non-researchers." "Not the least of the problems in evaluating the Indicator is to have it treated as any other personality test," one statistician wrote. "A veil of suspicion hangs over it. It had an unorthodox origin, it is wedded to a somewhat uncomfortable theory and the enthusiasm it has aroused in some people has provoked sterner opposition in others."

And then there was Isabel herself, whom Chauncey had hired into an official position as "ETS consultant," paying her an honorarium of $250 a month for her expertise. Depending on whom you asked around headquarters, she was either a harmless and idiosyncratic old lady, someone to be humored until she grew tired and went away, or an intolerable nag. She insisted that the ETS staffers take the indicator, and not only did she report their results back to Chauncey—"Persons engaged in psychometric research seem to favor an introverted role based on Thinking," he informed his staff—but she decreed whom she would work with based on their type. For the first five years of her collaboration with ETS, she refused to share the MBTI's answer keys with the statisticians. "She scored it with secret scales she said she could never release, for if the Russians got hold of them, the United States and civilization itself would be lost," Davis recalled. In a perpetual state of paranoia, a state befitting the dark, fretful days of McCarthyism and bomb scares, she prowled the hallways of ETS, her breath fouled by a homemade energy drink she called "tiger's milk": brewer's yeast blended with milk and sweetened by melted Hershey's bars. Every week, she would ask Chief to deliver a fresh supply of yeast, milk, and chocolate to Princeton, and, lacking a kitchen or a blender with which to liquefy her ingredients, she would pulverize the chocolate with her fists, pour in the milk, and swallow with determination.

She recorded very little of her impressions of the ETS staff, but one could imagine that her possessiveness over the indicator was more rational than they made it out to be. This was her creation, her life's work; they treated it like just another tool to be vetted and, should it not meet their obscure technical standards, discarded along with all the other old, useless tests of the past. When Chauncey promised her in the spring of 1959 that his staff would test the indicator on eleventh and twelfth graders in Massachusetts in the fall of 1960, she did not believe his staff would follow through on his plans. "I wanted the students right then, being ready for them myself," she wrote. That spring, unbeknownst to Chauncey or his team, she drove to each of the courthouses of the five counties around Philadelphia and instructed the county clerks to make her lists of all the high schools in their jurisdiction. There were thirty schools in all. She visited each three times: the first to convince their principals to let her administer the indicator to their students ("This was walking in cold," she recalled, "but, of course, Educational Testing Service is kind of a magic name"); the second to deliver the test booklets and answer sheets; and the third to collect her spoils. By the end of the summer, she had more than ten thousand student answer keys, which she scored by hand and, much to Chauncey's surprise and dismay, deposited with ETS for analysis. To celebrate, she and Chief took a vacation to Bermuda. She packed a modest black bathing suit and lined her suitcase with the printouts from the computer's statistical evaluation of the students' scores.

Yet her enthusiasm to amass more test subjects, to spread the gospel of type to the young was not born out of her commitment to lengthening and strengthening the test. While she believed in ETS's brand, its seal of approval, on some fundamental level, she did not believe in its practices of empirical validation. The staff's testing and retesting of subjects, its vetting of every item on the questionnaire she dismissed as a series of operational delays—a waste of time, she thought, given that people like MacKinnon and Hay had already adopted the indicator and were happy with its performance. Nor did she believe in the division of labor between creators and validators, not when it involved stripping her of the control she had once exercised over her creation. Her dogged individualism did not play well at headquarters. Her demands that ETS staffers stop whatever they were doing to attend to her workplace needs became so burdensome that, after several months, certain staffers begged Chauncey for the day off when they knew she was coming to headquarters. She believed the statisticians were conspiring against her, that they were keeping the indicator from succeeding by holding it to unreasonably high standards.

At the end of the day, when everyone else had retreated to his home and family, she stayed behind, working uninterrupted for hours on end. She ordered Jay Davis to stay with her, and he, too beholden to Chauncey to say no, stayed. "Isabel, I simply have to go home and get two or three hours of sleep," he begged one morning at three a.m.

She shook her head. "Nap on a table in the seminar room across the hall," she suggested. "I'll have some material for you to review in just a few minutes."

Sometimes she took advantage of the empty office to search the staff's private files for data she suspected they were withholding from her. On nights when she reached for her thermos of tiger's milk for sustenance, her intrusiveness was documented by the trail of sweet, sticky fingerprints she left in her wake.

. . . .

During her time at ETS, Isabel had many handlers: the young men whom Chauncey appointed to mentor her, tutor her, and wean her from her "horse-and-buggy-methods": the 3" × 5" index cards she had inherited from her mother's dream analysis, her rotary calculator, her mulish resistance to social scientific methods. From Form D to Form E, there was Richard Cordray, a young statistics tutor from Chico State in California, once a high school classmate of Isabel's son, Peter. From 1959 to 1960, he was earnest but combative. He accompanied Isabel on her drives to the Philadelphia courthouses and high schools in the spring of 1959 and fought with her over the summer about her shameless disregard for ETS's protocols. "Mrs. Myers indicated that she was unhappy about the lack of close contact with ETS," he wrote in a frustrated memo to Chauncey. "I have seen her at least once a week, at Swarthmore if there was no reason for her to be here. (Reasoning: She is working full time on type. It is better for ETS to waste my time driving than to waste hers.)" During his visits to Swarthmore, he begged her to stop scoring tests by hand. ETS's computer technicians had written a new scoring program for the RCA 501, which could now score one test every four seconds—nine hundred tests an hour. "I have been trying for years to convince Mrs. Myers that she should do as little clerical work as possible, on the grounds that her time was better spent elsewhere. Her reply has been that she is disappointed with accuracy," he complained to Chauncey.

They fought about everything, big and small: where they would meet and at what time, how old students had to be for the results of their personality assessments to be accurate. They fought about the publication of a newsletter showcasing the most recent research on type. ("I doubt that Mrs. Myers will be happy about a publication as informal as the one I conceive this should be," Cordray predicted.) They fought about whether to permit or even promote uses of the indicator that were not dependent on its validity, which ETS had yet to establish and which Isabel, despite her impatience, worried would be necessary to demonstrate before the test was circulated to the public at large. More acutely than even Chauncey, Cordray perceived that the language of type might have psychological uses that exceeded whatever its scientific merits might be. "In comparison with other personality tests, the questions [are] not at all threatening; likewise, the theory involves little in the way of judgement," Cordray observed. Employers could use the indicator to gift their employees a partial, encouraging result from a battery of cognitive and psychological assessments, many of which were, unlike the indicator, explicitly and harshly judgmental. "I remember a comment from one of the insurance companies that they were using the indicator for this purpose," he wrote to Isabel. "They had been bothered about people asking how they came out on the test battery when the result of the test battery was confidential and could not be told to the testee." But employers, human resources managers, and career counselors could use the indicator to "establish rapport and confidence" without "being threatening." "The indicator offers this ready-made," he concluded, some months before he left ETS and Isabel to return to California.

Cordray did, however, inadvertently inspire Isabel to design a second section for the questionnaire: word pairs. He was an ENTJ who "consistently frustrated me," she would later recall, as "he wouldn't come out on the questions the way I meant him to." Her long drives around Philadelphia gave her "prime time to think" about why he got "wrong answers contrary to his type with discouraging frequency." One afternoon, as she let her mind drift behind the wheel, she realized that he might respond better to her questions if she simply placed the two key words from answer (a) and answer (b) in front of him and asked him to choose between the words. Like the Jungian imagery game her mother had played with Tucky, she would write opposing pairs of words on index cards, line them up on her living room sofa, and ask Cordray to pick a word, then tell her what it brought to mind. When they tested the word pairs on high school students, she asked them to write on the back of the answer sheet what it was like to take the indicator. "One boy wrote with the word pairs, 'These are all nice words.' I thought that was a tribute," she said.

From Form E to Form F, there was John Ross, a psychometrician visiting ETS from the University of Western Australia, who had no interest in either Jung's theories or their applications, only in their truthfulness. "I think it is true to say that Mrs. Myers has been more interested in proving that her theory is correct and in achieving ever greater refinement on the use of the Indicator than in stopping to evaluate it," he informed Chauncey in November 1959. Despite professing his impatience with theoretical argument, Ross expressed serious doubts about Isabel's misappropriation of Jungian thought: her inaccurate definitions of "introversion" and "extraversion," her insistence that type never changed. His doubts extended to the very idiom of type itself, which, for him, suggested that a person's psychological makeup was an essential, natural feature of her psychological makeup and that one could describe a person as "being" one type or another much as one could describe an animal as belonging to a defined biological species. "The word 'Type' . . . might create misunderstandings and initial negative reactions," he wrote to Chauncey. He urged Isabel to start referring to type as "preference-type," to stress "the voluntary character (albeit unconscious?) of the preference of type functions." She refused; individual choice was not assimilable to Jung's theory, she argued.

Their relationship, which had never been good, worsened when Ross discovered some statistical irregularities in Isabel's work. Isabel had always claimed that her indicator, and Jung's theory more broadly, was premised on the statistical notion of bimodality. In any random sample of human beings who took Form F, there was a good chance that the data would reveal two distinct peaks or "modes" that corresponded with the two opposed personality types for each dimension, an equal distribution of extraverts and introverts, sensers and intuitives, thinkers and feelers, judgers and perceivers. But after testing thousands of high school students and college freshmen, the samples revealed little evidence of bimodality; most people seemed to hover somewhere in the middle, their personalities lost in the no-man's-land between Isabel's two platonic peaks. This was an unsettling development. Isabel believed that both the theory and the numbers were right and that their misalignment was some sort of fluke—a problem that ETS had introduced in their validation process. Ross disagreed, and they argued for months about how to move forward. "The crux of our disagreement," Ross reported to Chauncey, "was firstly that Mrs. Myers emphasized the tests for bimodality and sharp breaks in regression, which are intended to show that the theory is correct in supposing bimodality (or 'polarizing tendency'?), whereas I stressed finding out how well the Indicator functioned as a predictor and as a sign of other concurrent characteristics; and secondly, that Mrs. Myers continually introduced new ideas . . . just as we were reaching the position of being able to stop and say: 'This looks like a good enough bet. Let's stop here and see what we've got.'"

The desperate amateur and the dogmatic statistician—there was no real resolution to the impasse they had reached. Although Isabel and Ross continued revising the questionnaire and answer key together, each laboring in silent resentment of the other, Ross would not allow ETS to sell the MBTI at scale as anything other than an experiment. "I would suggest that it be published and listed as an experimental test," he told Chauncey, "and that a manual be prepared for release at the same time as the test itself. I think we should advance any claims about the test cautiously." The problems kept piling up: the E-I scale was "overweighted toward talkativeness"; the S-N scale, for both males and females, seemed to reflect "intellectual ability and intellectuality"; the T-F and J-P scales yielded wildly different distributions across the sexes. When he returned to Australia at the end of the year, Isabel rejoiced. Little did she know that the man Chauncey had tasked with drafting the MBTI manual would turn out to be her greatest nemesis yet.

His name was Lawrence Stricker. In time, she would grow from disliking him to hating him, so much so that at her home office in Swarthmore, she kept a secret file on his activities titled "Larry Stricker, Damn Him." He was a mere twenty-seven years old then, a slip of a boy—younger than Peter and Ann. A recent graduate of New York University's doctoral program in statistics, he was the newest addition to ETS headquarters in 1960. He enjoyed the support and protection of the "graybeards in the research division"—this according to Jay Davis, who was annoyed with Stricker for making his job as the mediator between Isabel and ETS more trying than it already was. "He took a year to trash the device completely as without psychometric merit," Davis recalled. "Mrs. Myers, of course, hit the proverbial ceiling."

In his autobiography, Davis would call the episode "dramatic," but his condensation of it did little to convey the drama: Davis's ashen-haired, gymnastic, and paranoid charge doing battle against a young man who, by all accounts, was so impassioned about statistical analysis that he grew angry, changing color when the numbers did not work out as he had predicted they would. They were an unlikely team to work together on the manual, but work on it they did, for the six excruciating months that spanned November 1960 and April 1961. Isabel trusted him with material she had not shown anyone else— "first draft stuff of some things I had written down for my own convenience," she claimed. What Isabel did not know was that Stricker was, in secret, preparing a separate document about the indicator: a memorandum addressed to the "graybeards" in the research department that attempted "to outline the major problems in the evaluation of the Myers-Briggs Type Indicator," Stricker wrote.

His position, he claimed, was one of utmost objectivity, untainted by any personal frustration or dislike for Mrs. Myers; his was the voice of reason, cutting through all the irrational clamor that surrounded the indicator, both positive and negative. "I am making an attempt to be, neither pro nor con, simply the dispassionate and impartial evaluator," he insisted. "I am also making the attempt to sift the positively enthusiastic and the hostile statements made about the test from the actual claims made about its virtues and the critical points advanced against it." To that end, his memo posed three simple questions. How good was the theory behind the indicator? How good was the indicator as a device for measuring this theory? How useful was the indicator at predicting human behavior, quite apart from its virtue as a device for measuring Jung's theoretical personality types?

Point by point, Stricker dismantled the indicator, destroying whatever claims it had made to either theoretical insight or empirical validity. The theory was "Jungian in character," he noted, "but much of it is novel"—spun from Isabel and Katharine's mythological imagination of how human nature was or ought to be. "It employs the notion of introversion-extraversion, which Jung did; it uses thinking, feeling, sensation and intuition, which Jung counted as the four basic psychological functions; but it uses a distinction between judgement and perception which Jung either did not use at all, or did not choose to feature in his typological system. And even though there is a considerable overlap in the terms used, there is less in the meaning of the terms and still less in the system of compounding the primary characteristics into a complex set of types." What Isabel and her mother had done was to take a complex philosophical explanation for human subjectivity and flatten it into unrecognizable caricatures of psychological theory: the self dwindled into a four-letter acronym, the world compressed into a 4 × 4 type table. As for the indicator itself, he decreed it all but useless. The questionnaire items did not reflect the theory even in its most diluted form. The four dimensions either measured something relatively unimportant ("E-I merely measured talkativeness," he wrote) or something better measured by another scale ("S-N was merely conservatism versus liberalism").

It was a punishing, injurious document—"a critique of the type indicator done in the tradition of the graduate school he had come from in which the more faults you could find with a piece of work the better critic you were," Isabel described it with rage. More than that, it was a treacherous one. Stricker's denunciation of the indicator blindsided her. She was "shaken," Chauncey observed, and "quite upset by what she regarded as misinterpretations, distortions, and omissions." She no longer skipped into the office. She no longer wanted to visit the office at all to confront the smirking faces of the young and old men who whispered about her clothes and her hair, the men who urged Chauncey to show her the door before ETS wasted any more time or money on her silly schemes. "I guess you feel as though you were waiting for the cavalry to come and rescue you and when they came they started firing at you," consoled William Turnbull, ETS vice president, whom Isabel called her "only friend" at the organization.

At Turnbull's insistence, she returned to ETS, and she was careful not to reveal her true feelings. In private conferences with Chauncey, she was even-keeled, gracious. "She undoubtedly felt very keenly about the whole matter, but was quite reasonable in her discussion and did not seem to generalize her presumed negative feelings to ETS generally," he reported, relieved that she had not a made a scene. But in the privacy of her home, her original laboratory of type, she damned Stricker for damning her, for damning her life's work without considering what it had meant to her, how hard she had worked for the past twenty years, or what parts of her life she had sacrificed for people—for men like him—to take her seriously. The pace of her work slowed. Saddled by fresh doubts, she could not bring herself to finish the manual or the book she had wanted to write on type. "She is a kind of modern Joan of Arc, and her cause is as sacred," Davis wrote to Chauncey, observing the changes in Isabel. "She simply doesn't anticipate being trapped and bound at the stake."

"The whole Larry Stricker imbroglio," as Chauncey took to calling the incident, left Isabel in a precarious position at ETS. On the one hand, the possibility of validating the indicator had grown ever dimmer; on the other, Chauncey, unwilling to give up on it, began to shift his conception of what the test could do if it was not, in fact, a valid assessor of personality. Once he had championed it as a simple, systematic language for mediating between the shadows of the self and a series of expressed preferences. Now type appeared as a looser, freer idiom for self-description, something even more appealing and more democratic than what he had once thought. "One ought to consider any virtues that the theory might have; even if one does not want to dignify the hypotheses by speaking of them as a theory," Chauncey explained to Stricker, who listened with skepticism. "The four-dimension system is relatively simple and easily understood. It can be described in words that have meaning to the layman and it isn't so complex or unusual that he throws his hands up feeling that he just cannot comprehend the whole matter." His language recalled not Isabel's technical descriptions of the indicator but her mother's cheerful distillation of Jung's theories for readers of the *New Republic* in her 1926 article "Meet Yourself." "In fact," Chauncey continued, "people generally, after learning a little about the theory, find that it is a convenient way of describing individuals. Frequently, people use J-P, S-N, or E-I in describing an individual to a third party." While he acknowledged that this was "kind of a dangerous basis for adopting a theory," he believed that "in considering the practical usefulness of the test, if it meets other requirements, this is a significant one." Scientific or not, the indicator had always managed to spark a sudden and ecstatic perception of self-knowledge in its subjects, no matter their age, sex, education, occupation, or political leanings, no matter their initial skepticism toward its operations. "The proof of the pudding is in the eating," Chauncey rhapsodized to Stricker. "Does the theory or the score of the Indicator, along with other test scores, in fact provide a platform that will enable us to scale the mount of understanding a little higher?"

It was on the back of faith, not science, that Isabel's work at ETS continued. But she was unwilling to accept its diminished status, its fall from grace. "She tends to fight her battles on the most difficult and dubious grounds," Chauncey worried. Nor could she free herself from Stricker's criticisms. It was one thing to question the indicator—the technical aspects of its design, the individual items—but it was another to dismiss the theory behind it, which had stirred the souls of those she loved with the promise of self-discovery. With deliberate and destructive cruelty, he had used his memo to invalidate her sense of who she was and what she had spent her life doing. He had attempted "to cut off the dog's tail behind its ears," she wrote in the only angry letter she sent to him. But he should watch his step, she warned. "The dog might turn out to be a champion."

. . . .

She finished the manual in 1963, but by then, her relationship with ETS had frayed badly. So too had her resolve. Her father, Lyman, had died earlier that year, and, in a reversal of roles no daughter can fully anticipate, she had become her mother's keeper. Katharine's mind—the same mind that had designed the cosmic laboratory of Isabel's childhood, the same mind that had drafted thousands of pages on Jung, religion, marriage, and motherhood—was failing. The responsibility for her daily care had fallen to Isabel, who had set aside her work to tend to her mother's needs.

The children, too, needed her now more than they had in the past thirty years. Both Ann and Peter were on the verge of unpleasant divorces. Peter was about to leave Betty, his wife of twenty years; Ann, an introvert, had married an extravert, Jim, who did not think she loved him unless she said so. "I didn't think I needed to," she confessed to her mother. Like Isabel, she had also committed herself to motherhood, but now she wanted to become an educator, designing better methods for teaching young children how to read. Such a project offered Isabel a welcome distraction from ETS. Just as mother and daughter had talked about the indicator twenty years ago at Isabel's kitchen table, now they sat at Ann's, designing games and writing poems for kindergarten curricula. Later, when Ann would present her and her mother's materials at a conference in Illinois, she would meet the professor of psychology who would become her collaborator and, much to her mother's dismay, her lover. The home Isabel had built around type seemed to be slowly crumbling.

But the details of Isabel's personal misfortunes mattered to the ETS staff only insofar as it affected her work. After seeing her soldier through the "whole Larry Stricker imbroglio," her ego and her work ethic bruised but never broken, they believed the indicator would precede everything else in her life, even the care of her dying mother. Plus, she had never thought to ask Chauncey for royalties on the thousands of tests he and his team had sold; all the money from the indicator was going straight in the ETS coffers. "Although she would surely find ways to continue this work under any circumstances, and although her responsibilities for her senile mother have slowed her down considerably, we have gotten a good buy for the research dollar," reported Chauncey.

But by the mid-1960s, the research division had moved on from her and the indicator. "We had a spell of hostility toward any test development activity," Davis recalled, "probably reflecting scars from the MBTI escapade." In 1964, Davis sent a memo to Chauncey titled "The Recent Life and Times of Isabel Myers," wondering if this chapter in her story—her long, tortuous affair with ETS—had come to an end. "How many more years will this continue?" he asked Chauncey. "What is your general feeling about our relationship with her at the present time?" On the one hand, the crude economics of their partnership were not encouraging. Although ETS had distributed the indicator far and wide, they had sunk too much money into validation; it was a commercial failure, especially when compared to the SAT and its $2 million annual revenues. Over two years, gross income from sales of the MBTI had totaled $10,594, a number well below ETS's expectations. In the mid-1960s, users tended to be small consumers ("counselors and personnel officers," Davis qualified), and the large accounts that ETS had coveted in the early days of 1956, like universities, corporations, churches, and government agencies, had never scaled. In hindsight, Chauncey's decision to pay Isabel a consulting fee instead of royalties seemed like a bad gamble. "We would have paid her $642 in 1962–63, and not over $500 for 1963–1964," Davis pointed out. "Her consulting fee will amount, in the two years, to about half the cash or outside income from sales and services. We are losing heavily on this operation." The numbers alone seemed to justify cutting ties. "Technical questions can be and are now answered by ETS staff, so we do not require her for this function," Davis concluded.

And yet, for all her eccentricities, Isabel was not an easy woman to shake. She might never have known it, but they admired her, however begrudgingly won their admiration might have been. "Her work," Davis reflected, "has been timely, appropriate, sound, and responsible. Personally, she seems to treasure the title of ETS consultant as much as the income, though she has never abused this relationship." (He may not have known about her secret trips to Pennsylvania high schools in the spring of 1959.) He marveled at her single-mindedness even if he did not agree with her theoretical commitments. She had "dedicated her life and the life of her family to the concept of type; she believes it to be a profound and extremely important social discovery," he continued. "Anything that may further the development and promulgation of the Indicator and its acceptance by the professional public transcends any other code of behavior" like office politesse or deference to expertise. The decision, he believed, came down to ETS's future investment in the test. "Do we want to maintain it, in spite of financial loss, and have a formal part in the continuing work?" he asked Chauncey.

The answer was yes—but only for one more year, before they cut her loose as a consultant. It was a good year, maybe the best year they had together. She and Davis traveled together to the American Psychological Association conference in Los Angeles, where, amidst the high sun and the dry winds that had once entranced her uncle Bert, she found a stronghold of West Coast Jungian analysts, all eager to hear more about the type indicator. The West acted like "a strong shot in the arm," Davis reported to Chauncey. At the conference, she fell in with a group of nurses who persuaded her to make their profession her next testing ground. "Mrs. Myers became extremely excited about the possibilities of using type to illuminate or predict professional ratings of nurses," Davis added. "No amount of caution, or requests for thinking through carefully, could deter her from coming home via a number of schools of nursing, where she will knock on doors to explore possibilities for administering the MBTI." Riding high on the promise of a new project, she took a long detour from Los Angeles to Palo Alto and Oakland (stopping in to say hello to Donald MacKinnon and his staff), then to Denver, Chicago, and finally Swarthmore, before she arrived in Princeton, where she was greeted with the sudden, strange news that her services were no longer needed.

She took the announcement in stride; she had known their days together were numbered. Out west, she had met people who, unburdened by computers and algorithms, had embraced a more open-minded approach to Jung. Out west, she had heard the siren song of self-care: the keen cry for physical and mental growth that sounded up and down the California shoreline, reverberating through meditation retreats and wellness institutes where people indulged in special diets, exercise regimes, purges, and tests of self-discovery. Out west, she had seen the future of type, and now it called her away from the East with a persistence she could not shake. In California, she had seen her grandson, Jonathan Briggs Myers, and they had had "a grand time talking type," she wrote to a friend. He had reassured her that her work was "too important to be made so inconspicuous."

She did not want to assess the fatal blow ETS had struck her. Without evidence to support its theory or its findings, the type indicator was, in the eyes of psychometricians, little better than a horoscope; she was nothing more than an old, unrelenting charlatan. But she knew there was more to the business of type than numbers and distributions; there was a faith in the theory and its promise of self-discovery that one could not reduce to statistical significance. She did not want to look back. She only wanted to look forward, awaiting the indicator's resurgence among people who shared her intuition for its truth.

Part Three

CHAPTER THIRTEEN

The Synchronicity of Life and Death

Katharine Briggs died in 1968 in Bishop Nursing Home in Media, Philadelphia. She was ninety-three years old, and her mind had long abandoned her body. In one of the last unpublished pieces she wrote, titled "Death and Resurrection— The End of the World," she expressed her satisfaction that she had "achieved the reintegration of the adult personality that Jesus coveted for all mankind." Her "frustrated Maker" may have brought her mind to a "sudden stop with a painful, disabling psychogenic illness," but for the most part, she had lived her extraordinary life on her terms. Even though her "worldly activities had come to an end," she took comfort in the idea that her spirit and her name would live on in her daughter and their shared creation.

Her mother's death spurred a grieving seventy-year-old Isabel to action. ETS may have killed off the indicator, but this did not mean it could not be reborn—"resurrected," as her mother wrote in her last piece, in a "shining, resplendent new form." The next twelve years would be the final, feverish years of Isabel's life as she sought to preserve her and her mother's creation. They would also be the years in which she would grow close to the young woman who would transform type into a global phenomenon, a surrogate daughter born not of Isabel's body but of her philosophical convictions. This woman was a psychologist at the University of Florida named Mary Hawley McCaulley, and it would be her fate to revive the type indicator and launch CAPT—the Center for Applications of Psychological Type— where Isabel's letters and diaries, as well as all the drafts of the type indicator from "A" to "M," would be kept under lock and key to this day.

In learning the story of Mary's life, Isabel must have glimpsed flashes of her own history in Mary's: a happy and protected childhood in a wealthy East Coast suburb; an autodidactical spirit that left her fluent in French, Spanish, Latin, and Greek by the time she entered the University of Rochester; an early marriage to man she had met even earlier in life, her high school ancient history teacher; a job at the school where her husband taught until the principal let her go, attributing his decision to something he called the "nepotism rule": "A husband and wife should not be teaching the same school." And then came World War II, which thrust Mary out of unemployment and into the workforce, first as a volunteer seamstress for the army, then as a caseworker for the Red Cross, and finally as an analyst in the personnel department of Provident Mutual, a life insurance company in Philadelphia. "So here I am, coming out of the humanities, always thinking business is the dullest thing in the world, in the middle of this wonderful place where I got to know everyone from the newest person up to the President," she would recall in the impatient, matter-of-fact tone she would take when talking about the history of type. "I was there for ten years, and being a woman, I wasn't going to go anywhere, obviously."

Working in the personnel department at Provident Mutual, Mary had already developed a habit for categorical thinking of the crudest sort. She may have known everyone from the newest hire to the president, but she knew them only by their job number. "I remember saying to somebody . . . I said, 'I know who you are: 420; you're 420,' and I thought, 'Oh, this is a terrible thing.'" She did not know that just twenty minutes away in Swarthmore, Isabel and Edward Hay were supplying Provident Mutual with dozens of the personality tests that Mary would slot into the company's personnel files every day, the small secretarial task that first piqued her interest in the emergent field of personality research. Her curiosity only amplified when she decided to go to graduate school for psychology in the early 1960s. "Tried out Penn and they were all into brain behavior and the clinicians seemed miserable, so that didn't seem right," she remembered. "Then thought of Columbia. My husband said, 'You are not going to commute to New York, for heaven's sake! That's ridiculous! So I finally went to Temple." It was at Temple that Mary met Dr. Zygmunt Piotrowski, the psychologist who would introduce the Rorschach ink-blot test to America. While she was impressed by how the inkblots compelled psychiatric patients to confront memories they had never acknowledged, let alone shared with anyone else, she found it took far too long to administer and assess for her large backlog of research subjects. So did Henry Murray's TAT, Silvan Tomkins's Picture Assessment Test, and every other projective test on the market. What she needed was a test she could administer to multiple people at the same time and score in under five minutes flat.

She did not find what she was looking for as a graduate student at Temple. Nor did she find it on her journey south to Gainesville, Florida, where her husband had insisted they go so that he might retire in warmer weather. Mary, not yet ready to retire with him, secured a job in the obstetrics department at the University of Florida's hospital, this despite her frequent profession that she had no interest in mothers or young children. "This hospital is very interesting because Gainesville has a very rural, unsophisticated group of people," she observed. The locals she met reminded her of the characters in Marjorie Rawlings's 1938 novel *The Yearling*: poor, simple black folk who did not know enough of the world to have either good or bad intentions toward it. She remembered with a sense of droll amusement her first encounter with a patient. "The first thing a patient ever said to me was a 15-year-old black woman, pregnant, saying, 'They tell me you strap us down on the delivery table because that's the way white people punish black people for having babies.'"

Over time, she developed an interest in the women she treated, not the "Women's Lib kind of 'women in the workplace' interest," she would qualify—she never bothered to conceal her disdain for second-wave feminists and their crusade for labor rights—but the intersections between women's personalities and their bodily acts of "menstruation and pregnancy and labor and delivery and motherhood and stages of motherhood." How did a woman's personality change when she had her period? How did it change when she gave birth for the first, the second, or the third time? Could one evaluate these changes in any systematic way? In a figurative sense, her discovery of type would echo Katharine's and Isabel's turn from their domestic institutions, their daily considerations of childcare and housework, to the public institutions in which typology now thrived: colleges, hospitals, laboratories. Maybe this was just a coincidence; maybe it was something more. Mary would come to believe that it was fate.

. . . .

Mary's favorite word to use when relaying to her friends the story of how she and Isabel met was the Jungian term "synchronicity": a "meaningful coincidence," according to Jung, who developed the concept in the 1950s. Synchronicity was Jung's attempt to explain the improbable pileup of happy accidents that had no causal or rational relationship to one another, a connecting principle that claimed to account for the existence of soul mates, the connection between identical twins, and all manner of paranormal phenomena, from hauntings to extrasensory perception to the sighting of flying saucers. "My life was synchronicity," Mary reflected when asked how she had discovered the language of type. She had stumbled onto her job as a personnel analyst at Provident Mutual through a passing connection—a woman she used to take the train with every day on her way to the Red Cross. That was synchronicity. By sheer happenstance, she had been invited to work with a group of behavioral scientists tasked with writing the first curriculum for high school sex education—a group whose interests in the differences between male and female sexuality had led her to the theories of Jung. That was synchronicity. While poring through recent publications that mentioned Jung, she had discovered an ETS catalog from the mid-1960s, which advertised a test called the Myers-Briggs Type Indicator—a test based on Jung's *Psychological Types*. "I saw 'Jung,' and on a fluke, an absolute fluke," she recalled, "I bought it, sent for it from Educational Testing Service. You had to sign a piece of paper to promise you would not use it for anything practical or applied, because it was a research instrument and they wanted your answer sheets." She went home and took the test herself before administering it to her husband. "My poor husband," she lamented. "All my time learning to be a psychologist, he had to take all these tests I was learning to give. He was an INFP and I'm an INFP." The discovery of the manual, the ordering of the test, the fact that Mary, like Isabel, was an INFP—all this was synchronicity.

She was skeptical at first of "this MBTI thing." But her skepticism began to wane when she started introducing it to her patients and she heard their reactions upon learning their types. "They said, 'Oh, there it is in black and white! My kind of person is okay? All my life people have been telling me to be different.'" She watched the indicator deliver self-discovery time and again, and she thought, "There's more to this MBTI than I realized. I haven't had any other instrument that did this!" The test offered its subjects more than just the possibility of meeting themselves; it offered them a chance at redeeming themselves, pulling them back from the shame of psychological abnormality, celebrating their differences while also preserving their similarities. She wrote a letter to Isabel at ETS, but she was no longer working there as a consultant. That was when "synchronicity hit again." When Mary was invited to a meeting of the Center for the Study of Sex Education Matters at the University of Pennsylvania, she wrote to Isabel's home address and arranged to meet her in the lobby of the hotel where she was staying. This was August 1969, and when Isabel arrived, her hair alloyed gray and white, a little slow in her step, she clasped Mary's hands and said to her, "Everybody who has fallen in love with the indicator without anybody else telling them about it has been an INFP. I am an INFP."

For a meeting that would turn out to be the most important one of Mary's life, very little transpired then and there. The women circled the lobby, talked about type a little bit, and as Isabel walked away, Mary, unimpressed by what she had heard, judged Isabel to be an amateur in the kindest sense of the word. "She hadn't been educated or contaminated by some of the clichés we psychologists have," she judged. Yet something compelled her to seek her out again. The next time the women met was in Swarthmore, in the former bomb shelter of the Myers home, which Chief had converted into Isabel's vault for all her type materials after Richard Nixon became president and the Cold War started to thaw. Mary stayed with the family for a week, and she felt at home amidst the stacks of answer keys, the old hand-crank calculator, and a dozen or so elephant figurines very precisely polished and arranged around Isabel's desk and file cabinets. Isabel was partial to her elephants, cleaned them daily, in fact—a ritual that Mary found funny and romantic given that the rest of the house was a mess. Her hostess, she reported to her friends back home, was a terrible housekeeper, a moderately good cook, and, in her midseventies, largely unconscious of her clothing. When Isabel had opened the door to Mary, she was wearing her favorite nylon dress—the same blue one with pink flowers she had worn the first time she arrived at ETS—only now the blue had faded, the flowers had drooped, and there was a hole under the arm from overuse.

For Isabel, it was like having a daughter come home for a long visit. "She made me think of Ann," Chief said to his wife as he watched how Mary shadowed her, speaking her language of type with an ease that seemed inherited. The visit concluded with an unexpected rite of exchange: not only did Isabel show Mary the scoring keys she had refused to show the men at ETS (lest they fall into the hands of the Russians), but she also made her a duplicate set of "special keys" so that Mary, too, could score tests when she returned to Gainesville. "That was very, very, very sweet," Mary would recall, marveling at how quickly Isabel had grown to trust her and at the magnanimity of her intentions in designing the indicator. "You psychologists, you're always trying to find out what's wrong with people," Isabel had told her, adopting the begrudging, loving tone she always did when maligning the profession she most admired. "And this is not what type is about. Type is about how people reach their own special kind of excellence. This research is just a way for us to understand if people are having trouble on their pathway, how do we help them?"

When Mary returned to Florida, she was determined to complete the mission that ETS had abandoned: to start a research center for type. In the beginning, she had her little obstetrics laboratory and a thousand dollars of discretionary funding from her department. Instead of attending to the labor pains of Gainesville's expectant mothers, she began seeing psychiatric patients—many of them also poor, black, and not fully briefed on what she was doing. She administered the indicator to them and scored their tests in exactly the time she had hoped—five minutes per test. The doctor who had the office next to her was advisor to the university's football team, and he offered to help broaden her sample by "getting Indicators on all of them." "They had better be sensing!" Mary joked to Isabel. "He also has been working with the black students and may be able to get data from them."

With stacks of answer sheets in hand, Mary would wander among the wealthier departments at the University of Florida, begging to steal a little time with their computers. She wanted to see if certain types were more prevalent among certain races and if certain races had different attitudes toward responsibility as measured by the J/P dichotomy. She found a "very undesirable pattern reflecting the shirking of responsibility" in her black test subjects, which "in minority groups," Isabel explained to her, "can mean simply that life is nicer before you grow up and run into the race problem, which must be true." It did not occur to her or Mary that the "race problem" was not something one suddenly ran into; it was ever present in the lives of their subjects. Nor did it occur to them that their conclusions propped up irresponsibility and laziness among minority students as a psychological destiny. Both women seemed too engrossed in their work to reflect on its implications for their subjects.

Every several months, Isabel took the train from Swarthmore to Gainesville to help Mary—her "dear partner in adventure," as she referred to her disciple—sort through her data. As she had done once before, when she was entering the workforce during World War II as an assistant to Edward N. Hay, she offered to work with Mary for free. "I don't like the idea of a consulting fee," she said, recalling the unpleasantness of her situation at ETS and the hoops she had to jump through, the abuse she had to endure, so they could feel comfortable profiting from her creation. Her vision of the future of type was kinder, more democratic, than what any corporate interests would allow. "I'd rather work on my own, creating materials that people anywhere can buy and use if and as they want to," she wrote. "If the materials are good, they will reach many more people than I would ever reach by 'consulting,' with the added advantage that they can go on operating without me, in both space and time." To save money, Isabel would stay at the student union and eat breakfast in the cafeteria. She loved standing before the tray disposal, smiling as she watched students slot their trays onto the conveyor belt that would whip them around the corner and into the kitchen, so that the dishwashers could clear them. On mornings when she felt particularly inspired, she would say her prayers over the dirty dishes. "She had a beautiful childlike appreciation of little things," Mary would recall, moved by the contrast between the complexity of Isabel's mind and the simplicity of her worldly desires. "She was really one of the few authentic geniuses I've ever known," she said, not knowing that Isabel's mother would have disagreed.

At the beginning, Mary and Isabel called their joint venture the "Typology Laboratory," and its setup was just as unassuming as Isabel herself—"a Rube Goldberg, put together with chewing gum and string," Mary described it. To draw attention to the Typology Laboratory, the two women would go "off MBTIing," as Chief referred to their escapades. They would attend conferences together, traveling from Gainesville to Swarthmore, Princeton, and Chicago in sleeper cars, Isabel in the bottom berth, Mary in the top, both working so hard on type that they forgot to look out the window to check what state they were in. At conferences, they shared a hotel room and, because they were both INFPs and thus inclined to overlook minor details, they invented a ritual where each woman would encourage the other to look in her purse before they went out, ensuring they had at least one set of keys between the two of them. They avoided restaurants that Isabel dismissed as "high class," the kind of places where you needed three or four table lamps just to read the menu, and opted instead for bar snacks and Isabel's favorite breakfast spot, McDonald's. They refused to apply for grants to finance their travel

THE SYNCHRONICITY OF LIFE AND DEATH | 235

or their research on the assumption that no grant agency or research board would appreciate—or perhaps approve—what they were doing. "You and I are too much alike—the project is more important than the money," Mary once observed to Isabel. "Men are more pragmatic."

Given the kinds of patients Mary had the easiest access to in Gainesville—pregnant women, young couples—the research the women did together soon began to shift from psychiatric disorders to family therapy. For one year, they typed all the pregnant women who delivered in Mary's OB unit to see if certain types were more prone to postpartum psychoses than others. With the support of three graduate students in psychology, they launched a survey of "marital enrichment," which used the type indicator to predict disagreements between couples. (Scandal erupted when one of the graduate students—an ENFJ, Mary noted in her report to Isabel—ran off with one of the husbands in the study.) Often, they attempted to advise psychiatric in-patients and their spouses alongside the hospital's social workers and doctors, a service they referred to as their "Counselor Program." Their counsel was not always welcome. One young woman's psychiatrists had diagnosed her as a "pseudo-neurotic schizophrenic" and suggested deep hypnosis to help temper her violent outbursts toward her husband. Mary and Isabel insisted that there was no need for such a serious diagnosis or such serious therapy; the woman was simply a feeler while her husband was a thinker and therein lay all the difficulties between them. "F types don't convince T types through histrionics—which is what she has been using," Mary told the patient, advising her to activate her thinking function, while her psychiatrists looked on uncomprehendingly. She scolded them for mismanaging the husband, an ISTJ, who reported feeling "very beleaguered by therapists all telling him he needed to learn to feel."

Over the decade they worked together, they accumulated approximately thirty thousand answer sheets from couples and families. As they began analyzing the data, they found that people were most likely to marry someone who shared two or three of the same type preferences. It was rare to marry someone of your type and equally rare to marry someone who was the opposite of you on every single type dimension. (They did not account for the fact that, if types were equally distributed, chance alone would account for an average of two shared types among couples.) They believed it was important to recognize that certain type combinations were more likely to lead to marital problems than others: the extraverted wife and the introverted husband, the intuitive wife and the sensing husband. "There is a real problem if the wife is an extravert and the man needs his peace and quiet," Isabel wrote in one of her early papers on type and relationships. She and Mary had counseled one couple—an introverted man, an extraverted woman with a job and five children—through the crises they faced because of their type mismatch. The wife was unhappy that her husband did not want to spend time with her and the children when he came home from work. The husband felt pressured, nagged. Isabel advised the wife to leave him alone until he wanted to be bothered. "When he comes home, he is not to be presented with anything in the way of companionship . . . until he has had peace in his own study and signifies that he is now ready to rejoin the family," she ordered her.

The intuitive wife with the sensing husband reported a similar source of friction. She felt like he was a "wet blanket," always poo-pooing her suggestions for romantic, spontaneous activities that would liven up their marriage. He resented her impracticality. What working man had time to go dancing on a weekday night? What did she mean, "Let's get in the car and just drive!" "Very often the sensing member of the marriage ends up feeling like they are always the wet blanket because the intuitive is coming up with these great new possibilities and they are always the one that tells them the grim reality and the facts," Isabel told them. "If you want to present a blazing new idea to your superior officer or boss or spouse . . . you must state it as a problem, a thing that needs to be remedied, needs to be solved." She and Mary dreamed of someday having explicit guidelines for couples of all type combinations.

By the mid-1970s, their Typology Laboratory had become one of the premier centers for marriage counseling in the state, run by two women who now seemed to feel a greater affinity for each other than for either of their husbands. "Here are some pictures of you—not that you don't know what you look like!" Mary had written to seventy-three-year-old Isabel one winter, and she described her mentor with vivid affection as "a self-fulfilled example of what a type, and a beautiful person, can be." In keeping with Isabel's vision of type's appreciation for the human spirit, she and Mary co-christened the lab the "Center for the Applications of Psychological Type, Concerned with the Constructive Use of Differences"—CAPT for short. "CAPT—it's Mary's dream," Isabel would later write on a stray piece of paper, just months before she died. But it was hers too, and she asked Mary to use the logo she had designed: a tiny, perfectly symmetrical type table that testified to her appreciation for the beautiful little things of the world.

. . . .

Isabel had just turned seventy-five when she discovered the body of her daughter, Ann, dead, on the floor of her bathroom, her life claimed by an embolism that had lodged itself in one of her stomach vessels the night after an elective abdominoplasty—a "tummy tuck." The surgery, which had left Ann pale and prostrate, had taken place at a private medical facility somewhere near Cambridge, Massachusetts, where Ann was living for the summer with her lover, Carl Bereiter, the professor of education she had left her husband, Jim, for several years earlier. Isabel, who, unbeknownst to her husband or son, had helped Ann arrange to divorce Jim, flew up from Swarthmore to take care of her daughter while she recovered. She met Carl for the first and only time that night—eight hours in total. There was a brief, easy exchange of pleasantries before he exiled himself to the living room sofa so that mother and daughter, both tired, both frail, might share a bed.

What thoughts must have assailed her when, sometime near dawn, after a series of increasingly urgent knocks on the bathroom door, she opened it and found death lying in wait? Did she think of her grandchildren, Kathy and Doug, relieved that they were not there to see their mother's body? Did she think of Jim, who had escaped to Brazil for work, or of Carl, who had heard Isabel's cries and ran into the bathroom to perform CPR until the ambulance arrived? Did she

think of Chief—"the Chief," as Ann had called her father? He and Ann
had had a terrible fight when she had notified her parents in a letter
that she was leaving her husband for Carl, a man with a wife and two
children of his own. "Since when does an honorable person decide to
chuck overboard a wonderful marriage, distress everybody who loves
her, and decide, at age 42, to pull up stakes; cut loose from most of her
'roots,' and take her children away?" he had written to his daughter,
his rationality contorted by deep disappointment. "It sounds like one
of those horrible movies! It is absolutely unbelievable." More unbelievable, more horrible still, was the phone call Chief would receive
from Isabel as dawn broke on the morning of August 24, 1972. "I don't
know how to tell you this," she wept into the receiver. "She's dead."
Chief appeared in Cambridge the next morning, his demeanor curi-
ously unchanged. He would handle everything in a "lawyerly manner," Carl would recall with a sense of disbelief. Did Isabel consider his
stoicism? Did she register it at all?

Or did she think what any parent who outlives her child must
think? *It was not supposed to happen; not like this.*

She had lost her mother four years earlier, but Katharine's habits of
grief haunted Isabel as she mourned her daughter. She began writing
long religious tracts, orthodox meditations on suffering and endurance that drew inspiration from the holy scriptures and John Bunyan's
Pilgrim's Progress. "The old idea that God and Devil are contending
for our souls can be comforting in times of confusion," she wrote,
"because it gives us the chance to take sides in the fight even before
we are out of the fog. Rejoice not against me, O mine Enemy! When
I fall, I shall arise." She began playing solitaire in the middle of the
night. She shuffled and dealt and exhausted deck after deck until she
had lulled herself into a state of hypnosis—the absence of all thought,
even the most grievous one. She tried as much as she could to forget.
She hid the urn with her daughter's ashes in the home of a friend. She
and Chief dissolved in water a clay bust her granddaughter Kathy had
made to fix her mother's likeness, a child's cold comfort disintegrating
in a matter of minutes between her grandparents' unsteady fingers.
Most astonishing of all, and most reminiscent of her mother's fren-

zied turn to the cosmic laboratory of baby training after the death of her infant son, she began to immerse herself in her work with a determination no one in her family had seen since the early days of the indicator—since she had sat at her kitchen table with Ann and her high school friends for hours, the girls laughing with wonder as Isabel typed each of them. Like her mother and Mary, Ann was—had been—an INFP: a self-reliant perfectionist whose greatest goal in life was to bring hope and happiness to others.

After Ann died, Mary's dedication to type gave Isabel a reason to live. She needed one, badly. Her mother and daughter were dead. The cancer that had first lodged itself in the lymph nodes of her right arm in 1956 had returned fifteen years later as a pair of tumors: one at the top of her right arm, one just under her elbow. After her doctor cut them out, she found the scar tissue unbearable to look at; the missing parts of her body were "sort of a spooky thing," Mary observed. She stopped wearing her favorite nylon dress, stopped wearing dresses altogether because of how they hung on her hollowed arms. She started wearing loose blouses and slacks, which she had never done before, and, because she liked the feeling of them, suspenders. When, in 1975, her oncologist told her a recent scan had revealed a tumor on every vital organ in her body, she started "coping and hoping" that she would secure a permanent publisher for the indicator. She thought she had one year, maybe two if she was lucky, left to live.

ETS, which had dismissed Isabel as a consultant in the mid-1960s, had continued to publish the indicator due to a combination of genuine interest in its findings and bureaucratic inertia. But now it wanted out of the personality testing business altogether—a symbolic act more than a practical one for the MBTI, whose distribution by ETS had dwindled to almost nothing. In the same week that Isabel met with her oncologist, the organization notified Isabel of its decision to sever all ties with her and her creation. "The purpose of this letter is to serve as an Agreement between yourself and Educational Testing Service (ETS) as to termination of the Agreement dated February 3, 1959, and amended on December 2, 1960, and September 1, 1962, concerning the Myers Briggs Type Indicator," the letter stated, a curt history of her vexed sixteen-year relationship with ETS. "In recognition of the fact that ETS is planning to cease operation of the Office of Special Tests, which handled publication of the MBTI, and that ETS has no other office or department to which it is able to assign responsibility for publication and dissemination of these materials, it is hereby agreed that the above referenced Agreement shall be terminated as of December 31, 1975."

"Stuffy bastards!" Chief exclaimed upon reading the letter, but he quickly assimilated his surprise to his thinker's point of view. "There's no point in being miserable about things you can't help," he told his wife. Mary, who had written to ETS some months earlier to tell them "what a goldmine they had with MBTI," was less surprised by their decision. She had suspected that ETS's withdrawal of support was a foregone conclusion—her letter had fallen on deaf ears—but she was worried about the future. Although royalties from sales of the indicator had dwindled to almost nothing by 1975, she speculated that without a reputable publisher the indicator would disappear from the annals of personality psychology forever. "Here is this instrument, the author is not a psychologist, it's never been in a catalogue," she told Isabel. "It'll die if you don't figure out what to do with it!" Isabel was struck by the twin specters of death: the lymphatic cancer that she expected would kill her in the next year or two, now outpaced by the death of her life's work at the hands of ETS. Together, these two "enemies," as she took to calling them, would ensure her total erasure from the world. "Everyone has the sword of Damocles [hanging above his head]," Isabel told Mary. "They're just not so aware."

But then—synchronicity hit again. Isabel was not the only researcher who had felt tossed aside by the Office of Special Tests. Just two years before Henry Chauncey had invited Isabel to ETS, he had asked IPAR's Harrison Gough if ETS could vet the California Psychological Inventory (CPI) that Gough had devised: a questionnaire with 434 true-false items that assessed personality on eighteen different dimensions. Although the CPI had struck ETS's psychometricians as "promising," ETS had concluded that the inventory needed "further validating evidence" before they could commit to publishing it.

This displeased Gough—an "Emersonian nonconformist," according to Chauncey's psychometricians, a pointlessly arrogant man, according to Ravenna Helson. "The CPI is not an instrument in need of elaborate additional symbols of respectability and status," he wrote to Chauncey, bristling at the skepticism of the staff. "It is already accomplishing the things that are only embarrassing impossibilities for most other inventories." When Chauncey refused to be pressured by him, Gough broke with ETS in 1956, and in 1957, with the support of his friend Dr. John Black, a clinical psychologist who would soon become the head of Stanford University's student counseling center, started a test publication company headquartered in Oakland: Consulting Psychologists Press (CPP).

Much to Gough and Black's disappointment, CPP remained a small shop for its first twenty years, operating primarily out of Black's garage. The CPI had endured a brief brush with notoriety in the mid-1950s, when parents in several California school districts had complained that the testing of their children was a violation of privacy, and again in the late 1960s, when angry second-wave feminists had written to complain that one of CPI's scales, "masculinity vs. femininity," was sexist. But with its 434 questions and its eighteen scales, CPI was perhaps too unwieldy and inaccessible to anchor a sustainable testing business. When Mary reached out to Black and Gough in 1975, it was as a last resort; the indicator had already been turned down by testing giant PsychCorp as well as several smaller, but still well-respected, assessment publishers. She had heard about CPP from some allies she maintained at ETS who, angered by the staff's cruel and sexist treatment of Isabel and her work, remembered Gough and thought CPP might be sympathetic to her plight. "There's this college professor at Stanford who's moonlighting with a testing company called Consulting Psychologists Press," they had told Mary. "Maybe you could call him."

When Mary expressed interest in bringing the indicator to CPP, Gough recalled his experience with the Briggs-Myers Type Indicator at IPAR as a promising one. MacKinnon had typed him when he had arrived at the IPAR fraternity house—"My first testing, in the early

1950s, showed me to be an ENTP," he recalled—and, when he had assessed himself again in the 1970s, he had come out an INTJ. ("In my work as a teacher, journal editor, and administrator, I think the judging function has indeed become stronger in the past 25 years," he said, explaining his test-retest unreliability.) Black, the business strategist, was the more cautious of the two partners. He would accept the indicator, he told Isabel, on several conditions. She had to shorten the questionnaire so it would not bore its subjects; Form F, which ETS had "lengthened and strengthened" at the behest of its psychometricians, would become Form G, a 126-item questionnaire that would pick from the best of the forced-choice questions ("*Do you prefer (a) or (b)?*") and word pairs ("*Select the word in each pair that appeals to you more*"). She had to edit her descriptions of the types so that they were "less dogmatic," ensuring that people could self-identify with any given type. She had to give Black full control over the aesthetics of her answer sheets and test booklets, which he wanted to make "more attractive and easier to read." When she balked at his cosmetic choices, he responded with a stern and condescending letter. "I would like to suggest that in an enterprise of this kind, it seems to me that the parties involved have to respect one another's competencies," he wrote. "Your unique and irreplaceable contribution lies in your intuitive ability to devise items with high potential for defining types . . . I think we know more about design, format, type selection, layout, paper and ink selection than you do. Furthermore, you have to remind yourself that I have as much interest as you in broadening the market for MBTI and I do not intend to produce materials that jeopardize that goal."

Isabel, never truly concerned with broadening the market or making money, worried that partnering with CPP would require reorganizing the distribution of the indicator along "business-man lines." Still, she signed her creation over to CPP in 1975; it is hard to imagine that her illness did not influence her decision. She continued to worry that the company was more interested in the indicator's value as a product—a simple, fun, and massively appealing commodity—than in understanding the intricacies of Jungian personality or the intimacies of human relations. But what was she to do when no one else wanted it? In 1977, when Mary visited Isabel after a recent hospitalization to treat her intensifying pain, she noted, "She is not much slowed down but is still a little cowed by Black. (& Peter)." Peter, Isabel's son, and his second wife, Kathy, a former employee of Hay and Associates, had both become involved in the efforts to find a publisher for the indicator once it became clear to them that Isabel would soon die. "We were her apprentices," Kathy later claimed. They had pushed hard for her to partner with CPP, not just approving Black's edits to the type descriptions but insisting that she soften them even further. Isabel could not know that her death would represent more than her relinquishing of control; it would set up the conditions under which the indicator, in its shorter and more appealing form, could truly flourish.

CPP exercised little of ETS's restraint in distributing the indicator; Black and Gough were only too happy to market their wares to anyone who asked, so long as they were willing to pay: psychologists, physicians, spiritual leaders, high school teachers, college career counselors, human resources managers, industry executives, astrologers, artists, writers. And pay they did, for the shorter, unverified Form G test booklet, which came in pretty pale shades of green and blue, bearing a three-dimensional type table on the front. To do away with the time and tedium of sending in answer sheets to CPP to be scored by a computer or hiring a trained psychologist to interpret the results, Black and Gough soon introduced a self-scoring version of Form G. This made the consumer—or "client," as they preferred to call the buyer—solely responsible for assessment and interpretation. "It might be argued that a self-scoring version embedded in an explanatory booklet would provide additional security," they reasoned in their marketing memos. "Correct interpretations would be in the client's hands even if incorrect explanations were given to the client orally . . . Proper uses of the MBTI in any of its forms, would, of course, be enhanced."

Once CPP had managed to silence all the ethical objections and obstacles to selling the indicator, the company's revenues climbed— from ten thousand dollars in 1975 to one hundred thousand dollars in 1979, a "strong and inexorable growth curve with no plateau in sight," boasted Black at the Third International Conference on Myers-

Briggs, which was held in Philadelphia on Isabel's eighty-second birthday, mere months before she died. The guest of honor was in attendance, too frail to stand or speak on her own. All she could do was listen. "It's not even that Isabel doesn't look her age," Black observed. "I think the reason we're here is that Isabel doesn't act her age." Just a year earlier, he recalled, he had thought any publisher was "crazy to get mixed up with an octogenarian author." But Isabel had proven him wrong, and the proof, as she liked to say, was in the pudding. By the end of 1979, CPP had sold more than a million answer sheets. "Imagine! A million people will have learned about type!" Black reported Isabel exclaiming when he had told her the good news. Isabel, pained but smiling from her place at the banquet table, had nothing to add.

The last time Mary saw Isabel was two weeks before she died in 1980. She had retained so much water from the cancer treatments that "she looked like she was nine months pregnant," Mary recalled. But her force of will remained intact—she would touch her swollen ankles, her wrists, her stomach, and say, "The enemy is here," but the enemy no longer hurt her as he once had. The indicator was safe if not entirely sound; she was ready to go. On May 5, 1980, the morning of her death, her remaining family—Peter and his wife, her grandchildren, Chief—gathered beside her bed, where she was resting underneath her favorite chenille blanket, patterned with marching Indian elephants and tigers. One of her grandchildren, offering a prayer of sorts, misquoted one of her favorite lines of poetry. She drew a breath, corrected him, and, shortly thereafter, died in her sleep. Some days later she was cremated and her husband, after retrieving the urn with Ann's ashes from their neighbor's house, scattered his wife and his daughter to the winds.

CHAPTER FOURTEEN

One in a Million

Some people start to live only when they die; others stay unrecognized, their labors lost to time. In the case of Isabel Briggs Myers, both posthumous states held true. The Myers-Briggs Type Indicator became the most popular personality inventory in the world; Isabel's names—maiden and married, forever conjoined—were shorthand for the whole strange business of personality testing. But only the smallest fraction of those who encountered the indicator knew anything about Isabel, Katharine, or the origins of type. If asked about the indicator's provenance, most people would have assumed that Myers and Briggs were the last names of two collaborating psychologists—two men, naturally—who had built their long, lucrative careers within the same institutions that had supported Henry Murray, Donald MacKinnon, Edward N. Hay, Henry Chauncey, and Harrison Gough. It was as if Isabel herself and her various personae—daughter, housewife, mother, writer, creator, entrepreneur—needed to die so that her creation could live.

Imagine the million people who, according to John Black, had learned about type by 1980. A million was a large, happy number, of course, but it was also an abstraction, free from any sense of consequence. Where did they encounter the indicator? What did learning one's type do for each one of these million people? No doubt it did different, incommensurable things from person to person. ("You are not one of sixteen. You are one in a million," declared CAPT in a 1990 marketing campaign.) But one could apprehend in ten, twenty, a hundred separate accounts of learning one's type the emergence of certain undeniable patterns: the first rush of self-discovery, the cheerful lull of self-acceptance, the comfort of solidarity. You may have been one in a million, but part of the appeal of type was imagining that there were others out there like you: people whose lives had arced toward type at different moments but who had all come away from it with understanding and affirmation.

Imagine, then, a child—a bright, impressionable little boy or girl enrolled in an affluent school district in Chicago or Los Angeles or New York, the kind of school where parents who have learned the language of type from self-improvement seminars or wellness retreats are eager to bequeath it to their offspring. Reporting from the auditorium of Irvine's Greentree Elementary in June 1982, the *Los Angeles Times* observed the youngest participants in the Social Thinking and Reasoning (STAR) program, an MBTI-based educational experiment funded by an $800,000 grant from the Department of Education. Nine- and ten-year-olds wearing sequined sock puppets on one hand and holding cue cards in the other nervously shifted from high-top to high-top, as their puppets ventriloquized statements like

> "I'm an introvert. I need to be alone to recharge my batteries. It's important for people to know introverts like other people."

> "I'm an NT. We NTs have a great desire to accumulate knowledge and wisdom. Sometimes I may appear cold. But I don't like to show my feelings. It makes me feel not in control."

> "I'm an NF. We're idealistic. We like meaningful relationships."

Now imagine that child three or four years later, after she has discarded her hand puppet and forgotten her lines. She is in a middle school home economics class, although no one calls it that in 1985, preferring more up-to-date titles like "Work and Family Studies" or "Family and Consumer Sciences." Her teacher distributes an MBTI questionnaire and answer sheet, and she tells students that knowing one's type will help them navigate difficult discussions around drug use and premarital sex—the students giggle and groan—and, in a less prurient vein, dating, marriage, work relationships, and parenthood. The test is "designed to meet the needs of the kids today [and] to help them to get ready to have strong families in the future," one middle school teacher from Fairfax, Virginia, explains to a reporter from the *Washington Post*. Knowing the positive and negative attributes of each type helps construct a thoroughly "modern view" of the family as a complex behavioral-economic unit; "both parents work and are trying to balance careers and personal lives" in different and often incompatible ways. Some kids rely on after-school specials or *Seventeen* magazine to hone their basic life skills. These kids lean on type to learn how to be healthy and wholesome.

A half decade later, the teenager who used her type knowledge to learn how she could just say no to drugs and alcohol and yes to the right man applies to college. When she is accepted, she learns that deans and counselors at many schools use the MBTI to match incoming students to their freshman-year roommates, hoping to "decrease odd couples" on campus. "Self-discovery is a significant part of the educational process," declares Cindy Crowe, a counselor at the University of South Carolina's Counseling Services Center. She warns students that the process can be "extremely difficult," but the MBTI, which Cindy is grateful to have discovered one summer in the late 1980s, offers a "painless," "easy," "non-intimate," and "psychologically patriotic" tool to size up one's personality. The student can clarify her sense of self—good for choosing a major and, eventually, a job—and smooth out difficult relationships with roommates by answering questions as simple as *"Do you prefer (a) small parties, or (b) large gatherings?"* or *"When the truth would not be polite, are you more likely to tell (a) a polite lie, or (b) the impolite truth?"* Sister Susan Randolph, the housing director at the College of Saint Benedict, a small midwestern women's college, claims that the MBTI has helped her assign 60 percent of students to their "ideal roommates": students with whom they matched on three out of four of the indicator's dimensions. "With the pressure a college student faces, dealing with an unacceptable roommate can be overwhelming," she says. The counseling team at the University of Wisconsin has even more faith in the indicator than Sister Susan; they offer a monthlong summer course for roommates based on Myers-Briggs called "I'm Going My Way, and You're Going Yours, How Can We Arrive Together?"

Four years later, the college freshman who embarked on her painless journey of self-discovery through type is, for all intents and purposes, an adult, eager to enter the white-collar workforce. She quickly learns that this is not her parents' job market. "It's a different world out there," warns a 1991 article in the *Chicago Tribune.* People in America no longer make products; they *are* products and they "can and should be marketed just like soap, luxury cars, and facsimile machines," one personality consultant tells the *Wall Street Journal.* Gen X job candidates must show up to interviews looking sharp—the author recommends suspenders and wire-rimmed glasses for men, blazers with shoulder pads for women—and brace themselves to take "the Myers-Briggs test, which determines your strengths and interests, what your style is and how you react in situations." Type is one of the best marketing techniques for selling yourself. It gives you a four-letter brand instantly legible to the white, well-educated professionals working the kind of job she wants to get. "There are as many office types as Mr. Potato Head has personas. Do you understand yours?" asks the *Times-Picayune.*

She must also anticipate that some people will not want to hire her based on her type. "Have you ever been so frustrated by some employees' inability to make quick decisions on really simple issues that you put those wooly thinkers on a list of no-can-do types?" asks an ENTJ columnist, a technology entrepreneur, in the *Wall Street Journal.* The MBTI is the best way he knows of to avoid these annoying hiring mistakes. "Insights provided by the MBTI are so extraordinarily useful that the test should be routinely administered to adults as they enter the workforce," he gushes. His sentiments are echoed by human relations teams in nearly every Fortune 100 company as well as CPP, recently the subject of some harsh criticism after studies by psychologists showed that people who take the test more than once, even just a few weeks apart, get classified as a different type more than

50 percent of the time. The MBTI's test-retest validity is well below acceptable levels of statistical significance. "Four of the 16 Myers-Briggs types account for 80% of managers," shoots back CPP executive Lorin Letendre, citing "extensive studies" conducted by CPP. "That's extremely statistically significant."

Yet disputes over statistical significance matter little to our job seeker when she enters her cubicle on the first day of work. She does not know that her office has been configured by Herman Miller, the world's leading office furniture designer, with a computer program that uses a modified version of the MBTI to analyze the personality types of white-collar workers to help engineers, designers, and architects allocate office space, ergonomic furniture, and technology among them. "We have found that only 8 percent of workstations fit the personalities of workers using them," proclaims John Berry, Herman Miller's director of communications, though he does not specify how the company has managed to arrive at such a precise number. The company's computer program administers a hundred-item questionnaire and identifies its subject as one of four personality types: the visionary ("one who looks at the big picture"), the catalyst ("a people person, a leader"), the stabilizer ("an efficient machine"), and the cooperator ("a friendly person"). It then assigns interchangeable furniture components to the worker's office based on his preference for privacy versus socialization, concentration versus distraction. The ideal office of a visionary, a man who "could never have enough books and liked a window with an interesting office view," has dark, elegant bookshelves, ample display space, and a corner work surface. The ideal office of a stabilizer is "cock-pit like"—neat, spare, silent.

Nor do the MBTI's empirical failings faze her if she decides, after several years of industry experience, to go to law school and become a corporate lawyer or a litigator. In 1993, the American Bar Association administers the indicator to more than three thousand lawyers to learn how different types dealt with coworkers and clients. According to Larry Richards, the former trial lawyer turned management consultant who runs the study, one of every two lawyers identifies as a thinking and judging type, "aggressive, vocal, time-driven and one who [likes to] cut to the chase," Richards summarizes. Richards left the profession some years ago when he took the MBTI and discovered that he was a feeling and perceiving type; he longed for adventure and spontaneity, not long nights at the office "battling deadlines, forced to be orderly." He has seen "feelers" like himself "get into trouble" in big law firms, where 77 percent of lawyers are thinkers, he notes. In his sample, military lawyers score highest on the thinking scale, followed by specialists in labor, patent, tax, real estate, and divorce law. The only clear feelers are woman lawyers who specialize in legal aid and public interest law, which Richards describes with pointed tact as "less conventional practice areas." One lawyer, a defense attorney for executives of financial institutions, is relieved to learn that she has a "good amount of empathy, but not enough to interfere with the ruthless behavior you have to exhibit when dealing with the government." Another woman going through a "minor midlife crisis" yearns for the test to tell her that she was never meant to be a lawyer so she can justify quitting her job. She is distressed to find out that her type makes her "a pretty good lawyer." So she stays.

Think, once more, of the child from the beginning, who now has spent the last decade of her life as a lawyer in a cockpit-like office and wants to try something new. But what are the right things for her? How can she find out? Perhaps she lives in New York City and can enroll in "Using Your Personality Type to Find the Right Job," a three-hour, sixty-five-dollar course at the New School, where attendees take the MBTI and receive a one-on-one counseling session. There, she might meet Susan, a Wall Street trader since the late 1970s, who discovers that she is an ESFJ—a "provider type," she is told by the course leader—and that the cutthroat world of high finance is ill-suited to her personality type. She might share a cigarette with Gary, an aspiring novelist who, upon learning that he is a "highly rational," "entrepreneurial" ENTJ, decides to return to his job as a management consultant; the "radical change" he wants for his life will have to wait. If she wants a deeper, more individually tailored analysis of her personality and her prospects than what Susan and Gary have experienced, she will have to pay more; the New School's course is on the very low end of MBTI consulting services. Many personality consultancies now charge upwards of five thousand dollars per session to administer the test and help a client strategize how best to market herself to a new employer based on her type. The world of the MBTI in the 1990s is a far cry from Edward N. Hay's office in 1943, but there is no way for her to know this, just as there is no way for her to know about the two women responsible for the direction her life has taken, the writers of her life story.

She markets herself and changes careers, working hard for the next twenty years or maybe more and rarely looking back. Upon retiring, she decides it is time to take care of herself, to get back in touch with who she is and what she wants of the years that remain. She knows she can find in almost any city, on almost any weekend, a church or synagogue or "spiritual life center" offering workshops on "living and loving" through the MBTI. She can participate in any number of luxurious, all-inclusive retreats or "personal development seminars," sitting for the indicator in the morning and learning how to care properly for her aging hair, skin, nails, and wardrobe in the afternoon. ("Would you rather die than wear a gaudy Hawaiian shirt? You may be an ISTJ. Have you dropped out of school or spent time in jail? You may be an ISFP," says the organizer of one such seminar. Another matches celebrity clients like Elle Macpherson and Kyra Sedgwick to exercise regimens that are "spiritually appropriate" for their MBTI type.) She can travel for these seminars, perhaps abroad to Florence ("Italy is an extraverted country," claims a CAPT research report on national types) or Paris ("We may think of the French, uncivil to tourists, contentious in the legislature, and the home of Descartes, and declare 'France is a nation of thinking types'"). Or she can sign up for an American "identity quest," paying thousands of dollars to take the test in the deserts of New Mexico or the mountains of Colorado. She can drum and dance under the moonlight to "enhance her Sensing Self." She can fashion a clay vessel in which to deposit her "New Found Self" and, possibly, her ashes when she dies, old and tired yet satisfied, after a lifetime of self-discovery.

. . . .

After Isabel's death, there no longer existed one beating heart, one tireless and exacting intellect to regulate the MBTI's emergence as a mass cultural phenomenon in the 1980s and 1990s. Unleashed by CPP on an eager and largely untutored public, the indicator traversed thousands of primary and secondary schools, colleges, workplaces, hospitals, and churches, as well as a vast network of Jungian enthusiasts; people who, after Isabel and her mother, started referring to themselves as "type watchers." Type watchers congregated in certification and training programs around the world, some sanctioned by CAPT, others homegrown affairs that took place in basements and backyard barbeques. They shook hands at health-care and education conferences, where they exchanged tips on how best to care for feeling types, how to motivate students who were introverts in classrooms dominated by extraverts. They embraced one another at wellness and healing seminars, where they discussed the sexual, emotional, and spiritual compatibilities of S's and N's, J's and P's. They wrote articles for the CAPT newsletter, which carried news of the indicator from Gainesville, Florida, to Melbourne, Australia. Among the most devoted type watchers were the nine thousand men and women who paid membership dues to the Association for Psychological Type (APT), a sister organization to CAPT that Peter's second wife, Kathy Myers, had assumed command of just before Isabel's death.

Even within this great and growing mass of type enthusiasts, certain individuals emerged as type's most impassioned spokespeople. "I believe that in the world of psychological theory, the '80s will belong to Carl Jung," prophesied Otto Kroeger, a round, red-faced, and emphatically upbeat Lutheran minister who, in the mid-1970s, had left the church to devote his life to spreading the gospel of type. Known around Washington, D.C., as "Mr. MBTI," Kroeger had started the most popular MBTI certification program in the world through his consulting firm Otto Kroeger Associates (OKA), a "mom-and-pop operation" that was committed to "helping individuals make breakthroughs, both large and small." When it came to teaching people about type, "the first big thing is self-insight," Kroeger declared in a 1981 interview. The second was "self-management." In his 1988 book,

Type Talk: The 16 Personality Types That Determine How We Live, Love, and Work, which Kroeger coauthored with his wife Janet Thuesen, an assistant director at the Department of Education, the couple identified the "fundamental gift" of type as "the ability to manage yourself more effectively by understanding yourself more completely in any situation." These situations included everyday scenarios like these:

- You're in the express checkout line, the sign says "10 Items or Less," and it appears that the person in front of you can't count;
- The very thing that attracted you to your partner or spouse is presently driving you apart; or
- Your boss has assigned you to work with (or for) someone whose style you find anywhere from mildly irritating to downright infuriating.

The marriage of self-insight to self-management was a highly profitable union, tapping right into the ethic of entrepreneurialism that posited personality as a product that could be inventoried, refined, marketed, and sold across multiple domains: the church, the state, the workplace, the marriage market. Kroeger secured lucrative contracts with clergymen and the army, with wealthy Washington couples seeking nuptials counseling, and with the National War College, the stomping grounds for America's "warrior elite." Most students tested as ISTJs, a type Kroeger described with great solemnity as "the guardians of time-honored institutions, and, if only one adjective could be selected, dependable." The rest were ESTJs, "outstanding at organizing orderly procedures and in detailing rules and regulations."

The quasi-spiritual convergence of self-insight and self-management appealed primarily to "corporate America," which, Kroeger and Thuesen claimed, now needed executives who were "more sensitive and flexible and less fixated on profits and productivity." The dizzying ascension of the service economy in the 1970s and the temporary, immaterial forms of labor it valued—"soft" or "transferrable skills" like networking and team building, leadership and communication—had put tremendous pressure on corporations to attend to, and even celebrate, the social and emotional dimensions of their employees. This was not, as Kroeger and Thuesen suggested, because profits and productivity were any less important to corporate America than flexibility or sensitivity but precisely because the flexibility of work and workers was what allowed companies to profit. "Work is elastic," observed Barbara Moses, author of the 1997 best-selling guide *Career Intelligence: Mastering the New Work and Personal Realities.* As workplaces were "increasingly organized around teams that coalesce around a project and dissolve once its objectives have been achieved," everyone labored under the same conditions of precarity and experienced the same need to "market themselves" once a project was complete. Extraverts had great success "networking their way into the best projects," while introverts excelled at "working from home or on the road"—a perfect fit, Moses claimed, now that companies were outsourcing more jobs to independent consultants.

Many corporations were happy to pay consultancies like OKA to help their employees become the best versions of themselves through type discovery; they believed in "investing in people." In a 1996 article entitled "Earning It: Personal Trainers to Buff the Boss's People Skills," the *New York Times* profiled several midlevel executives who had been asked to undergo MBTI-based career counseling when their personalities started interfering with their abilities to manage happy and high-functioning teams. "I was angry and humiliated at first," testified a woman whom colleagues had described as "a pain in the neck." She continued: "But I was also open to it. I said if the company wants to pay for me to get some coaching, I'm smart enough to realize this is not any different than if I went for computer training." Her coach asked her to take the indicator. "The more we talked, the more the light bulb went on," the woman reported after learning her type, which she chose not to disclose. "When my boss asks me to do something, I should say, 'Sure, no problem.' If I felt somebody asked me something stupid, I might still feel angry, but now I hide it. That's what I learned." Often, the best version of someone was the most complacent version, eager to please both the people she worked for and the people who worked for her. "My people skills needed to be polished," reported one woman, whose subordinates complained that she acted like "a dictator rather than a mentor." Learning how to be a mentor meant softening one's hard edges, making herself more available and pliable to the company's needs.

Personality testing and training was more than just a worthwhile investment in people; it was good public relations in workplaces increasingly committed to showcasing diversity and tolerance as profitable skills. "Many consultants first conduct what they call a 'corporate audit,'" reported the *New York Times* in a 1992 article on promoting diversity in the workplace. "They interview groups of employees about the company's corporate culture: the way employees are selected, assigned jobs and promoted; whether extroversion is valued over introversion, and whether employees' ideas are routinely sought . . . Some consultants have managers and employees take personality tests like the Myers-Briggs Test, which helps determine how certain personality traits lead to race or gender stereotypes." A 1997 guide for dealing with sexual harassment issued by Equal Opportunities recommended hiring a personnel consultant to assess employees' types so that they might learn "to appreciate the variety of communication styles" in the workplace, thereby avoiding embarrassing misinterpretations (or lawsuits) concerning sexist or racist "jokes" or "light hearted fun." OKA's offerings included articles and workshops with titles like "The Anatomy of Misunderstanding: Sexual Harassment & Type," "The Changing Face of Banking," "Bringing the Feeling Function into Top Management," and "Uncle Sam Wants All Types."

Kroeger and Thuesen's vision of better self-management through self-insight did not acknowledge any distinction between labor and leisure; where personality was concerned, what was true for the workplace was true for the home. In their second book, *16 Ways to Love Your Lover,* the couple drew on their marriage for examples of how knowing one's type could help husbands and wives manage each other, so that their behavior would converge on mutually satisfying outcomes. They described themselves as the typical sloppy woman/ neat man couple, a P married to a J. Although he identified as a "strong N," Kroeger admitted that he could be "very detail oriented in some areas" and that, as a J, he liked living a well-ordered life. He felt especially distressed when Thuesen forgot to polish the chrome faucets in the shower or put away the telephone book or make the bed in the mornings.

"I can't imagine a bed not made," he groaned.

Thuesen, who admitted to "not sweating the small stuff," said she did not mind accommodating Kroeger's fastidiousness. "I can wipe down the faucets after a shower so that they're shiny and not all spotted," she said. "I don't care and he does, so I'll give him that. It's a little concession that makes life easier for him, and I can do without calling him neurotic."

While some couples spent evenings at home, talking about their days, and others went out for drinks and dinner, Kroeger and Thuesen admitted to sitting in front of the television and "indulging in type watching just for fun." "We can't help it," they said in unison, and Thuesen added, "We apply it all over." They liked applying it to sitcoms, as many television writers used type to develop a well-balanced cast of characters, and especially to advertisements. "Like the ads for Hyundai cars," Thuesen explained. "They appeal to sensing types, which is very smart, since about 70 percent of people in this country are sensing types."

Both at home and at work, they appeared to be the perfect couple for the new service economy: receptive, flexible, always open to compromise, and, most important of all, self-governing.

. . . .

"Imagine! Over two million people *per year* take the type indicator," John Black might have said to Isabel if either of them had lived to see the dawn of the twenty-first century, when the MBTI secured its place as the most popular personality inventory in the world. One wonders what Isabel would have made of the indicator's creeping growth on the backs of type watchers like Kroeger and Thuesen: how its dizzying, indiscriminate diffusion through popular practices of self-management and business psychology expanded its reach while diluting her ideas, making the whole enterprise of personality assessment more vulnerable to criticism than it already was. She was an austere and ambitious person, determined to be taken seriously, and so she certainly would not have approved of the kitschy goods that CAPT, CPP, OKA, and other consultancies started manufacturing to make Myers-Briggs a household name: type T-shirts ("ENFPs give life an extra squeeze!" "INTJs can improve this T-shirt!"), lapel pins, mouse pads, playing cards, songbooks. How could she when they made the process of self-discovery into a silly slogan or a poorly rhymed song set to the tune of "My Favorite Things":

Flavors and colors and sounds of the seasons
Touching and tasting are certainly pleasin'
Check in with us if you want the details
You'll never find that our memory fails

O sensation, sweet sensation
You fill life with spice
You'll never know 'til you work on your "S"
That being can be so nice.

Yet before the 2000s, it still seemed possible to sing these words without a trace of irony, much as Katharine had once sung her paeans to Jung. Whatever else the type watchers of the 1980s and 1990s might have been, they were unflagging in their devotion to the indicator and the theory behind it. But the earnestness that characterized their culture of type would be difficult to sustain as its presence and influence grew. "Visibility brings its own challenges," cautioned Mary McCaulley in 1987. "The assumptions and construction of the MBTI are increasingly challenged . . . It is essential that we continue to work constructively to protect and expand a body of work which is literally improving people's lives around the world." Her call was echoed a decade later by Kathy Myers in a 1998 interview. "The MBTI has experienced such phenomenal growth that there is an increased danger of [it] being used superficially," she observed. "We need to maintain a critical mass of people dedicated to the integrity of the system and the inspiring vision of Carl Jung, Katharine Briggs and Isabel Myers. Otherwise the MBTI will be a fad and something valuable will be lost." Just two years away from the turn of the century, their fears were justified.

Imagine again a child, but of a different generation: a millennial. She does not need a test to encourage her to discover and appreciate her true self; her entire education, a carousel of customized curricula and creative projects, of bespoke apps and after-school activities, already revolves around it. Born into Web 2.0, she opened her Facebook account in ninth grade, her Instagram in tenth. Like Jay Gatsby, she too is constituted by an "unbroken series of successful gestures," only her gestures are archived in a litany of clicks, posts, likes, and shares that anyone can scroll through or search or scrape for data, projecting her personality from the work she has put into curating her online persona. She knows that a traditional education is important— she is part of the most educated generation in history—but she also knows that education is no substitute for experience when it comes to discovering and developing one's life story.

Unlike her Gen X counterparts, she seems to have a native fluency in the language of service work. After she graduates from college, saddled with more debt than her parents, she starts to speak matter-of-factly about "selling yourself," "optimizing your work-life balance," and "staying flexible." These words are, if anything, more central to her survival, as she has entered the workforce at an especially dismal moment. As the post-2008 economy has substituted permanent, stable employment for small, part-time gigs, she must sell herself over and over again just to pay her rent and keep food on the table. She is no stranger to marketing her personality. Her livelihood depends on it. "The Biggest Financial Asset in Your Portfolio Is You," announces a *New York Times* article that orders her to take a personality test to "engage your human capital at the highest level." She obeys, and she is not the only one. The market for workplace personality assessments is now a staggering two billion dollars, and according to a recent report from Facebook, online conversation has grown around the terms *Myers-Briggs Type Indicator* and *personality.*

Her relationship to her personality is wry and self-ironizing; she knows she is a product, just as she knows that there is nothing she can do about it except gently mock her conditions of production. When she is not searching the internet for freelance jobs, she is taking BuzzFeed quizzes with parodic titles like "What's Your Animal Personality Type?" or "Pick Some Hats and We'll Guess Your Personality Type." Her favorite type tables are the ones that speculate about the personalities of pop cultural icons or fictional characters. ("Who Are You? *Game of Thrones* MBTI." "Who Are You? *Harry Potter* Personality Chart.") If she is single, she reads terrible, banal dating advice in *Elle* and *Teen Vogue* about how different types approach romance: "ENTJ: You'll stay single until someone stops you in your tracks." "ISFJ: You want someone to sweep you off your feet." "ENFJ: You want to share everything with someone special." She cannot afford to take the actual MBTI, and so she hunts online for knockoff versions, websites advertising a "Free Personality Test" from 16Personalities or "MBTI/Jung Personality Test" from Psych Central. She posts the results of the test on her Facebook page and her OkCupid and Tinder profiles, hoping someone will notice and that it will spark his interest. "What's your type?" she imagines asking, half jokingly, on their first date.

It is one of the small ironies of history that Isabel died before she could see the extent to which mass culture hollowed out her creation, a sad irony or a merciful one, depending on one's perspective. There was always a danger that this was where type would end up, among the silliest, shallowest cultural products of late capitalism. After all, the logical extension of typological thinking was that type itself would stiffen and standardize in its bid for universality. The more rapidly type circulated through knockoff tests and advice columns, the more its descriptions of people's personalities would reduce to one-word caricatures. "The market is glutted with self-assessment tools," reports Bob Kaplan, a leadership consultant and author of *The Versatile Leader: Making the Most of Your Strengths Without Overdoing It*. "Everybody and their brother is putting them out there on some basis, or very little basis." (This was the case not only for internet versions of the indicator but also for purportedly serious follow-ups to it. Take, for instance, these type descriptors from David Keirsey and Marilyn Bates's popular 1984 book, *Please Understand Me*: "Pedagogue (ENFJ)," "Author (INFJ)," "Journalist (ENFP)," "Questor (INFP)," "Fieldmarshal (ENTJ)," "Scientist (INTJ)," "Inventor (ENTP)," "Architect (INTP)." The distortion of type was the first inevitable consequence of its dramatic decontextualization. Only a decade into the twenty-first century, it was no longer possible for an early adopter of type like Mardy Ireland, OKA client and psychologist at George Washington University's counseling center, to claim of the MBTI, "The more you use it, the richer it becomes. It never goes flat."

The consequence was that the indicator could no longer hide its classifying impulses behind the ideological veil of individualism. By the new millennium, CAPT's 1990 marketing campaign—"You are not one of sixteen. You are one in a million"—could not be uttered without skepticism, maybe even an eye roll, at the naïveté of the sentiment. The cultural logic of type was out in the open for anyone with a browser to see; it could no longer sustain the delicate fiction of striking a balance between individual uniqueness and social order. Would Isabel have despaired at the breakdown of the indicator's cultural logic? Or would she, in all her unflagging optimism, have taken this new language of type as proof that the indicator had greater appeal than she had ever known?

Here is one thing about which there can be no doubt. She would have been heartened by the testimonials of the thousands of people who, upon discovering type, claimed that it had helped them clarify not just who they were but who they wanted to be, the people who seemed untouched by irony even today. "I have run into people who have been pressured by their parents and family and tried to conform to being a particular sort of person, and then they run into the indicator and decide that this is a liberation and they are absolutely not going to be repressed anymore and they go ahead and be their own person," she said in one of the last talks she gave at the University of Florida. It was to these people that she would have turned when faith in the indicator ebbed, when sales declined, when knockoffs circulated, when the membership of APT dropped, as it began to do in the twenty-first century. Had she lived to see the days when type watchers began to peel away from the MBTI's guardian institutions, when the indicator became a parody of itself, she would have immersed herself in the people who had sustained her throughout the life of type: the true believers.

True Believers

To obtain a hard copy of Form M of the Myers-Briggs Type Indicator, the latest iteration of the questionnaire, one must spend $2,095 on a weeklong certification program run by the Myers & Briggs Foundation—the sister organization to CAPT. In 2015, there were close to one hundred certification sessions in cities ranging from New York to Pasadena, Minneapolis, Portland, Houston, and CAPT's hometown of Gainesville, where participants could get a $300 discount for making their way south to the belly of the beast. It was not unusual for sessions to sell out months in advance. People came from all over the world to get certified.

The session I attended to gain access to Isabel Myers Briggs's archives, and that launched me into the orbit of the MBTI to begin with, took place in New York in April 2015. There were twenty-five aspiring MBTI practitioners in attendance: a slick British oil executive who lived for half the year under martial law in Equatorial Guinea; a pretty blond astrologer from Australia, determined to "invest in herself," she told me, as her U.S. visa was about to expire; a Department of Defense administrator, a recent divorcée who went to Bloomingdale's during the lunch breaks and came back with shopping bags full of flimsy floral skirts and loud patterned tops; and a jovial high school basketball coach who, until recently, had worked as a manager at IBM. There were three college counselors from New York City public schools, five human resources representatives, and a half-dozen "executive talent managers" from various Fortune 500 companies. We sat at tables of five or six. Each of us wore a name tag with our first name, last name, and our four-letter type printed on it in large block letters. It was not unusual for people to lead with their type when they introduced themselves.

I said hello to the woman sitting next to me. Her name tag said ENFJ.

She looked at my tag (ENTJ) and sighed. "We're both E's," she said. "We'll get along great."

Once our instructor, Patricia, had reviewed the three rules of "speaking type fluently"—type is a valid Jungian framework of self-discovery, type is not a test, type is innate—she started her weeklong attempt to convince us that Katharine and Isabel's simple system of thought could account for nearly all our personal and interpersonal relationships, regardless of our backgrounds: our gender, our race, class, age, language, education, or any of the other contextual intricacies of modern existence. As she presented it, type was intensely democratizing in its vision of the world, weird and wonderful in its commitment to flattening the differences between people only to construct new and imaginary borders around the self. "As long as you have a seventh-grade reading level and you're a 'normal' person"—by which Patricia meant you were not mentally ill—"you could learn to speak type successfully." After all, the indicator's sole measure of success was how well your results aligned with your perception of yourself. Did you agree with your designated type? If you did not, then the problem lay not with the indicator but with you. "Maybe you were in a work mind-set when you answered the questions," Patricia suggested. Or maybe you had become so adept at "veiling your preferences" to please other people—your spouse, your children, your coworkers— that you had lost touch with your true self.

Beyond all the pseudoscientific talk of "indicators" and "instruments" was a simple but subtle truth: the questionnaire reflected whatever version of yourself you wanted it to reflect, whether consciously or unconsciously. You could quickly become attuned to the pattern of the questions, their basic idiom of sociability, creativity, rationality, impulsivity. If you wanted to see yourself as odd and original or factual and direct, it required only a little bit of imagination to nudge the answers in the right direction. I did not observe this in any overtly manipulative sense. People wanted to answer in earnest, for to lie outright would have been to derail the practice of self-discovery the indicator promised. But to succeed, the indicator had to introduce the test subject to the preferred version of herself and to claim this self as the "true you"—unchanging and whole. This was the only way to link its simple, sometimes hackneyed, questions ("*Are you inclined to: (a) value sentiment more than logic; or (b) logic more than sentiment?*") to the experience of meeting your unified and purified self.

What also became apparent throughout the training was that the impulse to treat personality as complete and innate was, in no small part, a convenient way of slotting people into their designated niches in a high-functioning and productive social order. This was another fiction—a dystopian fiction, to my mind—that most contemporary personality tests continued to trade in: the fantasy of the rational organization of labor. "The MBTI will put your personality to work!" promised a career assessment flyer one of the college counselors shared with the trainees, a promise that was echoed by the many leadership guides and self-help books that Patricia referenced during the week. "For companies today, business is all about the participative management of things," she claimed. "The old command-and-control approach doesn't work. You have to bring feeling into it." To believe that one was ideally suited to do one's job still meant to do it well and to do it willingly—to embrace one's work under the belief that everyone was exactly where he or she was meant to be. Or as one trainee belted out in the middle of an exercise, "Teamwork makes the dream work!" A half-century after Theodor Adorno's and William H. Whyte's blistering critiques of type's relationship to industrial modernity, the false consciousness perpetuated by the language of type remained almost impenetrable.

Patricia found dozens of ways to intertwine the fiction of the true self with the fiction of the happy, hardworking team. We were grouped with others of our type and prompted to share stories, to marvel at the consistent patterns in our "communication methods," our "leadership styles," and our "decision making profiles." At first I tried to stay as quiet as possible so that I could take notes from a distance; after all, I was there only to get access to the archive. But the invitation to talk about myself, to pick myself apart and have this room full of strangers put me back together in a reasoned, systematic way, was difficult to forgo, even for the introverts among us, which I most certainly was not. Sometimes I answered questions sincerely and was rewarded with overtures of friendship; my fellow trainees seemed eager to bond with others who were like them—who understood them. Other times I played an extreme version of my ENTJ self: brash, snobby, impatient, cocksure, a real bitch. I wanted to see who I could irritate and, more telling, how the conflicts that might arise between me and my fellow types would be resolved.

This role-playing came to a head on the third day of the training, when Patricia gave us each a marker and a large sheet of paper and asked us to draw our personalities as rooms. "What kind of room best represents who you are? Use your imagination!" She laughed. I felt annoyed by the assignment, not just the juvenility of it, but the crude interpretive protocols I knew it would engender. ("You drew a living room, which, as an extravert, testifies to your social nature," I could imagine Patricia saying.) I briefly considered drawing the Red Room of Pain from *Fifty Shades of Grey,* a phalanx of whips and harnesses and naked men, but I reasoned that cartoon nudity might get me kicked out of the training. Instead, I drew a stick figure with spaghetti hair and x's for eyes parachuting onto a tent in the wilderness—a tent flanked on all sides by ravenous wolves, which, in my clumsy hands, resembled chubby hamsters with sawtooth fangs. My only goal was to create an image that defied interpretation.

But I was foolish to think I could have succeeded. Patricia circled my drawing with a promising attitude of skepticism and asked me to explain. I did, trying hard not to stray from the literal: this is a parachute, this is a tent, these are wolves, this is me. Her skepticism disappeared. She began to smile and nod violently. "This makes a lot of sense," she said. "ENTJs are our leaders, our CEO types. Like this parachuting woman, you want to come in from the top and make all the decisions. You love taking risks."

I decided to follow her lead. "And the wolves are the people who want to get in my way," I said, letting some menace creep into my tone. The other trainees looked at me nervously, as if seeing me—the true me—for the first time. My drawing gave them all the confirmation they needed to know that I was not a good "team player."

The next room and personality belonged to an executive talent manager from the United Kingdom named Michael, my antithesis in training, a type enthusiast who spoke in a clipped, posh accent and (I thought unkindly) bore teeth too small for his mouth. According to a story he would share later that day, Michael was so good at managing people that once a man whom he fired thanked him for the unexpected opportunity to "self-actualize." This made Michael happy because there was nothing he hated more, he informed us, than people who "played the victim," refusing to assume responsibility for their lives. That morning, Michael had sketched in fine and elaborate marker strokes a nineteenth-century drawing room, which he had furnished with upholstered chairs, brandy decanters, and a wall covered with portraits of distinguished-looking men.

As Patricia admired his work, Michael pointed to the largest of the miniature portraits that he had drawn, a man who loomed, proud and handsome, over a reading chair. "This is a portrait of Dorian Gray," he announced. His reference was to Oscar Wilde's ageless libertine, the fictional character who sold his soul to pursue beauty and sensual experience for eternity. "I put it there," Michael continued, "because Dorian's portrait captured him at his most perfect. But I wanted to remind myself that he got uglier because his ego got in the way of him appreciating other people of different types." This was not exactly true—really, it was not true at all—but no one seemed to care about Michael's bad reading of Wilde. Our fellow trainees beamed and applauded his underlying point: it was important to remember that all types were created equal, even if the portrait exercise was silly and easy to mock. True to Katharine Briggs's metaphor of the personality paint box, Michael had stepped back from his portrait and met his ESFJ self. No doubt he liked what he saw.

After Michael's presentation, I decided to share my mistrust of

the test—I insisted on calling it a test as a small act of rebellion—
with Wesley, a thirty-year-old career counselor at Bethel University,
an evangelical Christian college in Arden Hills, Minnesota. Wesley
was brave enough to raise the question of the indicator's biases to
the room. After our drawing exercise, he gave a small and respectful speech, pointing out that the type indicator and its personality
profiles were only "representative of the white male leaders of the
U.S." But at an institution like Bethel, 70 percent of Wesley's students
were women, international students, underrepresented minorities,
and first-generation college attendees, many of whom saw the dangers
endemic to "managing other human beings." How, he asked Patricia,
could Myers-Briggs or any other personality test speak to his students'
experiences and their aspirations?

Patricia did not appear to appreciate the question. "That's the pool
they're going to be swimming in," she said, dismissing Wesley's concerns with a nervous shrug. "It may not be the worst thing in the world
for them to learn how to adapt to it."

"What about the way things like introversion are used to discrimi-
nate against women in the workplace?" rasped a laryngitic consultant
named Larissa.

"And what if what you want is to change the underlying system?"
asked Ashley, one of only two black women in training.

"I don't want to go there," Patricia said.

. . . .

Is the test a joke? A scam? Every six months or so a reputable news
source publishes what it takes to be a devastating critique of the type
indicator. Consider such recent titles as "The Mysterious Popularity
of the Meaningless Myers-Briggs," "Nothing Personal: The Question-
able Myers-Briggs Test," and "Goodbye to MBTI, the Fad That Won't
Die." The skeptics who write these pieces tend to repeat the same argu-
ments. They say the instrument is unreliable, that people often get
different results when they take it from one week to the next. They
say the type descriptions are loose enough to fit anyone, a flagrant
example of circus man P. T. Barnum's observation that the best hoaxes

are the ones that have "got something for everybody." They deride the test's origins as the hobby of two untrained women, even though they seem to have only the faintest sense for what its history really is. Their total skepticism makes it impossible for them to account for the astonishing effects that learning one's type has on people.

On the last day of my training session, the room filled with true believers, I witnessed flashes of epiphany that were not, in any sense, untrue; I saw things fall into place for people. The Department of Defense representative confided in me that the training had helped her make sense of her divorce, the pain of it lingering nearly five years after her husband left their home. Geoff, a kind and quiet IT executive who had come with two of his boisterous colleagues, whispered that type had given him the language to justify to his coworkers why he avoided office gossip; they are E's, he is an I, and he would prefer to keep to himself. The blond astrologer and I chatted about Jung while we waited for the bathroom. "Jung is my boy!" she exclaimed before inviting me to coffee so that we could continue to "network" as "strong E's." When we met up later that week, she would tell me that the training had given her the confidence to start looking for new jobs. She now knew that she belonged in customer relations, not product management. A consultant named Sarah (an S) told the room that she suddenly understood why she and her mother (an N) fought so much. "When I ask my mom for a recipe, she says, 'Just a dash of this, just a dash of that,'" Sarah said. "But I'm like—Ma, how much is that? Give me a real measurement." When the subject of marriage came up, which it inevitably did, many J type women in the room had stories about planning trips with their P husbands. "I just got back from Disney World and I really realized the difference between me and my husband," said Jody, who sat across the table from me. "When we're there, he plans it all out—the way I plan out the kids' schedules at home." Someone else chimed in, "When we went to Disney World, I forced myself to act as J as possible. That's just what you need to do to survive there." Everyone laughed, even me. In this moment, we were all believers.

Although the world has come a long way since Katharine opened her cosmic laboratory of baby training, the link the language of type helped forge between self-discovery and self-creation stays intact. Self-awareness remains a precious psychological offering no matter the end, and the painless knowledge peddled by the indicator can seem more appealing than other, more chaotic processes of self-excavation, ones that do not fit neatly into a 4 × 4 type chart or a four-letter acronym. For many of my fellow trainees, the five days we spent learning the language of type presented a rare opportunity to confront themselves, to speak their truths in a strange but useful tongue. For others, type offered a framework for justifying who they were, and who they would forever be, to others: the decisions they had or had not made, the fights they had or had not resolved, the careers and lovers and dreams they had pursued or abandoned. Despite all the challenges to its validity and reliability, despite all the criticism of its origins and its uses, despite its silly, ironic appropriations, the indicator continued to operate as a powerful technology of the self even in its twenty-first-century incarnation.

"As type spreads around the globe, I have come to see that it can have influences far beyond what I would ever have expected from a psychological test," Mary McCaulley once stated in a 1996 conference on type in South Africa. "It may even be subversive, if that term can be used in a positive way. It is a legacy from two giants of our century, a vision of how we can find better ways of living in peace on our planet, and a legacy for all of us to protect and develop." It is an exaggerated claim, to be sure. Yet for those who have been listening to and speaking the language of type for the past half-century, these words promise more than just the possibility of discovering and cultivating one's true self, more than the possibility of becoming "a more perfect type," to echo the words of Carl Jung. They promise a more perfect world to come—a world made by and for true believers just like them.

Acknowledgments

I never would have written this book without the encouragement and guidance of Alia Hanna Habib and Anna Dubenko—my first and greatest thanks go to them. I am grateful beyond measure to Yaniv Soha, Anne Collins, Sarah Porter, and Tom Killingbeck for their keen editorial input and to Daniel Novack and Natalie Cereseto for their valuable legal advice and good humor. I am thankful to everyone at Doubleday U.S., Random House Canada, and HarperCollins U.K. for all the hard work they did to transform my words into an object out in the world.

I owe so much to my earliest readers and friends: Sarah Chihaya, Michelle Cho, Ming-Qi Chu, Gabriella Coleman, Maggie Doherty, Eve Fine, Gloria Fisk, Shanon Fitzpatrick, Len Gutkin, Amy Hungerford, Evan Kindley, Sean McCann, Marcel Przymusinski, Sarah Rose, Poulami Roychowdhury, Rachel Greenwald Smith, Richard Jean So, and Rachel Watson. Kasia van Schaik read my manuscript several times, always with an exacting and generous eye. Thank you for making my work better, and thank you too for making the process of revision so enjoyable.

Once again, my greatest debt is to Christian Nakarado, whose list of personae might include: husband, father, reader, editor, weekend babysitter, and "neat man who has to contend with a messy woman." Aydin Berk Nakarado and Altan Emre Nakarado inspired my writing and thinking in ways I had not thought possible. Their grubby little fingerprints are all over this book. Thank you to Gulus Emre, Melis

Emre, and Sukru Emre, whose presence, even at a distance, makes me happy and keeps me motivated.

If, as Katharine and Isabel believed, every child is an experiment from the moment she is born, then that child's mother deserves most of the credit for the experiment's outcome. This book is dedicated to my mother Umit Emre: my inspiration, my model, my friend. By dumb luck, I was fortunate enough to grow up in her cosmic laboratory.

A Note on Sources

This project would not have been possible without the help of many dedicated librarians, archivists, and research assistants across the world: Jennie Russell and Katherine Grimes, who reproduced the Katharine Cook Papers at Michigan State University; Yvonne Voegeli at the ETH-Bibliothek in Zurich, Switzerland, who helped me navigate Carl Jung's correspondences; Emma Adler, who photographed the Henry Murray Papers at Harvard; Patrizia Sione, who scanned the Edward N. Hay Papers at the Kheel Center for Labor Management Documentation and Archives at Cornell University; Elizabeth Peele at the Institute of Personality and Social Research (formerly IPAR) at the University of California, Berkeley, where the materials of Donald MacKinnon, Frank Barron, and all the creative writers were housed; Jen Comins at Columbia University's Rare Book and Manuscript Library, who helped guide me through the Carnegie Corporation Papers; Nicholas Telepak and the legal team at ETS, which gave me access to the papers of Henry Chauncey; and Michelle Goldsmith and Peter Geyer, whose personal collection of MBTI materials in Melbourne, Australia, made it possible for me to write the last third of this book.

Due to the generosity of these institutions and individuals, I had a rich, varied, and highly disorganized set of materials that I combed through and combined to trace the lives of Katharine and Isabel, presenting them in their own words as much as possible. The only institution that did not respond favorably to my request for archival access was CAPT, which controls a large portion of Isabel's personal records. However, Frances Wright Saunders's authorized biography *Katharine and Isabel* contains excerpts of many of Isabel's letters, as well as useful information on her adolescence and early adulthood. While the biography, which was published by CPP in 1991, is a great way to encounter Isabel's inimitable prose, it is highly selective and contains inaccuracies. I relied upon it as little as possible, preferring to reconstruct events and timelines from my other sources.

Notes

INTRODUCTION: SPEAKING TYPE

xvi   **For some time too**: Theodor Adorno, *The Authoritarian Personality* (New York: The American Jewish Committee, 1950), 747.

xix   **Throughout the history of type**: Carl Jung, *Psychological Types* (Princeton: Princeton University Press, 1971), 83.

CHAPTER ONE: THE COSMIC LABORATORY OF BABY TRAINING

1   **"God was as real to her"**: "Why Live? Difficult Days," Folder 38, Box 4330, Katharine Cook Briggs Papers, Michigan State University (MSU) Archives. Hereafter KCB.

1   **For her, evolution**: "What Is Moral Character?" Folder 35, Box 4330, KCB.

2   **When guests came over**: "Katharine Cook Scrapbook," Box 2040H, KCB.

2   **"Even as a child"**: "Personal," Folder 20, Box 4331, KCB.

2   **She found herself "wrenched and shaken"**: "Why Live? Difficult Days."

2   **"The microscope"**: "Annual Report," Michigan Agricultural College (Lansing: State of Michigan, 1892).

3   **"I think science"**: "The Life Line," Folder 29, Box 4331, KCB.

3   **"Being impersonal and objective"**: "Why Live? Difficult Days."

3   **She thought that salvation**: "Up from Barbarism," Folder 34, Box 4330, KCB.

4   **"I write with love"**: "Katharine Cook Scrapbook."

5   **"This morning after bathing"**: Extracts from "The Diary of an Obedience-Curiosity Mother," Folder 17, Box 4330, KCB.

6   **"Is life worth living?"**: "Why Live? Difficult Days."

6   **Together, mother and daughter**: "Personal Evolution—When I Was a Child," Folder 9, Box 4329, KCB.

7   **"Give me a dozen"**: John B. Watson, *Behaviorism* (New Brunswick, N.J.: Transaction Publishers, 1998), 82.

8   **"There are few sights more pathetic"**: Rachel Kent Fitz, *Problems of Babyhood: Building a Constitution, Forming a Character* (New York: Henry Holt & Co., 1906).

8   **She cordoned off the living room**: Katharine Briggs, "Personal Evolution."
9   **They helped transform her home**: John Stuart Mill, *Autobiography of John Stuart Mill* (London: Longmans, Green, Reader, and Dyer, 1873).
9   **"For your child"**: "Children as a Hobby," *Saturday Evening Post,* October 5, 1909.
9   **"Not only psychologists"**: Donald A. Laird, "Debunking Child Psychology," *Sunday Star,* October 20, 1929.
10 **"As if every child"**: "Is Child Study Bunk?" Folder 6, Box 4329, KCB.
10 **"No! No!"**: "An Experiment in Education," Folder 40, Box 4330, KCB.
12 **"Now these are the Laws"**: Rudyard Kipling, *The Jungle Book* (New York: The Century Co., 1920).
12 **"Any mother who believes in"**: "Pre-School Education Questionnaire," Folder 3, Box 4329, KCB.
12 **"The futile, unauthoritative mother"**: "Obedience as a Regulator of Mental Tension," Folder 3, Box 4330, KCB.
12 **When one mother recoiled**: "An Experiment in Education."
13 **The ultimate purpose of baby training**: "Minding the Baby's I.Q.," Folder 3, Box 4329, KCB.
13 **"Multitudes of people"**: "Sentiment vs. Intellect," Folder 13, Box 4330, KCB.
13 **In his best-selling textbook**: William Hague, *The Eugenic Marriage: A Personal Guide to the New Science of Better Living and Better Babies, in Four Volumes* (New York: The Review of Reviews Company, 1914).
14 **For every child had innate preferences**: "Personal Evolution—When I Was a Child."
15 **"My child is not a genius"**: "An Experiment in Education."
15 **She was her piano teacher's**: Ibid.
16 **"I want you to tell me"**: "Teaching Obedience to Babies," Folder 27, Box 4331, KCB.
16 **"It occurs to me"**: "Publr's. KCB," Folder 25, Box 4331, KCB.
16 **Using the observations**: "An Experiment in Education."
18 **"The women who count most of all"**: Katharine Cook Briggs, "The Case for the Homemaker," *Woman's Home Companion,* December 1914.
18 **"Suzanne, my only child"**: "An Experiment in Education."
18 **"Mine is just the old, old story"**: "Personal."

CHAPTER TWO: WOMEN'S WORK

20 **"College of course"**: Katharine Briggs, "Getting Ideas," Box 4334, Folder 10, KCB.
20 **Each boy was impermanent enough**: Frances Wright Saunders, *Katharine and Isabel: Mother's Light, Daughter's Journey* (Palo Alto: Consulting Psychologists Press, Inc., 1991), 25.
21 **She called him "Myers"**: Ibid., 30.
21 **These questions worried Katharine**: Ibid., 29.
22 **"We know not"**: William James, *The Varieties of Religious Experience* (Minnesota: Dover Publications, 2013), 357.
22 **In addition to the Bible**: "An Experiment in Education."

23 **James argued that religion**: James, *The Varieties of Religious Experience*, 31.

23 **"We are no longer a Christian nation"**: Katharine Briggs, "Getting Ideas."

24 **"Your attempt to preserve"**: Saunders, *Katharine and Isabel*, 31.

24 **"Your mother grew up"**: "Personal."

25 **For the first time**: Saunders, *Katharine and Isabel*, 29.

25 **"Lettuce pray"**: "Sophs Present Comedy, Internal Relations," *Swarthmore Phoenix*, April 24, 1917.

26 **"For the greatest efficiency"**: "Louise Waygood Carries Off First in Women's Extemp," *Swarthmore Phoenix*, May 1, 2017.

26 **Men were not to be trusted**: Saunders, *Katharine and Isabel*, 31.

27 **Katharine would learn**: Ibid., 38.

27 **He told Isabel**: Ibid., 42.

28 **"The fact that your"**: Ibid., 43.

28 **"Isabel Briggs"**: "New Calendar," *Swarthmore Phoenix*, September 17, 1918.

28 **In the same home**: Saunders, *Katharine and Isabel*, 46.

29 **"What are the right things"**: Ibid., 49.

30 **"Though she came back"**: "Big Mass Meeting Thursday Evening," *Swarthmore Phoenix*, November 19, 1918.

31 **the social good**: Saunders, *Katharine and Isabel*, 65.

32 **Katharine had fallen**: Katharine Briggs, "The Stuff of Dreams," Folder 54, Box 4334, KCB.

32 **In a letter that she drafted**: Ibid.

33 **"Can a person understand"**: Ibid.

CHAPTER THREE: MEET YOURSELF

34 **"I loved the ideas"**: "Personal."

34 **Never a fan of psychoanalysis**: John B. Watson, "Jung as Psychologist," *New Republic*, November 7, 1923.

36 **"Dr. Jung symbolized"**: "Personal."

37 **She recalled the words**: James, *The Varieties of Religious Experience*, 196.

37 **"For five years"**: "Personal."

38 **She referred to him**: Katharine Briggs, *The Man from Zurich*, Folder 29, Box 4329, KCB.

38 **"In offering me this study of types"**: "Personal."

38 **This reputational imbalance**: Katharine Briggs, "Out of Zurich," Folder 6, Box 4330, KCB.

38 **"Psychoanalysis, which with Freud"**: Katharine Briggs, "Pleasure vs. Enterprise," Folder 21, Box 4331, KCB.

38 **Jung's theories**: "Out of Zurich."

39 **What defined Jung's introvert**: C. G. Jung, *Psychological Types* (Princeton, N.J.: Princeton University Press, 1971), 380.

39 **To the extravert**: Ibid., 377.

39 **On a blustery winter day**: Ibid., 333.

39 **The extravert "does what is needed"**: Ibid., 335.

40 **She was on a "quest"**: "Personal."

40 **In an exercise**: Katharine Briggs, "Using the Persona Idea," Folder 5, Box 4329, KCB.

40 **The sensing type**: Jung, *Psychological Types*, 364.

41 **"Thinking totally shuts out feeling"**: Ibid., 358.

41 **Jung's thinker**: Ibid., 347.

42 **"This new religion"**: Katharine Briggs, "The Dream of Death," Folder 6, Box 4331, KCB.

42 **"*Hodgepodge and fires*"**: Katharine Briggs, "Routine," Folder 23, Box 4331, KCB.

43 **To meet oneself**: Katharine Briggs, "Meet Yourself: How to Use the Personality Paint Box," *New Republic*, December 22, 1926.

44 **"Fortunate are they"**: Joseph Jastrow, *Plotting Your Life: The Psychologist as Helmsman* (New York: Greenberg, 1930), 361.

45 **In 1734**: Alexander Pope, *An Essay on Man* (Philadelphia: McCarty and Davis, 1821), 17.

45 **In 1750**: Benjamin Franklin, *Poor Richard's Almanac* (New York: Skyhorse Publishing, 2007), 58.

45 **In 1831**: Ralph Waldo Emerson, *Journals and Miscellaneous Notebooks of Ralph Waldo Emerson* (Cambridge: Harvard University Press, 1965), 75.

46 **"A new idea"**: Walter Isaacson, *Einstein: His Life and Universe* (New York: Simon & Schuster, 2007), 113.

46 **She asked him to clarify**: Katharine Briggs to C. G. Jung, August 23, 1927, Hs 1056:1083, C. G. Jung Papers Collection, ETH-Bibliothek (Zurich, Switzerland). Hereafter ETH.

48 **"Dear Madam"**: C. G. Jung to Katharine Briggs, September 13, 1927, Folder 16, Box 4331, KCB.

49 **She craved attention**: Katharine Briggs, "Up from Barbarism," *New Republic*, December 5, 1928.

50 **Her longest one was**: *The Man from Zurich*.

50 **"*Signs and symbols*"**: "Hail, Dr. Jung!" Folder 15, Box 4331, KCB.

51 **"Her pronounced femininity"**: "Minding the Baby's I.Q."

51 **Before she moved**: Saunders, *Katharine and Isabel*, 68.

CHAPTER FOUR: AN UNBROKEN SERIES OF SUCCESSFUL GESTURES

53 **"Rise from bed"**: F. Scott Fitzgerald, *The Great Gatsby* (New York: Scribner, 2004), 173.

53 **"If personality is"**: Ibid., 2.

54 **"Personality is more than character"**: Norris Arthur Brisco, *Retail Salesmanship* (New York: Ronald Press Company, 1920), 56.

55 **"The truth was"**: Fitzgerald, *The Great Gatsby*, 98.

55 **"There is probably no one"**: Katharine Briggs, "Personal," Folder 20, Box 4331, KCB.

56 **"Let us imagine"**: Ibid.

57 **"Very blue"**: Saunders, *Katharine and Isabel*, 75.

57   "I have the rest of my life": Ibid., 86.

57   "Your father and mother": "Getting Ideas."

57   "When number one was born": "Minding the Baby's I.Q."

59   "Even thE": Saunders, *Katharine and Isabel*, 85.

59   Then there was the third detective: Isabel Briggs Myers, *Murder Yet to Come* (Gainesville: Center for Applications of Psychological Type, 1995), 12.

60   "Had she produced a work of genius": "Minding the Baby's I.Q."

60   Gray-eyed, red-haired: Briggs, *Murder Yet to Come* (New York: Frederick A. Stokes), 12.

61   "You want to hear about me?": Saunders, *Katharine and Isabel*, 84.

61   "YOU WIN STAKES": Ibid., 83.

61   The celebration started: Ibid., 85.

62   The accompanying caption: "7,500 Is a Lot of Money," *Brooklyn Daily Eagle*, April 23, 1930.

62   In their Books and Authors column: Books and Authors, *New York Times*, December 15, 1929.

62   Happy to have her friends: Saunders, *Katharine and Isabel*, 85.

62   Debuting as: "Murder, Much Murder, and Murder to Come," *Honolulu Star-Bulletin*, January 25, 1930.

62   "It is a sound": "Books of the Week," *The Spectator*, March 1, 1930.

63   "It must, however, be admitted": *"Murder Yet to Come," Country Life*, February 15, 1930.

63   Gone was the playroom: Saunders, *Katharine and Isabel*, 97.

63   "I have some psychological advice": Ibid., 91.

64   After an unpredictable end: Ibid., 83.

64   "The work goes far more slowly": Ibid., 88.

65   "I want to write books": Ibid., 94.

65   Lawrence Jr.: "New Play to Be Shown," *Philadelphia Inquirer*, May 18, 1931.

66   Now it struck her: Isabel Briggs Myers, "IBM MBTI history 74," Peter Geyer Papers, Melbourne, Australia. Hereafter PGP.

66   Marriage and its temptations: Myers, "IBM MBTI history 74."

66   "Marriage? Big Job!": "Marriage? Big Job," *Philadelphia Ledger*, May 18, 1931.

67   "A philosophy of marriage": "Science as Male, Marriage as Female," Folder 37, Box 4330, KCB.

67   Every marriage represented: "Wifehood as a Life Work," Folder 37, Box 4330, KCB.

68   For Katharine, it represented: "Singles or Doubles (Woman and the House)," Folder 19, Box 4334, KCB.

69   Yet to acknowledge and accept: "Invitation," Folder 19, Box 4334, KCB.

69   "It has been proved to me": Isabel Briggs Myers, *Give Me Death* (New York: Frederick A. Stokes Company, 1934).

70   "Isabel Briggs Myers": "Mr. Quick Gets Fast Let-Down in Mystery Tale," *Chicago Daily Tribune*, October 20, 1934.

70   For the reviewer at the *Washington Post*: Theodore Hall, "No End of Books," *Washington Post*, November 2, 1934.

70   "I would ask her not": "New Novels," *The Observer* (London), December 9, 1934.

CHAPTER FIVE: DESPERATE AMATEURS

71 **In one strange and memorable dream**: "Dream Diary," Folder 1, Box 4330, KCB.
73 **"I and my two colleagues"**: Kristine Mann to Katharine Briggs, May 19, 1937, Folder 16, Box 4331, KCB.
74 **All Katharine thought about**: "Candy for Jill," Folder 25, Box 4330, KCB.
74 **There were the 3″ × 5″ index cards**: "Dream Cards," Box 4334A, KCB.
74 **There were the exercises**: "Candy for Jill."
74 **"You could always try an interpretation"**: "The Stuff of Dreams," Folder 40, Box 4334, KCB.
75 **She wanted to surround herself with**: "Persona Versus Soul," Folder 28, Box 4333, KCB.
75 **Just as she had opened her home**: Ibid.
76 **A wayward child**: Katharine Briggs to C. G. Jung, December 8, 1930, Folder 16, Box 4331, KCB.
77 **"I'm behind in my school work"**: "Persona Versus Soul."
77 **Touched by the girl's tears**: Katharine Briggs to C. G. Jung, June 18, 1931, Folder 16, Box 4331, KCB.
78 **"I have a poem!"**: "Persona Versus Soul."
80 **"My very dear Tucky"**: "The Jewel Bag," Folder 19, Box 4329, KCB.
81 **"Immortality"**: Katharine Briggs to C. G. Jung, June 18, 1931, Folder 16, Box 4331, KCB.
81 **"I'm changing!"**: Ibid.
82 **"No!"**: Ibid.
83 **"It is unethical"**: The American Psychological Association, *Ethical Standards of Psychologists* (Washington, D.C.: The American Psychological Association, 1953), 5.
84 **"In the absence of psychoanalysts"**: "Personal."
84 **"If I could wish"**: Katharine Briggs to C. G. Jung, June 18, 1931, Folder 16, Box 4331, KCB.
84 **"It is indeed an unfortunate"**: C. G. Jung to Katharine Briggs, July 4, 1931, ETH.
85 **"If you should write another letter"**: Ibid.
85 **His suggestion**: Katharine Briggs to C. G. Jung, July 24, 1931, Folder 16, Box 4331, KCB.

CHAPTER SIX: THE SCIENCE OF MAN

89 **"You can't think women away"**: Katharine Briggs, "Notes on Dr. Jung's Talk," Folder 15, Box 4331, KCB.
90 **"I feel as if I know you"**: Katharine Briggs to Carl Jung, May 8, 1936, Hs 1056:4314, ETH.
90 **Her dream club**: "Candy for Jill."
91 **Now there was "a very neurotic woman"**: Katharine Briggs to Carl Jung, May 8, 1936, Hs 1056:4314, ETH.

91 **"As I shall spend three weeks"**: Carl Jung to Katharine Briggs, August 2, 1936, Hs 1056:4319, ETH.

91 **She would note in her diary**: "Pleasure vs. Enterprise."

91 **A handsome**: Forrest G. Robinson, *Love's Story Told: A Life of Henry A. Murray* (Cambridge: Harvard University Press, 1992), 27.

92 **"Because Fascism"**: Lewis Mumford and Henry Alexander Murray, *"In Old Friendship": The Correspondence of Lewis Mumford and Henry Murray*, ed. Frank G. Novak Jr. (Syracuse: Syracuse University Press, 2007), 190.

94 *Psychological Types* **seemed to him**: Robinson, *Love's Story Told*, 94.

95 **Murray had to learn**: Ibid., 125.

95 **"One could characterize"**: Claire Douglas, *Translate This Darkness: Christiana Morgan, the Veiled Woman in Jung's Circles* (Princeton: Princeton University Press, 1993), 134.

95 **It took only three days**: Henry Murray, "Notes on meeting with Jung," HUGFP 97.8, Folder 1, Box 1, Papers of Henry A. Murray, Harvard University Archives. Hereafter HAM.

95 **To go on with what Jung has begun**: Douglas, *Translate This Darkness*, 140.

96 **They would call this discipline**: Henry Murray, *Explorations in Personality* (New York: Oxford University Press, 2008), 4.

96 **"Personality is a temporal whole"**: Ibid.

97 **Murray's experiments**: Ibid., 440.

98 **"But what living personality"**: Mumford and Murray, *"In Old Friendship,"* 67.

98 **She referred to Jung with tenderness**: Douglas, *Translate This Darkness*, 159.

98 **"Your function"**: Ibid., 151.

98 **Nor did his insistence**: Carl Jung to Henry Murray, September 21, 1931, HUGFP 97.8, Folder 1, Box 1, HAM.

99 **"Stories, like dreams"**: Henry Murray, "Uses of the Thematic Apperception Test," *American Journal of Psychiatry* 107 (1951): 577–81.

100 **When Isabel was little**: Extracts from "The Diary of an Obedience-Curiosity Mother."

101 **Murray would confess**: Murray, "Uses of the Thematic Apperception Test."

101 **"Les enfants"**: Paul Roazen, "Interview on Freud and Jung with Henry A. Murray in 1965," *Journal of Analytic Psychology* 48 (2003): 1–27.

101 **"Whatever I touch"**: Carl Jung to Henry Murray, October 6, 1938, HUGFP 97.8, Folder 1, Box 1, HAM.

102 **"Quite a number of Germans"**: Carl Jung to Henry Murray, August 29, 1938, Folder 1, Box 1, HAM.

102 **"Dr. Jung came down"**: "Yale Boola," Folder 15, Box 4331, KCB.

103 **"They asked C. G. Jung"**: "They Got What They Needed to Know," Folder 15, Box 4331, KCB.

103 **"I don't know"**: Saunders, *Katharine and Isabel*, 100.

103 **For Katharine, it was an unforgettable day**: Katharine Briggs to C. G. Jung, October 2, 1936, Hs 1056:4319, ETH.

103 **"Oh, you shouldn't have done that!"**: Mary McCaulley and Isabel Briggs Myers, "Making the Most of Individual Differences in a Changing World," PGP.

103 **"I understand from our interview"**: Katharine Briggs to C. G. Jung, October 2, 1936, Hs 1056:4319, ETH.

CHAPTER SEVEN: THE PERSONALITY IS POLITICAL

105 **On a 3″ x 5″**:"Type Moralities," Folder 62, Box 4334, KCB.

105 **"Feminine comportment"**: Henry Murray, "Notecards," HUGFP 97.45.4, Box 2, HAM.

106 **"I am planning to get my hands dirty"**: Mumford and Murray, *"In Old Friendship,"* 170.

107 **There was his suspected**: Henry Murray, "Analysis of the Personality of Adolph Hitler with Predications of His Future Behavior and Suggestions for Dealing with Him Now and After Germany's Surrender," October 1943, Box 1, Location 2000/06/02, Records of the Central Intelligence Agency, U.S. National Archives and Records Administration, Washington, D.C.

108 **There was Hitler the man**: Murray, "Notecards."

109 **Destiny had cast him**: Adolf Hitler, *The Essential Hitler: Speeches and Commentaries* (Mundelein, Ill.: Bolchazy-Carducci Publishing, 2007), 447.

109 **"Hitler speaking"**: Murray, "Analysis of the Personality of Adolph Hitler."

109 **The two characters shared**: Herman Melville, *Moby-Dick* (New York: W. W. Norton, 2017), 154.

110 **"That the Jews"**: "The Study of Dreams," Folder 41, Box 4334, KCB.

110 **"The proper interpretation"**: Murray, "Analysis of the Personality of Adolph Hitler."

111 **"This would complete the myth"**: Ibid.

112 **This was what happened**: Ibid.

113 **"If one is willing to lean"**: Murray, *Explorations in Personality,* 282.

113 **"How, then, can a psychologist foretell"**: Henry Murray, *Assessment of Men: Part 1* (New York: Rinehart and Co., 1948).

114 **"Between now and the cessation of hostilities"**: Murray, "Analysis of the Personality of Adolph Hitler."

115 **Instead, it preserved**: "Newspaper Clippings," Folder 14, Box 4331, KCB.

115 **"Whatever his peacetime sins"**: Saunders, *Katharine and Isabel,* 100.

116 **"This phenomenon"**: Albert Einstein to Theodore Roosevelt, August 2, 1939, Atomic Heritage Foundation, Washington, D.C.

116 **It promised to be an era**: Henry Murray, "World Concord as a Goal for Social Sciences," International Congress of Psychology, Stockholm, Sweden, 1951.

116 **"Nothing in the modern scene"**: "Type Moralities."

117 **"In the darkest days of World War Two"**: Mary McCaulley, "Person Behind the MBTI 1988," PGP.

118 **"Do you know someone"**: Dale Carnegie, *How to Win Friends and Influence People* (New York: Simon & Schuster, 1981), 12.

119 **"I made up my mind"**: McCaulley, "Person Behind the MBTI 1988."

CHAPTER EIGHT: SHEEP AND BUCK

121 **She was interested**: "People-Sorting Instruments," *Reader's Digest,* 1942.

121 **The article she had read**: Doncaster G. Humm and Guy W. Wadsworth Jr., "The

Humm-Wadsworth Temperament Scale," *The American Journal of Psychiatry* 91, no. 1 (July 1935): 163–200.

122 **"As to where"**: Saunders, *Katharine and Isabel,* 2.

124 **"It is the fashion to say"**: Isabel Briggs Myers, "The Myers-Briggs Type Indicator Manual," 1962, Palo Alto, Calif., Consulting Psychologists Press.

124 **"We often say of young people"**: "Getting Ideas."

125 **"The critique of"**: Adorno, *The Authoritarian Personality,* 746–47.

127 **She called herself**: McCaulley, "Person Behind the MBTI 1988."

128 **The feelers were**: Isabel Briggs Myers, "IBM typology 71 transcript," PGP.

128 **"If I ask complicated questions"**: McCaulley, "Person Behind the MBTI 1988."

129 **"Why do I have to learn these things now?"**: Isabel Briggs Myers, "IBM 72," PGP.

130 **"*Are such emotional 'ups and downs'*"**: Isabel Briggs Myers, "Form C of the Briggs-Myers Type Indicator," Folder 13, Box 3, Edward N. Hay Papers, Kheel Center, Cornell University. Hereafter ENH.

130 **"One of them was the editor"**: Myers, "IBM typology 71 transcript."

131 **"Every time you use your mind"**: Isabel Briggs Myers, "Thumbnail Description of the Type Indicator," July 1, 1945, Folder 13, Box 3, ENH.

131 **Her mother's J/P distinction**: Isabel Briggs Myers and Peter Myers, *Gifts Differing* (Mountain View: Consulting Psychologists Press, 1980), 9–10.

131 **She believed that J/P**: Ibid., 22.

132 **On one "disastrous occasion"**: Myers, "IBM 72."

132 **"I said to myself"**: McCaulley, "Person Behind the MBTI 1988."

132 **She condemned**: "Getting Ideas."

133 **"I have already given you a questionnaire"**: Katharine Briggs, "A Real Questionnaire," Folder 13, Box 4334, KCB.

133 **"What the Church called 'revelation'"**: Saunders, *Katharine and Isabel,* 116.

134 **What was needed**: Myers, "The Myers-Briggs Type Indicator Manual."

134 **"The more you know"**: Myers, "Thumbnail Description of the Type Indicator."

135 **Enchanted by her**: Saunders, *Katharine and Isabel,* 112.

135 **"This is not, strictly speaking"**: Myers, "Form C of the Briggs-Myers Type Indicator."

136 **"Quite a few questions"**: Isabel Briggs Myers to Edward N. Hay, August 30, 1943, Folder 13, Box 3, ENH.

136 **Questions that assessed**: Isabel Briggs Myers, "Contributions of a Man's Type to His Executive Success," Folder 13, Box 3, ENH.

137 **Each type was brought to life**: Isabel Briggs Myers, "Type and What It Tells You," Folder 13, Box 3, ENH.

138 **Her type descriptions**: Isabel Briggs Myers, "IBM construction," PGP.

139 **"Above all things"**: Isabel Briggs Myers, "Results on the Briggs-Myers Type Indicator," Folder 78, Box 4, ENH.

139 **It was all a very hush-hush operation**: Isabel Briggs Myers, "Briggs-Myers Test Account," Folder 13, Box 3, ENH.

CHAPTER NINE: A PERFECT SPY

142   "**It was evident that**": Myers, "IBM typology 71 transcript."
143   "**Will he be able**": OSS Assessment Staff, *Assessment of Men: Selection of Personnel for the Office of Strategic Services* (New York: Rinehart, 1948), 15.
143   "**No matter how substantial**": Ibid., 8.
144   "**Beliefs in themselves**": Ibid., 27.
144   **Above all, Murray wanted to avoid**: Ibid., 9.
144   "*Motivation for Assignment*": Ibid., 31.
145   "**We would never know**": Ibid., 9.
146   "**Our job**": Ibid., 64.
147   "**It might be unwise**": Ibid., 65.
149   **What was needed was**: Ibid., 14.
150   "**We are not interested**": Ibid., 169.
151   "**Mr. F.**": Ibid., 170.
152   **If E.**: Ibid., 175.
152   **In the scenario**: Ibid.
153   "**RECRUIT A**": Ibid., 192.
154   "**S was a society**": Ibid., 221.
155   **In his collection of prose**: Theodor Adorno, *Minima Moralia: Reflections on a Damaged Life* (New York: Verso, 2005), 104.
156   "**The task of fascist propaganda**": Adorno, *The Authoritarian Personality*, 10.
156   **What the postwar world needed**: Ibid., 476.
157   "*Obedience and respect*": Ibid., 255.
157   "*The sexual orgies*": Ibid., 239.
157   **Of all the items:** Ibid., 227.
158   **He believed that all men**: Ibid., 277.
158   "**People are continuously molded**": Ibid., 976.

CHAPTER TEN: PEOPLE'S CAPITALISM

159   "**Mr. Moe's**": Milton L. Rock to George Citron, March 24, 1950, Folder 13, Box 3, ENH.
160   "**Maybe I should sell GM**": Isabel Briggs Myers to Katharine Briggs, February 21, 1954, Folder 22, Box 4331, KCB.
160   **In 1955**: Theodore Repplier, "People's Capitalism," *V.F.W. Magazine* 43 (1955).
161   **Now that she had left**: Isabel Briggs Myers, Swarthmore College Alumni Questionnaire, May 1, 1951, Swarthmore College Archives, Swarthmore, Penn.
161   **According to sociologist**: William H. Whyte, *The Organization Man* (New York: Simon & Schuster, 1956), 174.
161   "**Let [us] ponder**": Ibid., 180.
162   **The mass testing**: Ibid., 3.
162   "**The function types**": Isabel Briggs Myers to Emma Jung, June 8, 1950, Hs 1056:16886, ETH.
163   "**As you have given the matter**": C. G. Jung to Isabel Briggs Myers, July 1, 1950, Hs 1056:17287, ETH.

164 **"The test is based"**: Edward N. Hay to O. A. Ohmann, July 19, 1949, Folder 13, Box 3, ENH.

164 **"Under all the shifting problems"**: Myers, "Contributions of a Man's Type to His Executive Success."

166 **"Our economy has been abundantly productive"**: O. A. Ohmann, "Skyhooks: With Special Implications for Monday through Friday," *Harvard Business Review,* 1955.

167 **The fact that it might also help enhance productivity**: Ibid.

167 **"The type differences"**: Isabel Briggs Myers, "The Measurement of Dissatisfaction as a Trait in Job Applicants and Its Differing Effect Upon Turnover in Type Suitable and Type Unsuitable Hirings," Folder 13, Box 3, ENH.

167 **From her experience**: Myers, "Contributions of a Man's Type to His Executive Success."

168 **"The expectation"**: Myers, "The Measurement of Dissatisfaction."

168 **The technical term for it**: Isabel Briggs Myers to Edward N. Hay, n.d., Folder 13, Box 3, ENH.

170 **Its tone is ruthless**: Whyte, *The Organization Man,* 171.

170 **"As in all applications"**: Ibid., 182.

171 **"The important thing"**: Ibid., 405.

172 **To commit**: C. Wright Mills, *The Sociological Imagination* (New York: Oxford University Press, 2000), 171.

172 **"While it is true"**: Whyte, *The Organization Man,* 406.

172 **Rather, Whyte advised**: Ibid.

173 **"To be considered"**: Ibid., 410.

173 **"The point of it is"**: Myers, "IBM MBTI history 74."

174 **"Medicine was a case"**: Myers, "IBM typology 71 transcript."

174 **With Chief as her chauffeur**: Ibid.

174 **"Type Indicator goes swimmingly"**: Isabel Briggs Myers to Katharine Briggs, February 21, 1954, Folder 12, Box 4331, KCB.

175 **Her study revealed**: Isabel Briggs Myers and Mary H. McCaulley, "Relevance of Type to Medical Education," PGP.

175 **"One medical student"**: Myers, "IBM MBTI history 74."

CHAPTER ELEVEN: THE HOUSE-PARTY APPROACH TO TESTING

178 **"The assessment of well-monitored individuals"**: Donald MacKinnon, "Proposal for an Institute of Personality Assessment and Research," March 21, 1949, Folder 18, Box 3, RG 1.2 (FA387), Series 01.0002/205: California; Subseries 205.A: California—Medical Sciences, University of California—Psychology—(Institute of Personality Assessment and Research)—(MacKinnon, Donald W.), 1946–1955, The Rockefeller Foundation. Hereafter TRF.

178 **"I contribute this reaction"**: Katherine Anne Porter to Frank Barron, November 21, 1957, Folder 4, Box 51, Katherine Anne Porter Papers, Special Collections, University of Maryland Libraries, Baltimore, Md.

178 **"Let's don't say personality"**: Eugene Walker, "A Rainy Afternoon with Truman Capote," *Intro Bulletin: A Literary Newspaper of the Arts,* December 1957.

178 **Upon his arrival at 2240**: Truman Capote, "Personal Interview," January 24, 1958, Institute of Personality Assessment and Research, Berkeley, California. Hereafter IPAR.

179 **Now human beings were traded on**: Erich Fromm, *The Erich Fromm Reader,* ed. Rainer Funk (New York: Humanity Press, 1994), 41–42.

180 **Now was the time for the Western world**: Ellen Herman, *The Romance of American Psychology: Political Culture in the Age of Experts* (Berkeley: University of California Press, 1995), 120.

180 **Like Isabel Briggs Myers**: Ibid., 120.

180 **It was time to set aside**: Ibid., 46.

180 **When he handed over the first installment**: Frank O'Hara, "Mayakovsky," in *Meditations in an Emergency* (New York: Grove/Atlantic, 1956).

181 **"A measure of the acuteness of the problem"**: MacKinnon, "Proposal for an Institute of Personality Assessment and Research."

182 **Each group occupied**: Ibid.

182 **"We did not take any Oriental students"**: Donald MacKinnon, "Interview with the Rockefeller Foundation," February 8, 1952, Folder 18, Box 3, TRF.

182 **As for women**: Ibid.

182 **Here was a group of elite white men**: MacKinnon, "Proposal for an Institute of Personality Assessment and Research."

183 **Yet inside the IPAR "fishbowl"**: Ibid.

184 **At the turn of the eighteenth century**: Jeremy Bentham, *Panopticon; Or, The Inspection-House* (London: T. Payne, 1791).

185 **Writing nearly two hundred years later**: Michel Foucault, *Discipline and Punish: The Birth of the Prison* (New York: Vintage Books, 1991), 196.

186 **"Everything is grist"**: Donald MacKinnon, "IPAR Annual Report, 1952–1953," Folder 18, Box 3, TRF.

186 **Harrison Gough, who would invent**: Harrison Gough, "Interview with the Rockefeller Foundation," February 8, 1952, Folder 18, Box 3, TRF.

187 **Successful students**: MacKinnon, "IPAR Annual Report, 1952–1953."

187 **For Gardner, America's secret weapon**: John Gardner, *Self-Renewal: The Individual and the Innovative Society* (New York: Harper and Row, 1964), 192.

187 **"We cannot believe"**: "Research into Creativity Booming," San Francisco *Argonaut,* December 16, 1955.

188 **"These are the fifties"**: Quoted in Frederic Prokosch, *Voices: A Memoir* (London: Faber & Faber, 1983).

188 **Their ascendance would have to wait**: Timothy Leary, *Turn On, Tune In, Drop Out* (Oakland, Calif.: Ronin Publishing, 1965).

188 **"*Life is devastating*"**: Frank Barron to Timothy Leary, May 22, 1956, Timothy Leary Papers, Box 10, Folder 13, New York Public Library, New York.

189 **"As a species"**: Frank Barron, "Putting Creativity to Work," in *The Nature of Creativity: Contemporary Psychological Perspectives* (New York: Cambridge University Press, 1988), 76.

189 **"The creative person"**: Frank Barron, "Proposal for Research on the Creative Personality," September 1954, Folder 18, Box 3, TRF.

189 **He—and Barron's creative person**: Ibid.

189 **"Better Testing"**: "Better Testing Sought for Creative Students," *Long Beach Independent,* November 24, 1961.

189 **"Can we teach"**: Gardner, *Self-Renewal,* 192.

190 **He was a man short of stature**: Capote, "Personal Interview."

190 **At thirty-three years old**: Norman Mailer, *Advertisements for Myself* (Cambridge: Harvard University Press, 1992), 465.

190 **"Since the colors were basic"**: "Mosaic Key," January 24, 1958, IPAR.

191 **"One felt that this world of literati"**: Capote, "Personal Interview."

192 **The next day, all the writers**: "Storytelling," January 24, 1958, IPAR.

192 **Burke, diagnosed by his staff psychologist**: Kenneth Burke, "Personal Interview," January 24, 1958, IPAR.

193 **"The apparently effortless"**: Capote, "Personal Interview."

194 **"So that's what I did"**: Ravenna Helson, interview with author, July 18, 2016.

195 **"With him one soon finds"**: William Carlos Williams, "Personal Interview," October 20, 1957, IPAR.

196 **"But the very circumstances"**: Simone de Beauvoir, *The Second Sex* (New York: Vintage, 2011), 725.

199 **"On applications"**: Sheila Ballantyne, *Norma Jean the Termite Queen* (New York: Penguin Books, 1983), 3.

CHAPTER TWELVE: THAT HORRIBLE WOMAN

201 **Finally, there was the woman**: Junius A. Davis, *Diary of a Curable Romantic* (Bloomington: Xlibris, 2008), 150.

201 **In their letters to one another**: Saunders, *Katharine and Isabel,* 155.

202 **He was heartened**: Henry Chauncey, "A Center for Research on Human Abilities and Personality," Folder 267, Box 24, Henry Chauncey Papers, Educational Testing Service, Princeton, New Jersey. Hereafter HCP.

202 **"The development of tests"**: Henry Chauncey to Dael Wolfe, May 15, 1953, Folder 267, Box 24, HCP.

202 **But Chauncey worried**: Chauncey, "A Center for Research on Human Abilities and Personality."

203 **His experience with the SAT**: Ibid.

203 **Just as his militant ambition**: Ibid.

203 **"I envisage a day"**: "Conference on Proposed Personality Research Center," April 7, 1953, Folder 267, Box 24, HCP.

205 **"Yes, she actually skipped"**: Davis, *Diary of a Curable Romantic,* 152.

205 **"It is based on theories"**: Henry Chauncey, "Reasons Why the MBTI Seems Promising and Particularly Useful in Connection with the Sloan Study," July 17, 1957, Folder 642, Box 61, HCP.

206 **The invitation from ETS**: "An Appreciation of Isabel Briggs Myers," PGP.

207 **At her instruction**: Henry Chauncey, "A Description of the Myers-Briggs Type Indicator," September 1957, Folder 642, Box 61, HCP.

207 **"Just by chance"**: Henry Chauncey to John Ross, "Conference with Mrs. Myers," February 10, 1960, Folder 642, Box 61, HCP.

208 **Like the army**: Association for Computing Machinery, *Communications of the Association for Computing Machinery* 2, no. 1 (1959): 108.

209 **Through the early 1960s**: Myers, "IBM MBTI history 74."

209 **"Neither of these authors"**: Chauncey, "A Description of the Myers-Briggs Type Indicator."

209 **"Indeed, many of the ideas"**: Ibid.

210 **"I sometimes kind of shook"**: Myers, "IBM MBTI history 74."

210 **"Mrs. Myers was not trained"**: Davis, *Diary of an Curable Romantic,* 163.

210 **"Not the least of the problems"**: Larry Stricker, "Evaluation of the Myers-Briggs Type Indicator," Folder 642, Box 61, HCP.

210 **She insisted that the ETS staffers**: Chauncey, "A Description of the Myers-Briggs Type Indicator."

211 **"She scored it with secret scales"**: Davis, *Diary of a Curable Romantic,* 152.

211 **"I wanted the students"**: Myers, "IBM MBTI history 74."

211 **She visited each three times**: Isabel Briggs Myers, "Reflections on the History of the Type Indicator," PGP.

212 **"Isabel, I simply have to go home"**: Davis, *Diary of a Curable Romantic,* 152.

213 **"Mrs. Myers indicated"**: R. E. Cordray to H. Chauncey, "Re: Myers-Briggs," August 5, 1959, Folder 642, Box 61, HCP.

213 **"In comparison with"**: R. E. Cordray to Isabel Briggs Myers, "Memorandum," August 21, 1959, Folder 642, Box 61, HCP.

214 **He was an ENTJ**: Myers, "IBM MBTI history 74."

214 **"I think it is true"**: John Ross to Henry Chauncey, "Myers-Briggs Type Indicator: Progress Report," November 5, 1959, Folder 642, Box 61, HCP.

215 **"The word 'Type'"**: Ibid.

215 **"The crux of our disagreement"**: J. Ross to H. Chauncey, "Myers Briggs Type Indicator," November 5, 1959, Folder 642, Box 61, HCP.

216 **"I would suggest that it be published"**: John Ross to Henry Chauncey, "Meeting on Friday, November 9," September 8, 1960, Folder 642, Box 61, HCP.

216 **In time, she would grow**: Saunders, *Katharine and Isabel,* 135.

216 **He enjoyed the support and protection**: Davis, *Diary of a Curable Romantic,* 151.

217 **Isabel trusted him with material**: Myers, "IBM construction."

217 **What Isabel did not know**: Stricker, "Evaluation of the Myers-Briggs Type Indicator."

218 **It was a punishing, injurious document**: Myers, "IBM construction."

218 **She was "shaken"**: Henry Chauncey, "Memorandum of Conference with Mrs. Myers," June 26, 1961, Folder 642, Box 61, HCP.

218 **"I guess you feel as though"**: Myers, "IBM construction."

219 **"She undoubtedly felt very keenly"**: Chauncey, "Memorandum of Conference with Mrs. Myers," June 26, 1961.

219 **"She is a kind of modern Joan of Arc"**: Saunders, *Katharine and Isabel,* 137.

219 **"The whole Larry Stricker imbroglio"**: Henry Chauncey, "Memorandum of Conference with Mrs. Myers," October 11, 1961, ETS, Princeton, N.J.

219 **"One ought to consider"**: Henry Chauncey, "Memorandum of Conference with Mrs. Myers," May 3, 1961, Folder 642, Box 61, HCP.

220 **"She tends to fight"**: Ibid.

220 **He had attempted**: Saunders, *Katharine and Isabel*, 135.

221 **"I didn't think I needed to"**: McCaulley, "Person Behind the MBTI 1988."

221 **"Although she would surely find ways"**: Henry Chauncey to William Turnbull, "Mrs. Myers' consultantship," July 14, 1964, Folder 642, Box 61, HCP.

221 **"We had a spell"**: Davis, *Diary of an Curable Romantic*, 156.

221 **In 1964, Davis sent**: Junius Davis to Henry Chauncey, "The Recent Life and Times of Isabel Myers," May 19, 1964, Folder 642, Box 61, HCP.

222 **In the mid-1960s**: Junius Davis to Henry Chauncey, "Mrs. Myers' Consultantship," May 22, 1964, Folder 642, Box 61, HCP.

223 **The West acted like**: Junius Davis to Henry Chauncey, "West Coast Trip," September 16, 1964, HCP.

223 **In California, she had seen her grandson**: Isabel Briggs Myers to Mary McCaulley, August 25, 1970, PGP.

CHAPTER THIRTEEN: THE SYNCHRONICITY OF LIFE AND DEATH

227 **In one of the last unpublished**: "Death and Resurrection," Folder 15, Box 4334, KCB.

228 **"A husband and wife"**: Peter Geyer, "Why is the future that's so clear to me so opaque to you? . . . and other issues. Mary McCaulley in conversation with Peter Geyer," PGP.

230 **Mary's favorite word to use**: Carl Jung, *Synchronicity: An Acausal Connecting Principle* (New York: Routledge, 2006).

232 **"She made me think of Ann"**: Saunders, *Katharine and Isabel*, 158.

232 **"That was very, very, very sweet"**: Geyer, "Why is the future . . . Mary McCaulley in conversation with Peter Geyer."

233 **"They had better be sensing!"**: Mary McCaulley to Isabel Briggs Myers, September 19, 1970, PGP.

233 **Every several months**: Isabel Briggs Myers to Mary McCaulley, March 16, 1972, PGP.

233 **"I don't like the idea"**: Isabel Briggs Myers to Mary McCaulley, July 4, 1970, PGP.

234 **"She had a beautiful"**: McCaulley, "Person Behind the MBTI 1988."

234 **At the beginning**: Geyer, "Why is the future . . . Mary McCaulley in conversation with Peter Geyer."

234 **They avoided restaurants**: McCaulley, "Person Behind the MBTI 1988."

235 **"You and I are"**: Mary McCaulley to Isabel Briggs Myers, April 4, 1970, PGP.

235 **With the support**: Mary McCaulley to Isabel Briggs Myers, September 19, 1970.

235 **One young woman's**: Mary McCaulley to Isabel Briggs Myers, December 11, 1970, PGP.

236 **"There is a real problem"**: McCaulley, "Person Behind the MBTI 1988."

237 **"Here are some pictures of you"**: Mary McCaulley to Isabel Briggs Myers, December 11, 1970.

237 **"CAPT—it's Mary's dream"**: Isabel Briggs Myers and Mary McCaulley, "CAPT—It's Mary's Dream," January 7, 1978, PGP.

237 **Did she think of**: Carl Bereiter, interview with author, June 3, 2017.

238 **"Since when does an honorable person"**: Saunders, *Katharine and Isabel*, 147.

238 "**The old idea**": Ibid., 150.

239 **After her doctor cut them out**: McCaulley, "Person Behind the MBTI 1988."

239 "**The purpose of this letter**": Educational Testing Service to Isabel Briggs Myers, April 17, 1975, Folder 642, Box 61, HCP.

240 "**Stuffy bastards!**": Saunders, *Katharine and Isabel*, 163.

240 **Mary, who had written**: McCaulley, "Person Behind the MBTI 1988."

240 "**Everyone has the sword**": Mary McCaulley, "Visit to IBM at Swarthmore," August 22, 1977, PGP.

240 **Although the CPI**: Memo from Henry Dyer to Henry Chauncey, March 8, 1955, Folder 432, Box 24, HCP.

241 **This displeased Gough**: Ibid.

241 "**The CPI is not an instrument**": Harrison Gough to Henry Chauncey, February 14, 1955, Folder 432, Box 24, HCP.

241 "**It is already accomplishing**": Ibid.

241 "**There's this college professor**": Geyer, "Why is the future . . . Mary McCaulley in conversation with Peter Geyer."

241 **MacKinnon had typed him**: Harrison Gough, "Studies of the Myers-Briggs Type Indicator in a Personality Assessment Research Institute," PGP.

242 **She had to edit**: Mary McCaulley, "Telephone Call with Isabel," December 7, 1975, PGP.

242 **She had to give Black**: Saunders, *Katharine and Isabel*, 165.

242 **Isabel, never truly concerned**: Isabel Briggs Myers to Mary McCaulley, November 25, 1979, PGP.

243 **In 1977**: McCaulley, "Visit to IBM at Swarthmore."

243 "**We were her apprentices**": Walter Joseph Geldart, "Katharine Downing Myers and the Whole MBTI Type—an Interview," *The Enneagram and the MBTI: An Electronic Journal,* February 1998.

243 **This made the consumer**: "APT Meeting Minutes," November 21, 1982, PGP.

243 **Once CPP**: "An Appreciation of Isabel Briggs Myers," *MBTI News* 2, no. 4 (July 1980).

244 "**It's not even that Isabel**": "An Appreciation of Isabel Briggs Myers."

244 "**The enemy is here**": McCaulley, "Person Behind the MBTI 1988."

CHAPTER FOURTEEN: ONE IN A MILLION

246 "**I'm an introvert**": Lynn Smith, "Adult-Type Training for Schoolchildren," *Los Angeles Times,* June 24, 1982.

247 **The test**: Tara Mack, "A Lot More Is Cooking in Home Ec: Updated Classes Reflect Changing Roles, Social Issues," *Washington Post,* December 15, 1996.

247 **Knowing the positive and negative attributes**: Ibid.

247 **When she is accepted**: "UA hoping to decrease odd couples," *Mobile Register,* August 27, 1989.

247 "**Self-discovery is**": Carolyn Haines, " 'Painless tests provide info about 'deeper' self,'" *Mobile Press Register,* September 11, 1983.

247 **Sister Susan Randolph**: "The perfect roommate? Just fill out this test," *Argus Leader,* September 1, 1985.

247 **The counseling team**: Sally Nelson, "It's unlikely you're just one personality type," *The Post-Crescent,* July 5, 1981.

248 **"It's a different world"**: Diane Lewis, "New rule on interviews is to expect unexpected," *Chicago Tribune,* September 8, 1991.

248 **People in America**: Elizabeth MacDonald, "Is There a Party Animal Lurking Beneath All Those Spreadsheets?" *Wall Street Journal,* January 24, 1997.

248 **"There are as many"**: Katy Koontz, "Know Your Work Personality," *Times-Picayune,* September 11, 1987.

248 **"Have you ever been"**: Ernest Auerbach, "Not Your Type, but Right for the Job," *Wall Street Journal,* January 6, 1992.

249 **"Four of the"**: Diane Goldner, "Fill in the Blank: Wondering what to do with your life? The first step: Take a test," *Wall Street Journal,* February 27, 1995.

249 **"We have found"**: "Visionary, Catalyst, Stabilizer, Cooperator: Which Type Are You?" *Washington Post,* November 7, 1991.

249 **According to Larry Richards**: Saundra Tory, "Thinker or Feeler? Test Offers Personality Insights," *Washington Post,* October 25, 1993.

250 **There, she might meet Susan**: Hilary Rosner, "Natural Aptitude: Testing for the Perfect Job," *Village Voice,* August 12, 1997.

251 **She knows she can find**: "Living-Loving Workshop for Couples Scheduled," *Los Angeles Times,* September 23, 1985.

251 **She can participate**: "Image Two: Personal Development Seminar," *The Oregonian,* March 6, 1986.

251 **"Would you rather die"**: Laura Ost, "Tomorrow: Health and Medicine: There's a system for describing your traits to a T," *Chicago Tribune,* August 16, 1987.

251 **Another matches celebrity**: Ellen Tien, "Pulse; Shrink Your Thighs," *New York Times,* August 30, 1998.

251 **"Italy is an extraverted country"**: Mary McCaulley, "Does a Country or a Culture Have a Type?" PGP.

251 **She can fashion**: Otto Kroeger Associates, "1998 Training Programs," PGP.

252 **"I believe that"**: Susan Scanlon, "Trends: The Way You Were," *Washington Post,* May 23, 1983.

252 **In his 1988 book**: Otto Kroeger and Janet Thuesen, *Type Talk: The 16 Personality Types that Determine How We Live, Love, and Work* (New York: Dial Press, 1988).

253 **Kroeger secured**: Emily Yoffe, "The National War College," *The Courier,* December 16, 1984.

253 **The quasi-spiritual convergence**: "Study: U.S. needs new executive type," *Trenton Times,* February 9, 1992.

254 **"Work is elastic"**: Barbara Moses, "Introverts break out in the new workplace," *Globe and Mail,* October 3, 1997.

254 **"I was angry and humiliated at first"**: Trip Gabriel, "Earning It: Personal Trainers to Buff the Boss's People Skills," *New York Times,* April 28, 1996.

255 **"Many consultants first conduct"**: Lena Williams, "Companies Capitalizing on Worker Diversity," *New York Times,* December 15, 1992.

255 **A 1997 guide**: Jeanne Maes and Robert Shearer, "Dealing with Sexual Harassment in the Workplace," *Equal Opportunities International* 16, no. 1 (1997).

255 **Although he identified**: Marta Vogel, "Tidying Up," *Washington Post,* September 14, 1989.

256 **While some couples**: Jim Fuller, "Know thy type: Are you an ESTJ, an INFP, an INTP? Give up?" *Chicago Tribune,* June 19, 1988.

257 "*Flavors and colors*": "From the Local Chapters of APT," *MBTI News* 7, no. 2 (Spring 1985), PGP.

257 **"Visibility brings"**: Mary McCaulley, "Relationship between CAPT and APT," PGP.

257 **"The MBTI has experienced"**: Geldart, "Katharine Downing Myers and the Whole MBTI Type—an Interview."

258 **"The Biggest Financial Asset"**: John Wasik, "The Biggest Financial Asset in Your Portfolio Is You," *New York Times,* February 11, 2013.

258 **The market for workplace personality assessments**: Facebook IQ, "The Annual Topics & Trends Report from Facebook IQ," Facebook, Menlo Park, Calif. 2017.

259 **"ENTJ"**: Jenna Birch, "Your Dating Style, Based on Your Myers-Briggs Personality Type," *Teen Vogue,* August 28, 2017.

259 **"The market is glutted"**: Kelley Holland, "What a Test Can Say About Your Style," *New York Times,* April 21, 2017.

260 **Take, for instance, these**: David Keirsey and Marilyn Bates, *Please Understand Me* (New York: Prometheus Nemesis Book Company, 1984).

260 **"The more you use it"**: Scanlon, "Trends: The Way You Were."

260 **"I have run into people"**: Myers, "IBM construction."

CONCLUSION: TRUE BELIEVERS

269 **"As type spreads around the globe"**: Mary McCaulley, "Building Harmony for a New Century: Jung's Typology and the Myers-Briggs Type Indicator," International Type Users Organization Conference, South Africa, 1996.

Index

Page numbers in *italics* refer to illustrations.

Illustration Credits

Page 47 Reproduction of the *New Republic* (December 22, 1926)

Page 72 Courtesy of the Katharine Cook Papers at Michigan State University

Page 138 (top and bottom) Courtesy of the Edward N. Hay Papers at the Kheel Center for Labor Management Documentation and Archives at Cornell University